Critique of Exotica

St

Critique of Exotica
Music, Politics and the
Culture Industry

John Hutnyk

Pluto Press

LONDON • STERLING, VIRGINIA

First published 2000 by Pluto Press
345 Archway Road, London N6 5AA
and 22883 Quicksilver Drive, Sterling, VA 20166–2012, USA

www.plutobooks.com

British Library Cataloguing in Publication Data
A catalogue record for this book is available from the British Library

Library of Congress Cataloging-in-Publication Data

Hutnyk, John, 1961–
 Critique of exotica: music, politics, and the culture industry/John Hutnyk
      p. cm.
Includes bibliographical references.
  ISBN 0-7453-1554-2 (hardback) — ISBN 0-7453-1549-6 (pbk.)
1. Popular music—Social aspects. 2. Popular music—Political
aspects. 3. Popular culture—History—20th century. 4. Asians—Social
conditions—20th century. 5. Intercultural communication. 6. Hybridity
(Social sciences) 7. Multiculturalism. I. Title.
  ML3918.P67 H88 2001
  306.4'84—dc21
                                00-009745

ISBN   0 7453 1554 2 hardback
ISBN   0 7453 1549 6 paperback

Designed and produced for Pluto Press by
Chase Publishing Services
Typeset from disk by Gilbert Composing Services, Leighton Buzzard
Printed in the European Union by
T.J. International, Padstow, England

Contents

Part I
Alliances

1
Dub: Introduction

'Which do you prefer: Music or ham?' (Erik Satie)[1]

Poetry or potatoes? Culture or politics? Dancing or meat? These are not just t-shirt slogans. Satie says a brutal choice must be offered just when the hors d'oeuvres arrive. He wants to upset bourgeois palates. 'Music or ham?' Asking neat, sharp and tasty questions like this raises issues of class, distinction and hierarchy while targeting polite society. An urgent economy slices through protocols of entertainment and opens onto a critique of 'trade' and of the commercial imperatives that drive the Culture Industry. Where frequency of representation cannot annul the complicity of critics, the self-declared impresarios of distraction, the purveyors of content, the advocates of lyrical and sonic seduction and the facilitators of fabulous 'flavours of transnational capital' (Banerjea 1998: 395), all owe a great deal to the multicultural trick that sells exotica as race relations and visibility as redress.

For starters, scholarship, creativity and activism seem too often to drift apart and across a socio-political divide. This drift is never more present than in the conflicted triangle bounded by academic study, the cultural industries and political organisations. This book responds to questions about how in an ever more popular and well-publicised way, certain cultural forms – specifically exotic, 'world' or 'South Asian' inflected musical ones – become 'flavour of the month'. Why?

The 'visibility' of culture in 'politics' has become a crucial site for theory – not only within cultural studies, communications and anthropology, but more and more in the mainstream media and in debates generated among practitioners themselves. Perhaps it is time serious attention was paid to the intersections between and contradictory interests in the scene and beyond. As cultural product and cultural 'flavour' become the seasoning for transnational commerce, there are engagements with very high stakes that cannot be left to a politically naive academicism. Who discusses the new 'visions' of Asia in Britain which are then exported to the Americas and abroad? What returns from these exports? In 1998, with her new album released simultaneously across the globe, Madonna donned a *bindi* for bad imitations of *bharatanatyam* dance moves on a chart-topping video. Academic discussions of appropriation do not offer any moves towards a transformatory politics capable of a response to this. Nor does cultural cringe at the antics of George Harrison hippie reruns give us much, as starry-eyed minstrels Kula Shaker offered retro 1960s pop songs and travelogue returns to the magical mystery tour via MTV, the English football fraternity sang along to a tune that acknowledged *the* national dish as 'vindaloo'. In this scene, articles by well-tenured 'Marxists' on 'culture' articulate only a mild disquiet and colonial and neo-colonial continuities are glossed as 'postcolonial', and so erased. Hybridity sells difference as the logic of multiplicity. Despite the effervescent cultural industries, the 'hybrid' visibility of Asian cultural forms has not yet translated into any significant socioeconomic redress of multi-racial exclusions within Fortress Europe. Granted we see the high profile of some ventures like *2nd Generation* magazine, Asian Dub Foundation or the high street curry house, but the marketing of things Asian is more readily available to a well-resourced material girl than to South Asians themselves. It seems that the fashion for *bindis* and sitars is not a guaranteed market option for the majority of *desi* diasporics even as it is they who have a large share in producing the cultural content of a refashioned multiculti Britain, exported as the latest 'cool Britannia' consumer product for the avaricious global culture-munching machine.

There is clearly a need for a critical and political assessment of the possibility of a transnational cultural studies that would respond to this smorgasbord (platter or banquet). This would examine the tools and concepts we might use to ensure a more adequate understanding of cultural production than has hitherto been offered. This will be one of the major framings of this book, which is conceived in terms of a wider cultural politics that uses the various global incarnations of World and South Asian musics and appropriation as examples. But the slogan: 'For a Transnational Cultural Studies?', even with a possible qualifier: 'the politics of hybridity and appropriation', would not work as a depiction of what this book is trying to do as such a characterisation probably errs towards the too theoretical and general for what is contained here. Avoiding the reification of 'transnational cultural studies' as a singular category and at the same time offering a critique of that nascent 'object' seemed critical. Then possibly the not wholly inappropriate 'dub' foundation metaphor might evoke an orientation much wider than the obvious reference to the music of the Asian Dub Foundation. This band is discussed in several chapters, and perhaps if some play could be made on 'dub' and 'dubious' as a general analogy (for cross-over, hybridity, layering, and for wider complications) some of the sense of this project's convolutions could be conveyed. A critique of exotica, however, is my preferred overall description because this idea can be read several ways – as a critique of those who peddle exotica, as a critique of exotica itself, and as a critique of exotica as desire that we all, to some degree, fall for (hence my complicity as an employee of the disciplinary apparatus, training critical thinkers for future deployment in the culture industries or with the international agencies of exploitation – service work, infotainment, charities at best, the World Bank/IMF/UN just as likely). As to the specificity of Asian Dub Foundation (ADF) in the book as a whole – well, the band and the collective community music project are important as they are central to two chapters, in quite different ways (one on their UK work, one on West Bengal revolutionary politics), and these differences are necessary to the development of the argument and the politics I want to illustrate. Yet while ADF often travel easily outside the UK context (well-known in Europe, popular in the USA, stars in Japan, etc.), it is not only *their* politics that I would celebrate as the potential site of valorisation in my version of a transnational cultural studies. Before ADF, Aki Nawaz and Dave Watts' Fun^da^mental were, and are, front runners of a wider cultural 'trend' – however contested, even by themselves – and as with all things 'Asian' in the youth culture market at present, they have also been 'flavour of the month' in complicated ways. But having toured the US with Oasis, been nominated for the Mercury Prize and with three successful albums, ADF are perhaps more flavoursome now. Though much of this book centres around different and diverse musics not readily or easily ascribed under the problematic hold-all category 'Asian', cultural production such as that of Fun^da^mental, the very different fantasy Asia of Kula Shaker and the general heterogeneity that surrounds the world music circuit are the favoured 'objects' of this analysis. It is still useful however if the dubious 'dub' of ADF also enables a self-critique of my own involvement as a commentator/writer – something neither to be hidden nor overplayed. The critique of exotica must also examine the advent of my own interests and motivations. Of course it helps to like these sounds. From the start I have to tell you that I am not *against* cross-over, mixing, dub or whatever. The dubious critiques offered here are then compromised by my personal involvement in the to and fro of ... well, of a white boy[2] writing about black music and, as one report to a government agency puts it, showing an 'exclusive interest ... in the politics of the Left'.[3]

I am not the only one compromised in some way here of course. The preparation of content for the liberal multiculturalism of the cultural smorgasbord implicates both well meaning Third Worldists and livelihood-seeking Third Worlders. Good intentions caught within a sometimes quite restricted and apolitical horizon transmute into an advertising programme for international capital hegemony. Hybridity and cultural diversity become much more than a relativist abdication or rejection of Enlightenment progress, but rather the diminutive version of a dominant ideology that works better than ever through complexity. This is why renewed thinking on appropriation and transnational cultural production may be needed now. The call would be for a new theoretical approach to cultural politics and music designed to shift debates beyond celebrations or condemnations of 'hybridity' and fusion or cross-over. Thus the argument is that although hybridity and other such buzzwords of cultural theory are 'dubious', there are ways in which other political agendas can be read, or rather should be read, into the cultural work produced by so-called hybrid selves. Of course the double argument for and against hybridity would need to be signalled. As this critique of exotica is elaborated, each chapter of this book addresses some form of cultural politics in performance, music or video, whether this be the 'hybridity-talk' and exoticism of world music festivals (Womad) or the anti-Islamic reaction to Fun^da^mental in the context of their self-defence proselytising. The book includes a critique of appropriation as a dubious concept or category deployed by influential US writers on cultural creativity, and critiques of the appropriations made by the white left of exactly these 'cultural' contents in the interests of popular anti-racism. Along the way tele-technological factors impact upon cultural production as much as upon theorisations of diaspora and identity – and some may detect a Marxist criticism resident somewhere here too. The book is – like *Rumour* perhaps – about how well-meaning Other-love (anti-racism, esotericism, anthropology) can turn out to be its opposite, can be complicit at best, counter-productive at worst, part and parcel of the evil dynamic of capitalist exploitation, more often than not.

The book is not 'about' culture, though possibly slips, here and there on purpose, into sentences that reify. It is not comprehensive, complete, an authoritative introduction to any bounded scene (some may find sections where the tone seems authoritative, but please try to leave

McCarthyite gut reactions at the door). The book is not always prescriptive. In essaying a series of stops along the way, this book perhaps works best as a partial, historical and personal – biased, perspectival, interested – accounting of several years of research and activism. It is a documentary record of sorts, rethought across changes of place and time. Transformations lurk here, not least in the styles of writing. Why the record is worth keeping in view is, I think, that the task of thinking through (negotiating seems too judicial a term) the complicities and complexities of cultural politics (this term seems not judicial enough, these days anyway) is one that has to be made public or visible, however contingent. The complexity cannot be an excuse for avoiding analysis; it is its rationale. Complicity cannot be an excuse for remaining mute; it is the condition of its expression.[4]

In the end, what I am looking for in approaches to cultural production is something like what Theodor Adorno called the 'secret omnipresence' of resistance (Adorno 1991: 67).[5] This can be seen as the possible inverse of that 'visibility' of culture which is not yet a sufficient politics. The argument is that more than visibility is required if co-option is not to be the beginning and end of cultural politics – visibility is a first and necessary move, a possible base, but upon this only a 'transnational literacy' (Spivak 1999: 357) that would trade visibility up into redress is adequate. I know that some friends will find this too much. I am thinking of Anamik Saha's excellent discussion of the band Cornershop and their contribution, or Raminder Kaur's sometimes more sympathetic line on Apache Indian (other takes on Apache Indian are scattered throughout the text, my own view is guarded).[6] However, in offering a critique of the ways well-meaning *scholars*, well-meaning *exotics* and well-meaning but under-organised *politicos* all too often succumb to logics rather more violent than can be kept in focus, the task is to strive for a political literacy that disengages the metropole equivalent of the elite comprador restitution of colonisation that prevails today. (Either the capitalist roaders or the landlord class nationalists betray the promise of anti-colonialism, while in the 'centre' anti-racism is betrayed by performed illusions of equality and tolerant rhetoric which masks business-as-usual. Multiculturalism is the nominated face of the latter. Post-colonialism the former.)

A more focused question that breaks visibility into components might be to ask, in the context of diaspora, to what degree Birmingham remix maestro Bally Sagoo's cultural pride and assertion of a strong Asian identity is premised on the sophisticated militant organising power of anti-racist and self-defence activism and its record in Britain? Here the organising moment is known under the campaign names of those killed or maimed by racists – Stephen Lawrence, Rohit Dugall, Brian Douglas, Amer Rafiq[7] – or of the organising groupings themselves – Asian Youth Movement, Indian Workers Association, Southall Black Sisters, Newham Monitoring Group, Satpal Ram Campaign. Certainly the work of ADF, Fun^da^mental or Hustlers HC does more to acknowledge the heritage of struggle that has played a major part in clearing a space within the British polity for such cultural innovations as what Sanjay Sharma called the 'new Asian dance music' (Sharma 1994). What then of the obligation of high profile stars to do more than celebrate visibility? Bally announces the goal of achieving a Hindi-language number one chart hit on *Top of the Pops* (in Housee and Dar 1996), but the cultural politics of this visibility belongs to a history that is more complicated than such markers. Aki Nawaz of Fun^da^mental and Nation Records has several times complained that the start afforded various so-called 'Asian Kool' acts – such as Talvin Singh – at the Nation label has been disavowed, possibly because Nation's politics are a little too hot for chart success (see Chapters 3 and 6). At a level less relevant to egoistic grandstanding, the community and mass movement character of audience-centred performativity and political engagement (I don't mean to affirm the priority of the dance hall here, but that of participation at multiple levels) has meant a lesser level of personality cult than that with which commercial culture usually finds it convenient to deal. This in turn leads to a certain invisibility of those less easily manipulated forms of cultural production – we have long endured the astonishing eclipse of drum and bass, rave and dance culture's political context in the texts of commentators, journalistic and academic, and avatars of the 'scene'.

It seems that talk of complicity is rarely welcome news, even if we are all caught somewhere. The visibility of some South Asian stars in the Culture Industry is, in itself, potentially useful but not guaranteed progressive – a favourite trick co-opts a few high profile names to foster the illusion that everyone else is ok (the classic here is the prime-time TV interview with some successful Gangsta Rapper who comes 'Straight Outta Compton', a place where newscasters still fear to tread). All this said however, how does a book like this one contribute to both a refinement of the argumentation around the politics and poetics of visibility and remember an historical and political context that will bring lessons forward for today, for interventions in practice that transform ill-informed and academic good intentions into struggle adequate to win?

Authenticity and visibility based upon tactically affirmed cultural specificity are only part of any political project capable of posing a challenge to hegemonic Culture-Industry-enhanced-quite-late-capitalism. Post-authenticity, and a move to expression within a universalism of differences where action works against exploitation, possibly goes further. Against those that mobilise their economic resources to sell cultural product 'plundered' from elsewhere – we might name this gambit after Madonna, now as mercantile girl – there might also be a critique of those who dress up their 'own' culture for necessary rent-paying and survival strategy success, and cannot make a full accounting of the consequences when this refracts across airwaves and pixel-vision. That Talvin Singh's success is founded upon a subsumption of the years of bhangra is only one aspect of the to and fro of complicity and occlusion that comes with vision. It would of course be inappropriate to complain that appropriation was evil because of some cultural inauthenticity, as if ownership of cultural form were attributable and immutable, and that then such owners are obliged to reproduce unchanged and authentic pre-colonial forms (so long as these are not lost and forgotten). The thing about appropriation is not authenticity or not, but rather the capacity to profit from culture. This profiteering is also not simply to be better distributed, or merely redistributed, but rather production for profit – I have by now declared my hand – must be replaced with as yet unmanifest alternatives.

Appropriation matters also where academic work approaches culture. The old Elvis Costello line about the absurdity of writing about music being like dancing about architecture would apply.[8] Pity those cultural studies scholars who imagine we are up to date with the cutting edges of culture and are at the same time the avant-garde of theory – not noticing that radical posturing within the institutions of higher education infects, with a parasitic and colonising glee, the role of all apologists and ideologues in the teaching factories. Culturally hip academics are the ones to watch out for, the agents of incorporation, domestication and pacification in the service of new elitism. On the other hand, it should not be thought that dedication to the exotic or esoteric might not be serious. There are of course superficial and casual approaches to exotica – weekend mystics – but a great many well-read people transform their entire lives through a 'vocation' for the East and the like. In other cases this might take the form of full commitment through external signs – the followers of Iskon who shaved their hair and danced down the metropolitan centre, or those who forsook routines of capital to take up lives in an Ashram or temple in India or some such, would be the extreme examples: the equivalent of 'wiggas'.[9]

Today, as much as in the 1960s, there are well-meaning people who do sometimes exhibit a strong commitment to the idea of, or versions of, the heterogeneity of cultures different from their own: anti-racists, new-agers, fellow travellers, socialists, liberals. The examples in academic work that follow this path – despite an injunction to not 'go native', and so to maintain distance in expertise – are elevated to approval in ways that gain institutional resources. This often manifests as history-defying Indology, or is authorised through the immersion fetish of realist ethnography. Virinder Kalra notes that anthropologists working in Britain have always written 'for "the Other" rather than reading or listening to their texts' (Kalra 2000a: abstract). It could be argued that this is an import of an older anthropological attitude that continues to work within a paradigm that considers the rest of the world as the site of documentary difference and fantasy, and has merely replicated this in conditions of transmigration. Notwithstanding the political correctness that forbids calling these different 'Others' primitive or savage, the structure which assigns civilisation and normalcy to white supremacy remains strong in an attitude that benevolently concerns itself with the 'non-West' within the West. This attitude is unable to conceptually grant citizenship or belonging to people of colour within the West – calling them migrants even after four generations, calling them Other, fascinated with multi-difference – and is only another dimension of 'propertied whiteness' (Banerjea 1999: 18) or, again, still, white supremacy. Kalra's insightful critique of anthropologists who fail to attend to what 'the natives' actually say, rather than tending to their curiosity value as 'others', is well brought out in his critique of the very often exemplary writing of Les Back analysing collaboration between Apache Indian and Maxi Priest – along the way introducing a more sensible reading of so-called 'hybridity' in the context of bhangra performance:

> Bhangra texts are primarily sung in Panjabi, but given the colonial encounter, they have long contained words borrowed from English in both folk and reproduced forms. In the context of the academic attention afforded to bhangra, the use of Panjabi mixed with English is read by Back (1996) in terms of an example of a new theoretical approach to hybridity. Back comments on the collaboration of reggae singer Maxi Priest with Apache Indian, a British Asian artist who successfully entered the main stream charts: 'The tune constituted an extraordinary and historic moment because not only did Apache Indian perform in his combination style but Maxi Priest sung part of the lyric in Punjabi taking the motif of cultural translation to new

heights' (Back 1996: 222–3). In this example, the actual content of the Panjabi lyric is not made apparent and indeed it is not important for Back's argument, which concerns 'cultural translation'. Thus, Back's analysis falls into the same mould of other ethnographers, not taking the actual content of Apache-Maxi's collaboration as a significant aspect of the event, but reading hybridity into the analyst's own 'cultural translation'. In fact, Maxi is singing in Panjabi, he is not engaging in an act of literal translation and his words are not translated in the song, but form part of the lyrical flow. (Kalra 2000a)[10]

At least Back writes with an ear for the music, rather than some sort of sociological or ethnographic thickness – though he does claim he is doing 'ethnography' and I am not sure that even if he had sorted the 'translations' out that this would have made the texts he examines into the cultural revolution he wants. Musings about sampling and bricolage (an old anthropology word), and about intermezzo cultural creativity, syncretism, hybridity and crossroads, etc., seem a little forced. Do regulation glossed intros telling us that bhangra originates in the Panjab (1996: 219), and has been 're-invented' in Britain, really provide all that much that is new? Why is it still heresy to suggest that, even back in the 1980s, an album like *Aaja* by the Sahotas could owe less to rural Panjab harvest festivals than to house music, electro or dub? Everyone has heard the not so syncretic voices of Baumann (1990), Gillespie (1995), and other domesticators of hybridity-talk, harping on in a refrain that ends up reasserting the theoretical importance of syncretism and mixture by way of positing a prior originary purity. It is not that bhangra didn't 'originate' in Panjab (fixed, stable, original, immutable, 'otherly' Panjab – see Kaur and Kalra 1996), it is rather that the research project that wants to find complexity and creativity in the new has to assert and construct the old as prior reference. The creative contamination that is the claimed preserve of metro-British cultural sites is given authorisation here, but along the way the importance of the contemporary metropolitan experiences of bands like Azaad, Apna Sangeet or Achanak are relegated to the status of 'curious' displacements. Malkit Singh meets Bally Sagoo and 'fusion' is noticed – but is this staged stylisation of the mix a sufficient description of what was going on? The return of anthropological interest in syncretism research is part of a systematic, and institutionally authorised, re-appropriation of thriving hybridities as the great hope of culture under capitalism (to the exclusion of more politically charged forms perhaps – Apache Indian here is no threat to the Culture Industry, rather its staple fodder). The idea that there are liminal cultures (another old word with a burden) and 'new forms of identity' (Back 1996: 245) that, with due acknowledgement of the stresses impinging upon their expression, are to be championed by ethnographers, and which indicate the ways in which 'the meaning of England is being recomposed in the heart of its cities' (Back 1996: 250), is resonant with possibilities. But singing the praises of 'vibrant culture' (isn't vibrant so often used as an apology for the much maligned – vibrant Calcutta, vibrant underground scene, etc?) and 'polyphonic explosions' (Back 1996: 250) also resonates with a somewhat utopian score – the musical metaphor here might be taken too far if it is thought that the compositions of Apache Indian would be adequate to a transformation of the racist, imperialist Britain we have here now.

The work of Mary Gillespie, in her study of ethnicity and television in Southall, offers an example of the kind of liberal exoticist enthusiasm I have in mind when she describes the music of Apache Indian as 'subversive' (Gillespie 1995: 47). The proffered evidence is that his bhangra-reggae cross-over style songs:

> present forceful social critiques of issues from drugs to AIDS to the dowry system ... allow[ing] for an assimilation of the values of urban British youth culture in combination with a continued attachment to the values shared with parents and rooted in the subcontinent. (Gillespie 1995: 46)

There are many who would contest the 'force' of Apache Indian's social critique, pointing instead to a commercialism and an opportunism that is not very radical at all. 'Assimilation' *to* British values is offered without regard to the politics *of* assimilation as a form of racism and this assimilationism is made more significant when Gillespie then takes the work of Apache as 'powerful testimony' to a dynamic culture 'responsive to the social world' (Gillespie 1995: 47). That this links directly to 'questions of ethnographic fieldwork and the potential it offers for *capturing* such processes of cultural change' (Gillespie 1995: 47 my italics) clinches the deal. This is the standard form of thinking in ethnicist anthropology, always referring Asian cultural production, whatever it is and wherever it is in the world, back to benchmark values 'rooted in the subcontinent' (here embodied as the unchanging parents) – or rather in a forever inscribed (Dumont-ian) anthropological version of caste, tribe, village and family (wholly inadequate for India today or for any notion of diasporic Asias).

Approaching from another angle, a colleague of Kalra's, Ashwani Sharma, who works in London and was also a contributing editor of *Dis-Orienting Rhythms* (Sharma et al. 1996), suggests a context for the dubious appropriations of academic interest in South Asian cultural production in the West. He asks the question: why matters 'Asian' are considered 'local', not universal, as is nearly always the case when discussion turns to matters 'white' (Sharma, lecture at 'Subcontinental Britain' conference, Goldsmiths 1999)? The focus that is required, surely, in work that would depart from the returnee orientalism of anthropology 'at home' would not be on Asians in Britain as 'native informants', as would happen in unreconstructed anthropology texts. Instead such work would seek exchange with practitioners and commentators on a range of musics, and cultural politics, which actually intersect with 'really existing' Asian people, and which would have significance for everyone, including whites, just as much as any cultural practice worthy of analysis should do. It is the case that in this book 'informants' are chosen for their politics, but also no doubt there is some influence of subjective preferences (my notion of Madonna and Crispian Mills as the two sides of the white supremacist's dream date might be grounds for critique of another kind of essentialising).

There is a host of new work that breaks with the voyeurism of a repatriated anthropology that unquestioningly turned its 'at home' gaze at so-called minority groups and found them – constituted them – in the image of the imaginary bounded social forms of its earlier project. Unreconstructed anthropology would just not do for a generation that read a politicised cultural studies alongside this more traditional ethnography. It is a matter of record that the politics of the cultural studies formation was desiccated by an ill-digested Gramscianism and, despite an inspirational early history (see especially *The Empire Strikes Back*, CCCS 1982) a wholesale drift into postmodernism and audience empiricism (a kind of market research tendency that ends up just watching TV). Thus, the edge of the newer work learns from, and over against, this situation, bringing an involvement in a more immediate and committed political engagement out of the difficult circumstances of a racist public sphere. Partly because access to academic tenure was not readily granted; partly then there was time for and dedication to off-campus politics, including off-campus Marxisms, campaign politics, anti-racist and anti-imperial struggle, struggles around identity and representation etc.; and partly because alternative resources, readings of history and reorganisations of alliances were available and deployed in a parallel formation: a block of mutual support sustained itself as a kind of secret resistance in the wings; a secret omnipresence. At conferences, seminars, in smaller publications and in the back pages of obscure journals, in sessional teaching, in postgraduate study groups and drifting into organisational politics, a new and angry sentiment was honed.[11] Another style of cultural political writing is now announced in the work I have been mentioning here and forthcoming – that of Virinder Kalra, Raminder Kaur, Sanjay and Ashwani Sharma, Tej Purewal, Sean McLoughlin, Joyoti Grech, Vijay Prashad, Amitava Kumar, Sunaina Maira, Sarbjit Ghattaura, Anamik Saha, Koushik and Partha Banerjea, Dipa Basu, Shirin Housee, Mukhtar Dar, Muserat Dar, and Parv Bancil – a frisson from left field.

Many in this group of writers would trace some of their inspiration to an older generation of scholars who cleared important ground within academic critique, but who oftentimes appeared somewhat more isolated within institutionalised space and, as a consequence, might sometimes be seen to have had a more radical edge dulled in favour of communicability. This is not a criticism, but recognition that maintaining a politics while in isolation within institutional space seems to impose necessary compromises. For both advantage and disadvantage this is less likely to be the trajectory of younger researchers if the conditions remain favourable for maintenance of mutual collaborative group support. Among the names in the older cohort who can continue to carve out spaces, and provide influence and direction, much respect is due to Ali Rattansi, Avtar Brah, Paul Gilroy, Stuart Hall, Gayatri Chakravorty Spivak, Arjun Appadurai and bell hooks. Theoretical inspiration by Karl Marx, styling by Vladimir Lenin and Comrade Mao. This book also draws upon writing by Theodor Adorno, Félix Guattari, Antonio Negri, Jacques Derrida, Rey Chow, Lisa Lowe and Gilles Deleuze, among others – it's a star system. The bibliography is the real credits, read the texts as itinerary.

Written over the last five years, some of the essays in this book, or parts of them, have appeared before and I thank the publishers, editors and co-conspirators for letting them loose again: Zed Books for versions of Chapters 2 (1997), 3 (1996) and 4 (1999); *Amer-Asia* for some of Chapter 5 (2000); *Theory, Culture & Society* for parts of Chapter 7 (2000). I'm glad to get the rest out, and all of it into one package, at last. Chapter 2 was formed at the workshop 'Culture, Communication and Discourse: Negotiating Difference in Multi-Ethnic Alliances' (Manchester 1994), an early version was published in the conference volume *Debating Cultural Hybridity: Multi-Cultural Identities and the Politics of Anti-Racism*, edited by

Werbner and Modood 1997, London: Zed Books, and it also appeared in the journal *Postcolonial Studies* 1(3), 1998. A version of Chapter 3 first appeared in *Dis-Orienting Rhythms: The Politics of the New Asian Dance Music*, edited by Sharma, Hutnyk and Sharma, 1996. Chapter 4 was first published in *Travel Worlds: Journeys in Contemporary Cultural Politics*, edited by Kaur and Hutnyk 1999, London: Zed Books. For Chapter 5, I especially thank Virinder Kalra for co-writing an earlier version (published in *Postcolonial Studies*, Kalra and Hutnyk 1998) and Vijay Prashad for his transatlantic (and beyond) influence and editorial clarity (for a short version published in the journal *Amer-Asia*). A small section of Chapter 6 was lifted from an article co-written with Sanjay Sharma and Virinder Kalra for *Dis-Orienting Rhythms* and I thank Barnor Hesse for his comments there. Chapter 7 was first presented, in much different form, at the conference on 'Music and Globalisation' at the Centre for Studies of Social Science in Calcutta in 1998. I owe much to Sugata Margit and Partha Chatterjee for their hospitality, and to Hillegonda Rietveld for the triage she performed on a version presented at a session Jon Beasley-Murray organised at the *New Statesman* conference at LSE in September 1999.

Along the way I've accumulated lots of debts, and not all to the bank. I acknowledge the financial assistance of the English Social Research Council through a post-doctoral fellowship held at the ICCCR in Manchester University's Anthropology Department. The encounter with Dick and Pnina Werbner suggested where to go, and I owe thanks to Tim Ingold, John Gledhill, other staff and all the students for making teaching in Manchester fun. The Asia Committee of the European Science Foundation funded a year of this work as a Research Fellow in Heidelberg, where Klaus Peter Koepping, Shobna Nijhawan, Michael Juach, Karoline Herring and Stefanie Menrath were among the many hospitable people who kept me plied with coffee and alcohol.[12] Visits from Sanjay and Vanita Seth, Ishita Banerjee, Suarabh Dube, Ramona Mitussis, Michael Dutton and Liz Van Dort were crazed enough to keep me close to sane. Other Charterhouse group members and associated interlocutors not already mentioned contributed their bits: Musa Ahmed, Bobby Sayyid, Meeta and Prita Jha, Kinni Kansara, Lynne Humphries, Damian Lawson, Chris Raab, Uma Kothari, Curtis Liburd and the always revolutionary-glam Eli Wong. Among the many who helped or hindered in useful ways, great or small, were Nikos Papastergiadis, Marcus Strom, Danny Sullivan, Gerard Goggin, Katharine Tyler, Laura Turney, Kate Goad, Drew Hemmet, Louise Murray, Kawori Iguchi, Don Miller, Julie Stephens, Emma Grahame,

Cmd. Saifuddin and the cadre at S.N. Banerjea Rd in Calcutta, John Pandit and ADF, the Khatam Music Crew, Imran Khan and all at *2nd Generation* magazine, Josie Berry and Hari Kunzru@Mute, Aki Nawaz, Dave Watts, Esther, Rich, and all the Nation crew for vinyl and CDs, Melanie from the Sparts, and in 'such much' style, Kaori Sugishita. In so many ways Goldsmiths colleagues and students have made the last two years a buzz – especially Rebecca Graversen, Atticus Narain, Anna Har, Ellie Jupp, Nicola Frost, Helen Morris, Sally Brewer, Ewa Jasiewicz, Kevin Davis, Steve Nugent, Olivia Harris, Anna Whitworth, Jenny Gault and Cris Shore. Also never forgetting the *Capital* reading group which was always a joy, if somewhat ill-disciplined and engulfed with smoke and booze – thanks Howard Potter, Jo-anne Bichard-Harding, Simon Cohn, Tillie Harris, Sarah Playden, Jean-Yves Guiomar, Matt Kelly and Rebecca Wright, with Kapital Letters: mush! Working with Pluto Press has been a pleasure, with special greetings to Sophie Richmond and Anne Beech. And, finally, the times I can get back to Australia to visit family and friends are too few, but I enjoy them too much – so maybe it's a dialectical thing – Ben Ross, Suzie Fry, Peter Phipps, Cass Bennett and Angie Mitropoulis thank you all. Lal Salaam.

Notes

1. In *Memoirs of an Amnesiac* circa 1914 (in Satie 1996: 106).
2. The plays on multiple meanings of the term 'dubious', as in cross-over dub music *and* the critique of appropriation – the dubious nature of Kula Shaker and Madonna's 'Asian' turn and the dubious 'application' of theory to the popular – also appeals because this usage has the modest benefit of poking some fun at the all-too-grim seriousness of my own critique. Can't dance, can't sing, etc., but that doesn't mean I'll inflict confessional anxieties about whiteness all throughout the book. A paragraph from a recent issue of *Transition* provides an out:

   > In scores of monographs and edited collections, critics have described the inevitable silence of whiteness, its 'transparency', its status as the unexamined norm against which all differences are measured. While much of the work on whiteness is intriguing, there is a danger of insularity, a narcissistic temptation intensified by the often confessional nature of writing about one's own white skin ... One can't help but register a concern that 'white studies' by, for, and about white people might displace examinations of groups that have only begun to be considered legitimate subjects of academic inquiry in the last thirty years. (editorial *Transition* 73: 5)

   I think this paragraph comes close to my own feeling about writing about whiteness, except rather than worry about the possibility that legitimacy as a subject of academic inquiry might disappear, I'd want to be more specific.

The making of subjects of academic inquiry is also differentially distributed across race in academia. Coming out of anthropology (coming out as an anthropologist?) makes it very clear that it matters who is asking-writing about these subjects. And this matters across race, class and gender not in a way that would exclude certain people from writing, but in a way that would question certain ways of writing about subjects. I think white privilege has often meant a 'freedom from having to think about race' and the study of whiteness of, for and by itself might displace critical thinking on all these 'unsolved' issues – race, class, gender. I'll confess a few other identifications and complexes along the way no doubt – an unsavoury fascination-hostility towards Kula Shaker for example – but I think the issue of race stays on the boil, however much I want to distance my take from sanctioned liberal 'anti-racisms'.

3. This was the assessment of my work by an employer when I held a post-doctoral research post in Manchester; the phrase was inscribed in an unpublished report to the English Social Research Council. From that quarter, red-baiting works as a compliment.

4. I am acutely aware that other complicities may feature here: the fact of the international book trade as ideological apparatus; the institutional context; the accountability and disciplinarity that codifies; an idea that ethnography could be changed into something more than it has been. Space demands that these emerge or irrupt as we move along.

5. 'It is a delicate question whether the liquidation of aesthetic intrication and development represents the liquidation of every last trace of resistance or rather the medium of its secret omnipresence' (Adorno 1991: 67).

6. Anamik Saha wrote a fine dissertation, 'Asians Can't Rock' on Cornershop at Goldsmiths College in 1999 and is proceeding towards publication. Raminder Kaur's option on Apache fandom is less strict and comes from a personal communication, see her nuanced article with Virinder Kalra in *Dis-Orienting Rhythms: The Politics of the New Asian Dance Music* (Kaur and Kalra 1996).

7. This list is only a few, the absolute excess of the statistics is, I find, far too tragic for mere typography, see CARF for the details: <www.carf.demon.co.uk> – an excellent site. Amer Rafiq was blinded in Police custody in 1996, as I discuss at the end of Chapter 6.

8. Such performativity might have its architectural side: Abbie Hoffman and the Yippies, dancing about the Pentagon in protest at the US aggression in South-East Asia, claim that they did manage to levitate that bastion of military power up into the air, and Ho Chi Minh was said to have commented that it showed the internal weakness of the running dogs. Things have changed much since the 1960s however, the 'Magic Bus' of fantasy trips across America or over to India transmutes into the discount privatised transport bus service in Manchester. Almost cut my hair.

9. This term obviously from Norman Mailer, but for a recent elaboration in the context of 1990s British youth interest in hip-hop see Calcutt (1998). This counter-reactive white identification with black culture occurs in the face of the rise of identity politics in general and takes on a hyperbolic tone where we see the articulation among hegemonic whites of a sense of not having an 'ethnicity' and of experiencing this as a kind of loss. Worrying about this

should not lead to applause for the old invisible white supremacy of the pre-identity politics phase, but the desire for ethnic character – manifest in moves as diverse as wannabee wiggas through tribalism-celtic nostalgias to ultra-Aryan fascisms – is no excuse for another round of Britpop national jingoism.

10. In the track 'Fe Real', Maxi sings in Panjabi: 'Everybody knows to listen to us, dance and shout loudly' (translated by Virinder Kalra).

11. Various meetings – both academic and campaign groups, sometimes overlapping – contributed to this process. From Community Consultation/ Confrontation with the Police at Longsight over Amer Rafiq (see Chapter 6) to disruptive enthusiasms at academic conferences such as the British Sociological Association meetings (especially the one in Coventry organised by Avtar Brah), and the British Association of South Asian Studies (especially the one organised in Manchester by Bobby Sayyid). Singular or one-off events like Transl-Asia in Birmingham (organised by Virinder Kalra and Rajinder Kumar), Identity Papers at the Institute of Contemporary Arts (organised by Ashwani and Sanjay Sharma), Vindaloo at the Vibe Bar in Brick Lane (organised by Rebecca Young) and Subcontinental Britain at Goldsmiths were especially productive.

12. Work, work, work – there were many that thought standing at the back of smoky nightclubs chatting with DJs and musos was no sort of work at all. Consider how difficult it is to claim pints and spliffs on research expense forms. Later, standing on the other side of the decks having cracked the secret of playing records in a row without gaps, I did manage to get paid a few times, but just a little (see Basu 1998). We – the crew I worked with – were never good enough to not need day-jobs, and of course these are hard enough to maintain anyway. What a bonus it is that they give some time to write (in between teaching, which is the real fun). In any case, the creative part that appeals most is putting the tracks together, and perhaps even more than that, performance and musicianship. A long, long time ago the Rickenbacker was traded for an international air-ticket (and partial payment of a still mostly outstanding higher education debt). I hope I'll get back to that sometime. In the meantime, it might be worth noting that just because this book contains single-authored papers, this does not mean that they are not wholly indebted to collaborative work, ongoing, whatever atrocities my sloppy politics may have introduced to the texts themselves.

2
Adorno at Womad

> The more total society becomes, the greater the reification of the mind and the more paradoxical its effort to escape reification on its own. Even the most extreme consciousness of doom threatens to degenerate into idle chatter. Cultural criticism finds itself faced with the final stage of the dialectic of culture and barbarism. (Adorno 1983: 34)

In his essay, 'The Culture Industry Reconsidered', Theodor Adorno writes: 'To take the culture industry as seriously as its unquestioned role demands, means to take it seriously critically, and not to cower in the face of its monopolistic character' (Adorno 1991: 88). Thus, while noting, with Horkheimer, that 'culture now impresses the same stamp on everything' (Adorno and Horkheimer 1944/1979: 120), Adorno also recognised that the standardisation of mass products had even to 'standardise the claim of each one [product] to be irreplaceably unique' (Adorno 1991: 68). These were, however, 'fictitiously individual nuances' (Adorno 1991: 35), examples of the rule of the 'iron grip of rigidity despite the ostentatious appearance of dynamism' (Adorno 1991: 62). Today the multiplication of differences has become repetitive to the point that diversity and difference as commodities seem to offer only more and more of the same. In this chapter I consider this claim in the light of the rise to popularity of 'world music', in order to evaluate the current vogue in culture commentary for hybridity.

Paul Gilroy writes that the 'hybridity which is formally intrinsic to hip-hop has not been able to prevent that style from being used as an especially potent sign and symbol of racial authenticity' (Gilroy 1993a: 107). In 'so-called World Music', he suggests, 'authenticity enhances the appeal of selected cultural commodities and has become an important element in the mechanism of the mode of racialisation necessary to making non-European and non-American musics acceptable items in an expanded pop market' (Gilroy 1993a: 99). There seems, at first glance, to be a possible convergence here between the critiques of Adorno and Gilroy. The commodification of black musics proceeds by way of a racialisation that has long been a part of the marketing of black musics such as jazz, disco and rap to white, Euro-American audiences. Gilroy adds that this has also served as a means of presenting identities for self-confirmation and internalisation to black communities themselves. If pointing to the artifice of this is 'not enough', as Gilroy suggests, then neither is just dispensing with 'authenticity' debates in order to unblock 'critical theorising' of much consequence either. The point is to take this a step further with the critique of cultural production. But this commodification in cultural production is also something in which we are complicit. For me this complicity escalates with attendance as a spectator consuming cultural 'difference' at Womad.

Womad

Womad Music Festivals, Reading, Morecambe, Adelaide and elsewhere, are huge events no longer confined to llama-wool jumper, bicycle-camping, tea-head greenie hippies and weekend travellers on weekends without a rave, but now successfully drawing in a cross-section of people not immediately or easily consigned to niche marketing categories. Even with the grab-bag categories it is difficult to specify the world music audience today – beyond the generalities of middle-class (it is a bit expensive to get in), young-ish (predominantly under 40) and Western. Unlike most specific music genres, say rock or bhangra, there is no obvious disproportionate cultural or racial audience mix vis-à-vis proportional representation in, for example, the UK. Indeed the audiences of Womad are markedly diverse. After more than ten years, the product recognition of Womad and the category of world music may not have achieved music industry dominance, but it has captured a significant, and growing, slice of the industry. Bands and musicians from all corners of the world are brought to Europe – on occasion Australia, Japan – to perform for appreciative audiences. Thus, for me, Womad looks interesting as a site for the playing out of capitalist cultural production at both ideological and economic registers. The commercialisation of music and the evacuation of politics at such events deserves comment and goes hand in hand (in a pastoral, folksy, face-to-face sense) with an aversion to the technological (or a pastoralising of it) and an absolutist and authentic singularism (not always nationalist) which needs to be unpacked.

World music has come to be considered by the music industry – its commercial production and promotional arms – as a potentially profitable, and so exciting, expansive and popular way forward in contemporary music. There has been little critical work produced on any aspect of this development at a time when what is required is a multi-perspectival examination of the world music phenomenon, ranging from a critique of the concepts and terminologies deployed, through the employment practices, marketing of 'ethnic identities', com-mercialisation and so on, to the attempts at explicit politicisation of Womad audiences by disparate political groupings. A multi-perspective approach to Womad would enable a focus upon world music as a kind of commercial aural travel-consumption, where the festival, with its collections of 'representative' musicians, assembled from 'remote' corners of the world, could be a reconstructed version of the Great Exhibitions of the nineteenth century. Womad gatherings have for the past decade offered musical 'multiculture' sampled according to the ethnic marketing categories which pass for intercultural relations today. The theoretical importance of an investigation of this would be in the conjuncture of local studies in a global context, addressing the potential for cultural creativity and political activist work within an international media economy.

Although there is space within the Womad ensemble for more 'traditional' forms of South Asian music such as bhangra or Qawwali, in the UK today it is post-bhangra performers who are in the ascendant within the Asian popular music scene. Thus, Womad is a venue for several different, but complementary forms of Asian-influenced musical production, ranging from folk bhangra to urban punk jungle sounds, yet before the audience and in the eyes of popular commentators and critics all these forms can too easily fall into a traditionalism mitigated only by an eclectic global sampling. A comment from one of the Nepali mask-wearing members of the 'trip-hop' band, Transglobal Underground (TGU), illustrates: 'World Music for me is anything from "Headbutt" (a band who use bass players, fire extinguishers and shopping trolleys) to Dimi Mint Abba. The term has been misused to refer to anything liked by old hippies in sandals, but to me, it's a street level vibe' (Man-tu, TGU). Natasha Atlas, the front person for Transglobal, wanted to distance world music from terms like 'traditional' which were 'corny' and 'an imitation of something that belongs in the past' (Atlas, TGU). Yet much of the Womad festival's attraction relies upon exactly this 'traditionalism' (or primitivism, see Hesmondhalgh 1995), placed alongside more explicitly 'contemporary' cross-over acts like Transglobal, to sell its global package. (Hesmondhalgh notes a bevy of terms: radical global pop, global techno, ethnic techno, ethno-trance, tribal dance, world house and world dance fusion, this last is his preferred choice to describe Transglobal Underground.) Womad's more explicitly cross-over acts often come from the UK, but there is an unacknowledged hierarchy factored into the preferred Womad mix – not too much old style, not too much cross-over: what some would call easy-listening.

It is through Womad or similar festivals that Asian musics in Britain gain 'mainstream' exposure. Without these events it is likely that the only 'known' Asian performers would be Apache Indian and Sonya Aurora Madan from the indie band Echobelly. Womad brings acts to Britain that would otherwise not be widely seen, and in this sense it serves a progressive and explorative, innovative role unlike any other organisation in the UK. It achieves this, according to Natasha Atlas, because 'the world is getting smaller'. Hence Atlas wants the music of Transglobal to 'cross over to as many cultures as possible' (Atlas, TGU). Cross-over. One of the first impressions of Reading I have is that audiences today are largely uncritical of world music. In the face of what must be a largely incomprehensible exchange, however much Qawwals or bhangra or whatever can be described as being able to cross over, it is stretching the notion of the universal language of music and rhythm a little to think that there are no lacunae here.

Surely there is something more to it than intercultural harmony and surely there are contradictions which might evoke consideration of the politics of difference? How is it that white British performers can wear Nepalese masks on stage, abstracted from their social cultural context, without critical comment? Such a global sampling has come to be accepted as 'normal', as a part of the benefit of global communications, as a consequence of a 'smaller world' and as something that mass audiences can comfortably appreciate on a sunny weekend (at a 'reasonable' price, where festivals are sponsored by beer corporations). This marked absence of any audience anxiety (compared to the anxiety for authenticity of anthropologists and ethnomusicologists) is particularly perplexing at a time of increased awareness of the politics of music in Britain – at least since the Criminal Justice Act's legislative banning of 'rave' music festivals at which 'music characterised by a succession of repetitive beats' is played (see Chapter 3 for discussion).

Womad festival in Reading offers the commercialisation of everything, where stalls set up in a circle around the perimeter of the festival site sell multicultural fast foods (rapid ethnicities of the gullet), political persuasions – from aid for Indian wells to petitions for Tibet (no organised left parties), campaigns to defend the cassowary from poachers to John Pilger speaking tours about Indonesian aggression in East Timor – and Womad merchandise (the Womad CD, the Womad book, magazine, t-shirt, cap), as well as sundry other merchandisers – often hardly distinguishable from the stalls and displays for various political causes – selling everything from oriental rugs to brass coffee-pots, jewellery, candles, incense, anarcho and techno small-label recordings, and even a weird drumming puppet rhino 'drumming up' support to save soon-to-be-extinct species.

It should not be thought that I am hostile, or mocking attempts to raise awareness about the plight of various mammals designated as aphrodisiacs, meat or game in less liberal cosmologies, nor that the campaign to expose Indonesian military atrocities, as funded, supplied and alibied by Western governments, is without urgency. The problem is that some point of connection and organisation seems missing in this context, and inappropriate 'appropriations' and half-understood orientations seem more the norm despite the best of intentions. No one seemed too embarrassed at the irregular dancing of the waif-like hippie woman spiralling in front of the devotional Islamic Qawwals of Hussain and Party: at the same time no one seemed to want to join in with her despite her exhortations to the crowd to 'get up and dance'. The importance of this performance for Hussain and Party, however, is a possible recording contract with Womad's Real World label, and an appreciative audience of Western buyers (a segment of the market not to be ignored). The Bauls of Bengal attracted a similarly curious and appreciative audience – a most cynical understanding of the audience– performance relation here would assess performances only on the criteria of whether or not the crowd can tap their feet and sway to a rhythm. I am particularly interested, and even 'anxious', about the appropriations, and questions of appropriate behaviour, in such a scene where authenticity operates through incomprehension and fracture of context.

Real World record company marketing of essential exoticas is the staple commercial angle of Womad. Working for Real World can be no easy task for the A&R reps and design-wallahs, because of quite inconsistent and differing demarcations of the authentic and the complications arising from having multiple 'national' musical traditions – so that Bauls of Bengal occupy a genre which sits uneasily alongside Qawwali and UK Asian rap and no clear-cut resolution into traditional and modern is plausible (not even the 'traditional' classical Indian forms are so neatly traditional in this context). Womad seems to maintain a form of nationalist cultural essentialism that must remain blind to the inconsistencies of its own designations. At this time cross-over articulates as world music, which in white hands often also loses its political edge. Yet Gilroy suggests that in the late 1970s it was the reggae of Bob Marley which provided a cross-over music able to articulate a critique of colonialism and repression, and which gave young audiences in England a chance to 'make sense of their lives in post-imperial Britain' (Gilroy 1987: 171).

Gilroy suggests that the possibility for some UK post-punk and ska bands to take up this cross-over work was short-lived, but perhaps this needs more careful consideration (see Chapter 6). The influence of (small) initiatives, such as Public Image Ltd, continues to percolate throughout the scene in the 1990s in diverse forms such as techno, dub, jungle and trip-hop. Understandably, in the context of a book written during the first half of the 1980s, Gilroy seems bitter at the loss of up-front cross-over which gave way, after Marley's death, to 'a new wave of post-punk white reggae musicians' (Gilroy 1987: 171). He directs his barbs elegantly at a target symbolically appropriate for all that came with the election of conservative government in Britain, 'The Police':

> The best known of these [white reggae bands] inverted the preconceptions of Rasta by calling themselves The Police and armed with 'Aryan' good looks and dedication to 'Regatta de Blanc' served, within pop culture at least, to detach reggae from its historic association with the Africans of the Caribbean and their British descendants. (Gilroy 1987: 171)

Whether or not The Police can be held responsible for this disarticulation, there was a period in which white musical hegemony again asserted itself through appropriation of non-European rhythms. The long tradition of appropriation reaches back to before even the early Beatles and Rolling Stones began playing that devil negro music unashamed. Nevertheless, whatever the antics of Jagger and Richards and co., there is reason to think that the protest politics of reggae and punk were not lost forever in the bland of The Police, and indeed return with hip-hop, house and techno in another cycle in the late 1980s and early 1990s. Whether or not this is encouraged or corralled on the Womad stage is another matter altogether.

In asking questions about how certain forms of music come to be designated and promoted as world music it is necessary to provide a critique of a number of institutional levels at work conjointly: (1) the commercial manufacture of the genre 'world music' and commercial considerations within the mainstream music industry; (2) the parochialism and biases of the 'mainstream' music industry and its public; (3) the influence of certain individual entrepreneurs, Western or not, with a 'foot in the door' of the music industry; (4) notions of tradition and authenticity, as maintained by the media, and often deployed by 'world' artists themselves; (5) the wider context of international politics, market forces and imperial relations; (6) exoticism, new-age-ism, the tree-fetish lifestyle-hippiedom and feral/folk market opportunism which provides cottage-capitalist support for the 'Womad' sector; (7) cyclical media ethnic feeding frenzy, lack of interesting rock-and-roll, we'll-try-anything-once experimentalism, commodification of everything, etc.; (8) technological development, in the music industry and in communications and transportation, facilitating the performance of those from faraway locations, their recordings distributed worldwide, their images beamed globally via satellite television.

The political task of a reading of Womad at Reading might include attempts to ascertain levels of educational and organisational impact, against commercial gain and consumption of target audience. The possibility of identifying what could be called 'cottage capitalism' throughout the Womad ensemble is real – punters browse past tent-stores and campaign tables as they would past display windows in shopping malls. Music from the corners of the world is provided as unique entertainment in the same way that food or clothes work like wallpaper, in endless aural, visual or tasty simulacra. What sort of coherence might be found in the different politics on the display tables remains unclear: some sign a petition or buy a badge to wear upon their lapel, or scarf or funny hat. Many more buy funny hats – and express an 'alternative' appearance and a well-cultivated grunge fashion (several varieties thereof). Honest and intense activist commitment also coincides with such lifestyle shopping. It could seem that the struggle of musicians and artists from the South to be heard amidst this din offers a metaphor for the cacophony of all world struggles drowned out in the on-the-spot reporting of CNN *World News* – on screen, but not heard.

A CNN report on Womad in 1994 stressed little of the grassroots politics and made much of the most 'exotic' of the musicians – the band Hussain Qawwals were shown in detail, with the requisite CNN correspondent speaking over the top of their image. The reporter celebrated Womad as an example of human harmony and togetherness, and the tone was one of tribute to the organisers and the people who attended. The one non-musical aspect of the event mentioned was an aid collection for hospitalised children in Bosnia. Such liberal music politics and Womad's breadth, from CNN Bosnia relief to cassowary campaigns, has been noted before: 'It is more than a coincidence that the development of charity rock, with its primary focus on Africa [Band Aid, Live Aid, etc.], paralleled the emergence of "world beat", a marketing category dominated by African and African-influenced sounds' (Garafalo 1994: 286).

What this restricted and edited marketing of 'oppositional' cultures does is to bring contradictory impulses into the happy relationship of a capitalism that can sell – and usually neutralise – everything under the sign of value. Everything can be equated to everything else (the beat of authenticity stimulates the rhythm of charity). The efforts of intellectuals to facilitate the entry of marginal discourses, like black musics, into the commercial and public sphere are fraught with exactly this contradiction – one that is shared with both the impulse to charity and the sponsorship of the state and of CNN itself. Despite all good intentions, the consequences are often inevitably incorporation and co-option because there has been no disruption of the overarching system. Another aspect of this double-play is taken up later in this chapter, where I argue that Gilroy overstates the role of performance in his analysis of black cultural forms (Gilroy 1993a: 75). While his enunciative stress is quite sound against textual narratives, it seems less useful to let this displace attention to mediatised forms of articulation and the role of the technological.

The problem of the privilege of live peformance is complicated, since it is often acknowledged that tele-technological flows (of which CNN is part) are essential to Womad's commercial success. Artists do, of course, want to sell their products. A complicated choice is marked out for any evaluation of world music by – to take one possible formulation of the parameters of this debate among many – Wallis and Malm (1984/1990) who (excerpted in the collection *On Record*) note first of all that:

> Music industry technology has found its way, in a very short time, into every corner of the earth. Both software and hardware can be found in even the remotest village in every country, irrespective of social or economic system. No other technology has penetrated society so quickly – what is more the rate of penetration appears to be accelerating ... [so that we also now see that a] transnational form of

nationless culture develops. Through a process of integration and concentration ... At the same time, the amount of music in our environment has increased to such a level that, even if a saturation point has not been reached, it is getting harder to experience silence! (Wallis and Malm 1984/1990: 161)

They also hold out optimistically against the transnationalisation of culture, because:

This scenario, however bleak it might appear at superficial glance, is not entirely negative. The sound cassette [for example] has given thousands of people the opportunity to hear more music. To a certain extent users can decide what music they want to hear ... cassettes can even be used for recording the sound of the small peoples themselves. The very accessibility of music industry technology has brought about another common pattern of change, particularly noticeable in smaller cultures. It has provided the prerequisite for a counterreaction against the transnationalization of music – even if no local music cultures have been totally unaffected by international music products. (Wallis and Malm 1984/1990: 161)

Despite some uneasiness about the propriety of metaphors of 'accelerated rates of penetration' and the rather ridiculous ethnographic recovery project phrasing about 'recording the sound of the small peoples themselves', the two poles here set out opposed uses of music technology: both as a force for the homogenisation of culture, and as an opportunity for resistance and creativity. The difference sketched in this model is between the integration and concentration of the music industry to the point of saturation ['any music may now be heard any time anywhere' (Simon Frith, personal communication)], and the counter-reactive possibilities of the cassette, user choice and local music cultural resistance to transnationalisation.

These two ends of music technology, and the concomitant imbrication of such technologies with socio-economic and political questions about the technological expansion of the international market and/or the possibilities for autonomy within or against this, have also exercised many writers, critics and the practitioners themselves. There is still much to be said for a critique of technologically rampant capitalist expansion. Although nostalgia sits less easily among wary critics, the music-as-alternative narrative is alive and well. Laments for a pre-industrial music manifest in many ways, not least of all in the rhetoric of

Womad, even at the very moment when it is the technological extension of market economies that is the ground of possibility upon which it is staged. Widespread familiarity with 'Indian' music, from Ravi Shankar at Woodstock to Nusrat Fatah Ali Khan on the Real World label, would not be possible without this extension. The technologies of capitalist music export Hindi film songs to communities in Britain, Canada, the USA, Australia, Fiji, Mauritius, Malaysia and so on and on – it is almost a cliché to mention this.

Popular Culture

The parameters of a discussion of world music might be recast in terms derived from the much maligned Adorno if we take up his comments on popular culture. What is important in Adorno's discussion of the Culture Industry is his interrogation of the relations between mass culture and capitalist imperatives of profit; he notes that with mass production in the Culture Industry 'cultural entities are no longer *also* commodities, they are commodities through and through' (Adorno 1991: 86, my emphasis). This comment, in an essay written to 'reconsider' the culture industry argument, maintains an uncompromising and unpopular position that exposes novelty and difference as illusion and commodity fetish (Adorno 1991: 87). There is a homology between a focus upon the skeleton of sameness behind commodity differences and the critique of 'hybridity' which, along with a questioning of the authority to comment of the critic, is offered below.

Scott McQuire argues that Adorno and Horkheimer have been used in much recent media theory as 'convenient whipping posts':

> A quick reference to *Dialectic of Enlightenment* today suffices not only to dismiss it, but also to counterpoint the 'advances' of contemporary theory with its (enlightened) concern with popular culture and audience ethnography. (McQuire 1995: 203)

Singled out for attention is the work of Mark Poster who refers to Adorno's 'revulsion' for popular culture. The litany against Adorno has it that he is motivated by a 'disgust for the common' (Poster 1994: 63), sees no worth in the products of mass media and sees them as homogenising rather than as potentially democratic (I am paraphrasing here). This is to give 'short shrift' to Adorno, as McQuire notes:

> Even in such a pessimistic text as *Dialectic of Enlightenment*, Adorno

and Horkheimer are less monolithic in their analysis than Poster suggests. While frequently scathing towards popular culture, they nevertheless grant the culture industry a positive role as the dialectical corrective of 'serious art'. What stalls the dialectic is neither the mass nature nor the technological mediation of the culture industry, but its gentrification ... One might well dispute their analysis, but this should not mean simply ignoring their attempt to relate these different domains, instead of declaring an absolute preference for one over the other. (McQuire 1995: 204)

Poster fails to understand, McQuire argues, the full significance of his own citation of Adorno and Horkheimer's analysis of 'the twin scourges of the twentieth century': the Culture Industry and fascism (Poster 1994: 57) – or in McQuire's gloss, of 'Hollywood and Hitler' – not that Hollywood was fascist, but rather that it is a mistake to think that fascism was 'simply an exception to the political culture and the political rationality of modernity' (McQuire 1995: 205). Such a discussion plays out across the all too easy acceptance of a strict opposition and incompatibility between democracy and fascism, and leads to serious errors 'when relating social and political transformations to transformations in technologies of representation and communication' (McQuire 1995: 205). The standard reference here is to Hitler saying that the National Socialists would never have conquered Germany in 1933 without the loudspeaker (but also see Visvanathan's play on this regarding Gandhi in Chapter 8). Interestingly, Adorno and Horkheimer note that it was by disseminating certain buzzwords like, say, 'blitzkrieg', that the power of this loudspeaker was brought to people's attention on both sides: they add, 'The blind and rapidly spreading repetition of words with special designations links advertising with the totalitarian watchword' (Adorno and Horkheimer 1944/1979: 165). The point is that debate about technological change and the music industry's homogenising effects are not simply consequences of cassette availability, of hardware and software, but parameters that need to be placed in political context.

There are reasons to be less sympathetic where Adorno gets denunciative of jazz as a 'cult of the machine' which 'necessarily implies a renunciation of one's own human feelings and at the same time a fetishism of the machine such that its instrumental character becomes obscured thereby' (Adorno 1941/1990: 313). But what is denounced here is not the machine *per se*, but the subjugation of human feeling to instrumental ends. There are, conceivably, other possible instrumental uses for these machines, but it is the domination of the commodity system of the Culture Industry that is prominent here. Adorno is not denouncing machines or culture, but rather, capitalist production – Poster conflates these.

This conflation is not only a fault of apolitical postmodernists. Reception of Adorno is skewed on all sides, and seems to exact a damning punishment for the presumption of calling entertainment and commodity desire to account – even those arbiters of critical theory fashion who should have been comrades appear keen to dissuade close attention to the specificity of his critique. Jurgen Habermas warns that Adorno and Horkheimer were too Nietzschean (Habermas 1987: 120), translators such as Ashton elide Adorno's Marxism and references to communist co-thinkers from the English version of his *Negative Dialectic* (reading 'exchange system' as 'barter' and turning Adorno's rival Karl Korsch into something of a non-person), and even Fredric Jameson, in his study of Adorno called *Late Marxism* (1990), wants to reconstruct him as an avatar for postmodern times.

By contrast, Robert Young points out (Young 1995: 30), that Adorno's understanding of the relation of high art to popular culture is more complicated: both coexist in a dialectic, he quotes:

> both bear the stigmata of capitalism, both contain elements of change ... both are torn halves of an integral freedom, to which however they do not add up. It would be romantic to sacrifice one to the other. (Adorno et al 1977: 123, Adorno's letter to Benjamin, in Young 1995: 30)

It may also be a kind of idealism to think that the adding together of these two, plus the removal of the stigmata of capitalism, would bring 'freedom', but as with Lukács' notion of free creativity, it allows an opening for evaluations of cultural production in terms of a movement away from the reification and alienation of human production under capitalism, towards liberation. What cultural life would be like after the abolition of the market cannot be specified in advance, but unlike most discussion of culture, which operates an impossible relativism, here is a perspective that gives at least some criteria for making judgements of the avowed 'cultural politics' and egalitarian popular intent that lies behind the idea of Womad as global musical celebration.

So is it possible to ask in a new way (in old Adorno's way) what is the political achievement of a Womad cultural politics that sees people like Nusrat Fatah Ali Khan and Bally Sagoo collaborating on 'cross-over' production for the Asian and Western market with a degree of success that attracts the attention of music industry majors like Sony-owned Columbia Records (who offered Sagoo a £1.2 million deal in 1994)? Much of the trajectory that launches certain musics into the market is attributable to the visibility of these artists provided by the commercial arm of Womad. Is this a part of a dialectical creation of a space for something 'liberatory' that may escape the dominance of commodity fetish forms? There are those who would valorise the success of Bally Sagoo as the creation of an Asian presence or 'space' within mainstream public culture. Here Sagoo's music itself takes on a fetish character – it offers an abstract or spectacular negation of mainstream music and its racially marked exclusions, but it does so through the capital market itself.

While it is still possible to imagine the oppositional use of certain commodities – and the illegal festivals of the anti-Criminal Justice Act campaign offer an example – the practical and material negation of the social relations of capitalism requires more than this. I would argue that Sagoo's 'Asian space' is a space wholly within the commodity system and is not in any way a necessary dysfunction or disruption of that system. Such dysfunctions there may be, and the promotion of Asian underground junglist and 'original nutter' UK Apache may be an example of a performer less easily accommodated within the music industry machine, but this too is insufficient challenge.[1] The potential for any oppositional politics seems wholly curtailed under the auspices of Sony Corp, even though the contract signed with Sagoo included clauses which, according to the artist, guaranteed against any compromise on 'Asian' content. This ghettoisation of purity and authenticity serves only to corral the 'ethnically' marked performer yet again. The double play, wherein space claimed for cultural expression becomes a constricted and restrained space within a wider system, is the recurrent theme of co-option.

Hybridity-Talk

In this context it is instructive to look towards what contemporary commentators might make of it all. Hybridity, diaspora and postcoloniality are now fashionable and eminently marketable terms. The authors who deploy them as key concepts have become the institutionalised social theory equivalent of household names, marketed with a brand recognition that is an advertiser's dream. In many ways they have broken new ground and forced reconfigurations and reappraisals that have enlivened and irrevocably transformed academic debate. Yet at the same time the transformations introduced seem also to have left the system intact. The point of taking a critical stance towards the deployment of these terms is not to insist upon true historical antecedents or debates about strict reference that would, for example, trace the term diaspora back to Jewish, Armenian, Greek, Indian, Chinese, African or even Black Atlantic units. The point is to question how these terms gain contemporary currency in the universities, academies, disciplines, history, publishing, political and social forums where things seem to carry on as if by remote control. Although we see a championing of experimentation, creative collage and multiple identities, it could be argued that the new contexts remain conventional: the same routines rehearsed, well-known tunes replayed – which is to say that the radical critiques signified by these celebrated names soon turn oxymoronically into 'new conventions' of scholarship and our valorisation of these critiques sometimes comes to nullify critical thinking itself. The same old record.

Or perhaps more confusing yet, the celebration of hybrid cultural activity promotes a seemingly rampant and chaotic mode of creativity. This in itself would be no problem if it did not also allow an abdication. In the context of a valorisation of mix, creole, mulatto and mongrel emergence (these are not *quite* the same things), it sometimes happens that a lesser place is accorded to intentional and targeted forms of politicised cultural production, ignoring both resistance to specific structural and institutional constraints and the almost inevitable hegemonic incorporation of random creativity through diffusion and dispersal of difference and its marketability. In this context the *political* work of bands like Fun^da^mental (who are regulars at Womad events) or ADF, can be obscured by a focus on the hybrid nature of their productions. Yet, hybridity-talk in favour of wild creativity and transnational, inter-racial, intercultural, hybrid mix could become interesting when conjoined to a political programme of the kind that ADF produce (this is discussed later in this chapter and in Chapter 7).

For pseudo-progressive, conservative (multiculturalist) forces, the convenience of this moment is clearly the fun and creativity, even radical cool, of fusion forms. What most often seems to be taken from the critical discourse of hybridity and diaspora are those aspects which repackage and reinscribe difference, juxtaposed exotica (hybrid as exotically mixed) and otherness as marketable categories. This is the appeal of someone like Apache Indian. Interestingly, then, hegemony, despite its homogenising cultural reach, now accommodates (circumscribed and carefully marketed) cultural differences. Difference within the system is the condition and stimulus of the market – and this necessarily comes with an illusion of equality, of many differences, and in the bastardised versions of chaos politics which results, the image is of 'crossed' cultural forms merely competing for a fair share. Among things that are forgotten here is the fact that it is often embourgeoised groups that can avail themselves even of the space to articulate a demand to go to market. In this respect, hybridity-talk might also be suspected of a collusion with state policy-making in that one of the things it can sometimes be is a call for access – a recognition that certain otherwise marginal, overlooked or previously excluded activities are now creative cultural practices of sufficient merit to attract a small share of Arts Council funding, state subsidy, commercial acclaim and critical attention.

Hybridity-talk, creole and so on, seem to imply a bogus notion of the prior and the pure – pre-hybrid cultures. This is a consequence that is inadequately solved by the insistence that all cultures are hybrid, since this is well and good in theory but is not the case in the face of absolutist and essentialist groupings and ideologies. Common parlance assigns hybrid cultural production to the – usually ethnic – margin, thus implying a wishful vision of future integration into a supposedly homogeneous West. For too many, South Asia remains a site of mystery, aroma, colour and exotica, even when it appears in the midst of Britain. In highlighting such themes, hybridity-talk obscures the aporias of official multicultural policies and, through inaction, in effect gives an alibi for the over-policing of inner-urban Britain, excessive and racist immigration control and the maintenance of white privilege in education, the workplace and the public sphere.

Stuart Hall identifies what he calls 'the end of the innocent notion of the essential black subject', recognising that a politics of representation has opened up an important, and ongoing, debate. If I read his argument correctly, his most crucial point, and the source of my troubles with it, declares: 'What is at issue here is the extraordinary diversity of subjective positions, social experiences and cultural identities which compose the category "black"; that is, the recognition that "black" is essentially a politically and culturally constructed category' (Hall 1996: 443; see also his 1989, 1995). It seems to me that this point is as important as it is banal. Was this really something that was not recognised by all except the most trenchant dogmatic participants in political struggle? In any case, what now needs to be debated is whether or not this recognition of the *constructed*-ness of the category 'black' and its political importance is any less constructed than any other categories, and if so, what it means to become less 'innocent' and 'essentialist'. What sort of politics flow from this? – as Hall also asks. The recognition of diversity that Homi Bhabha has denounced (Bhabha 1988) as the relativistic tolerance of exoticising multiculturalism is not that far away here – it could certainly slide into play in the hands of some commentators who can see a gain in such usages of anti-essentialism. Further, the slippage from a critique of an innocent homogenising politics to a further essentialising refraction is a real possibility. This politics may not be so innocent, tempered as it was, or is, in a common experience of racism. Sanjay Sharma argues that political identification with the category black need not mean that being different, or Asian, or Afro-Caribbean, or a woman, or working class or whatever, is incompatible with such a black politics (see Sharma 1996). Nor need the politics of black dissolve on the recognition that not all black people are the same. It is, as Hall notes, still no easier to 'build those forms of solidarity and identification which make common struggle and resistance possible' (Hall 1989). Yet the slippage that would make this task more difficult would be one that extrapolated negatively from premature declarations of the end of an 'innocent notion of the essential black subject' (Hall 1989), taken to mean the end of any black subject position in politics. This latter need not dissolve so fast.

Hall notes that 'some sectors of the mobile (and mobile-phoned) black youth' have taken advantage of Thatcherism and the enterprise culture of 1990s Britain, while 'a particular variant of black cultural politics' which had to do with campaigning, representations and media 'has had its cutting edge blunted in the 1990s' (Hall 1995: 16). This rightward shift, which goes along with the general trend of much cultural 'politics' in Western nations, corresponds to the one aspect of multiculturalism that Hall would applaud: 'the racial and ethnic pluralisation of British culture and social life'. This process is 'going on, unevenly, everywhere' and through television and other media the 'unwelcome message of cultural hybridisation' is being brought into 'the domestic sanctuaries of British living rooms' (Hall 1995: 18). The same process can also be seen going on in youth culture where 'black street styles are the cutting edge of the generational style wars' (Hall 1995: 22).

Hall wrote that 'black popular culture of the 1990s was more internally differentiated, by locality, neighbourhood, generation, ethnic background, cultural tradition, political outlook, class gradation, gender and sexuality than [older] models allow. It was far less "collectivist" in spirit' (Hall 1995: 16), and there can be no doubt that popular culture can be characterised in this way. But when he refers to those many people who 'are still trying to capture its [the dark side of black popular culture] contradictory diversity within older cultural models, honed mainly in the 1970s' (Hall 1995: 16), the suggestion that the black politics of the 1970s was superseded fails to escape his declaration that he is not trying to periodise. Diversity is now recognised, and older models were inadequate. But surely this does not necessarily mean abandonment of any 'collectivist' spirit since one can retain this and still be differentiated, by locality, neighbourhood, generation, ethnic background, cultural tradition, class gradation, gender and sexuality – as if it were ever any different in the 1970s? To imply that the 1970s was a time marked by only a collectivist black anti-racism would seem to underplay the political and cultural currents that enabled these differentiations to come to notice in the first place.

Gayatri Chakravorty Spivak says that a critique of hybridity is relevant at the present moment because that which hybridity-talk was useful for (for example, fighting the cultural absolutisms of racism in the First World) now tends to inhibit other, also necessary struggles demarcated differently. She suggests that as hybridity implies as its logical extension the hybridity of everything, this means also that contradictions and struggles that were in a certain way prior to those raised around the term still require urgent attention – imperialism, capitalism, exploitation, oppression. She argues that a negative word from socio-biology, hollowed out and reclaimed, is politically useful as a position from which to question the racism of the culturally dominant. But it is 'troublesome since it assumes there would be something that was not hybrid, or if you were to say that hybridity is everywhere, irreducible, then all of the old problems apply' (Spivak, Keele seminar, 1995).

Hybridity-talk is certainly useful in bringing to attention the ways in which cultural constructions can maintain exclusions. But why talk hybridity now rather than a more explicitly radical language? Another way to state this more bluntly is to ask why some 'postcolonial' discursive efforts seem to do very well at avoiding any discussion of Marxism, or indeed can even be considered an elaborate displacement, a way of keeping Marx out of the academy at a time when a materialist method has been never more relevant? The ways in which hybridity displaces other languages, and other ways of seeing and organising, deserves attention. Young's work suggests that something could be said for taking the meanings of hybridity away from the previous century's 'miscegenation' discourses, but this political project seems too often to have given way to an analysis of textual construction. As with Hall, a pro-hybridity stance does not seem to me to offer any guarantees of a revolutionary project, since the place for articulation of hybridity is also a space which already seems all too easily articulated with the market. Hybridity and difference sell; the market remains intact.

My charge against hybridity is thus that it is a rhetorical cul-de-sac which trivialises black political activity in the UK over the past 30 years, diverting attention from the urgency of anti-racist politics in favour of middle-class conservative success stories in the Thatcher-with-a-*bindi*-spot mould. What this means is that, rather than continue to fight for a solidarity amongst anti-racists and anti-imperialists, building upon the histories of those struggles of the 1970s and 1980s, the fashion for hybridity theory takes centre stage. Theorising hybridity becomes, in some cases, an excuse for ignoring sharp organisational questions, enabling a passive and comfortable – if linguistically sophisticated – intellectual quietism.

Despite this, some might have thought that a plausible approach would have attempted to make sense of phenomenon like world music, Womad and the new Asian dance musics via an operationalisation of the terms 'hybridity' and 'hybrid cultural production'. To ask if hybridity is helpful in elaborating explanations of world or South Asian musics at the same time would offer a chance to make an evaluation of this recently rehabilitated theoretical construct. However, hybridity is inadequate to a description, let alone an explanation, of these musics, and indeed invites celebration of bad examples in a rerun of cultural relativist unities. Abandoning the operation of hybridity, it would be a more practical political choice to begin with the terms which practitioners, and their audiences, deploy themselves in explanation of what they are doing. Of course, there are obvious problems with this – for example the way audiences, and critics, tend to internalise the commentaries provided by practitioners and offered in the music press by A&R reps and artists.

Abandoning the theoretical construct of hybridity or diaspora or whatever, would never guarantee that the analyst is also without baggage or dependencies. The point here is to commit to this political choice. Thus, beginning with the circumstances and struggle of the people involved at least circumvents any notion that an adequate politics can emerge from having the correct 'theory', as some seem to believe.

Technology and Hybridity

As with the infrastructural facilitation of world music festivalism like Womad, one of the lines of argument running through the works of Gilroy, Hall and Bhabha attributes significance to the role of technology in the production of hybrid, postcolonial, diasporic consciousness. One way to get more specific about these matters would be to critically examine the recent work of the one writer who is, perhaps, the most prominent and interesting of the varied purveyors of hybridity talk, Paul Gilroy. Gilroy notes that 'the musical components of hip-hop are a hybrid form nurtured by the social relations of the South Bronx where Jamaican sound system culture was transplanted during the 1970s', placed in this local setting in 'conjunction with specific technological innovations' and able to 'flaunt and glory in its own malleability' enough to become 'transnational in character' (Gilroy 1993a: 33). At the same time it becomes 'interpreted as an expression of some authentic African-American essence' sprung 'intact from the entrails of the blues' (Gilroy 1993a: 34). Questioning the assertive nationalism which seems to close down upon diasporic cultural forms leads Gilroy to see 'embarrassing' similarities in the practice of an essentialist black elite whose racial politics shares something with the 'pseudo-precise, culturalist equations' of the racist right (Gilroy 1993a: 34). The employment of hip-hop as symbol of racial authenticity fits a long tradition which uses music in such a register – that black people have rhythm is a stereotype found at both ends of the political score.

For Gilroy, an investigation of the 'cultural absolutism' and essentialism that attends controversies over the origins of hip-hop has to proceed through examination of the ways exclusivist notions of race, ethnicity and culture operate. What he appears to give less prominence to in his evaluation of hip-hop and black cultural histories, but which underlies much of the *Black Atlantic* argument, is a promise to reveal the transnational and technological coordinates within which these histories and identities are now played out. At the end of the book it is the idea of 'global circulation through the most sophisticated means that technological postmodernity can furnish' (Gilroy 1993a: 194) which exercises his thoughts. More work would be required here as the promise of the technological remains unfulfilled: hybrids, translations and transnationals do not all circulate in an equivalence or at the same speeds. While Gilroy might well note that 'transnational entertainment corporations unwittingly supply a vehicle for circulating these [radical black, heterogeneous, regenerative, etc.] ideas in the form of black popular music' (Gilroy 1993a: 194), it is also the case that the specific technological processes are left somewhat apart from the more literary and folksy interests and concerns of his book. An excellent formulation summarises work which is yet to be done:

> These means of distribution are capable of dissolving distance and creating new and unpredictable forms of identification and cultural affinity between groups that dwell far apart. The transformation of cultural space and the subordination of distance are only two factors that contribute to a parallel change in the significance of appeals to tradition, time and history. (Gilroy 1993a: 194)

These two factors – culture and distance – are crucially important, although Gilroy carries a strong nostalgia for the face-to-face relations of the local community and the dance hall scene (his continued valorisation of call and response restricted to this context rather than followed into technological mediations would count as evidence). It is not clear why he claims that the 'emergent culture of the black image offers no comparable experience of performance with which to focus the pivotal ethical relationship between performer and crowd, participant and community' (Gilroy 1993a: 203). This means that journals like *Black Film Bulletin*, and even Gilroy's own books, as well as numerous documentary, discursive and other mobile mediating forms, are rendered somehow invisible or transparent as constituent parts of identity formation (although they are all possibly more suited to 'ethical' relations than loud, smoke-filled, music clubs and such, however much fun).

Sidestepping the more mediatised varieties of cultural production that also form a community, Gilroy presents the performer dissolving into the crowd as his favoured example. It is the antiphonal, the communicative, the storyteller role of the musician and active listening that is characteristic and ubiquitous in the cultures of the African diaspora and which, he suggests, may make up the minimal coordinates of what should perhaps be reserved for the term 'tradition', in that these are what makes diaspora conversations possible (Gilroy 1993a: 199–200). He says the idea for much of the book *Black Atlantic* was conceived while 'watching and taking pleasure in the way that African-American and Caribbean singers would win over London crowds and dissolve the distance and difference that diaspora makes' (Gilroy 1993a: 201). It might be important to remember that these are not exclusively African pleasures – the translating dissolution of distance certainly has its Asian counterparts, Hussain Qawwals at Womad or at the Bradford Mela, for example (for discussion of this see Kaur and Kalra 1996).

When Gilroy does get around to mentioning Asian musicians, it is in terms that can be read as somewhat begrudging of Asian creativity and participation, though it cannot be ignored:

> In reinventing their own ethnicity, some of Britain's Asian settlers have also borrowed the sound system culture of the Caribbean and the soul and hip-hop styles of black America, as well as techniques like mixing, scratching, and sampling as part of their invention of a new mode of cultural production and with an identity to match. The popularity of Apache Indian and Bally Sagoo's attempts to fuse Punjabi music and language with reggae music and raggamuffin style raised debates about the authenticity of these hybrid cultural forms to an unprecedented pitch. (Gilroy 1993a: 82)

These words carry a specific tone: reinvention, borrowed, invention, attempts, debates, authenticity, unprecedented ... they are hedging words which would probably not be deployed to explain the same processes accompanying junglist innovations in the UK, so why single out Asian cultural production in this way if not to dismiss it?

Yet Gilroy's politics are usually fine.[2] He wants to 'invert the relationship between margin and centre' in a 'reconstructive intellectual labour' that examines black cultural history in a way that has 'a great bearing on ideas of what the West was and is today' (Gilroy 1993a: 45). Where such a project gets bogged down for me is in its aversion to any extended investigation of the new global tele-technological cultural conduits within a context of capitalism in crisis that recognises 'culture' over and over as hegemony and product. Cultural difference crossed with the new marketing configurations of another round of technological innovation only furthers the reconversion cycle of capitalist production in ways that could be more clearly spelled out. Gilroy continues to identify areas that would begin this critical work but he never delivers on the technology side. This does not mean his work is not the most suggestive we have in the field, especially where he points to current debates about the relationship between politics and aesthetics or about science and domination, noting that 'few of these debates operate at the interface of science and aesthetics which is the required starting point of contemporary black cultural expression and the digital technology of its social dissemination and reproduction' (Gilroy 1993a: 77). But while I agree that this is an important point, keeping in mind

Adorno's critique of the danger entailed in technological enhancement of the commodity system, I do not understand, then, how or why Gilroy immediately needs to differentiate himself from postmodernist textuality by means of what he calls an 'esoteric' interest in 'fleetingly experienced' black musical forms – most often signalled in his references again to 'antiphony (call and response)' (Gilroy 1993a: 78). The textuality he avoids is certainly well worth avoiding, but then I think it is through this esoterica that the project of comprehending tele-technological politics and the science/aesthetics nexus is also jettisoned. The question remains:

> How are we to think critically about artistic products and aesthetic codes which, though they may be traceable back to one distinct location, have been changed either by the passage of time or by their displacement, relocation, or dissemination through networks of communication and cultural exchange? (Gilroy 1993a: 80)

Surely, it is defeatist to think that technological mediation poses a threat to those long-standing, nurturing alternative black public spheres; and in a context where both the ghettoisation of black cultural production, and its extension into all areas of popular culture via the music industry, seems stronger than ever, this nostalgia appears to misconstrue what is going on. What is important is to analyse and evaluate the flows of displacement, dissemination, communication, and the hierarchies and exclusions maintained within the political coordinates of diasporic engagement with digital capitalism.

It could be suggested that an insistence on cultural particularities like the 'democratic moment enshrined in the practice of antiphony' (Gilroy 1993b: 138), the 'oral character of the cultural settings in which diaspora musics have developed', 'traditions of performance' (Gilroy 1993a: 75), and the dance hall scene, entails an anti-absolutism that produces only new essences by default and reaction. Gilroy takes pains to point out that he does not want to present the pre-modern as the anti-modern, nor to 'recover hermetically sealed and culturally absolute racial traditions' (Gilroy 1993a: 223). He is for the 'legitimate value of mutation, hybridity, and intermixture' which 'keep the unstable, profane categories of black political culture open' (Gilroy 1993a: 223), in preference to a reifying cultural or ethnic absolutism that must be rejected. He does want to evaluate not so much the 'formal attributes of these syncretic expressive cultures', but rather the problem of how critical '(anti)aesthetic judgements on them can be made' and 'the place of ethnicity and authenticity within these judgements' (Gilroy 1993a: 75). Authenticity, however, seems already marked out on a dance hall floor that has stronger roots in Africa and Jamaica than in the experiences of black politics in the UK. In this context, his comments on antiphony as a shrine to 'new, non-dominating social relationships' (Gilroy 1993b: 138) tend towards a celebration of Afro-centric particularity and ignores other cultural possibilities.

Gilroy's reluctance to work with a notion of black that includes Asian politics in Britain raises difficulties. Examining what he identifies as a 'retreat from a politically constructed notion of racial solidarity' (Gilroy 1993a: 86) in the context of the tele-technological reach of certain intellectual vanguards might indeed produce a different picture. The alleged 'retreat' asserts a 'compensatory recovery of narrowly ethnic culture and identity' (Gilroy 1993a: 86) and is most clearly visible for Gilroy in the break-up of the unity of the 'commonality' of racial subordination in the UK (for a contrary narrative see Sharma and Housee 1999). For Gilroy this legacy has dissolved as constituent elements of the previously singularly configured peoples of African, Caribbean and Asian descent 'rejected' the 'unifying notion of an open blackness' in favour of 'more particularistic conceptions of cultural difference' (Gilroy 1993a: 86). In another work he places this dissolution under the signs of hybridity and bhangra when he notes that 'there are now important signs that ... processes of cultural and linguistic syncretism are beginning to take in "Asian" culture too' (Gilroy 1993b: 61). Setting up a hierarchy and history of hybridities he prioritises Caribbean and African-American hybridity as 'no longer the exclusive raw material for cultural experimentation and synthesis', and to this prior, and by implication, original and authentic mixing he announces the emergence of bhangra which fuses 'traditional Punjabi and Bengali music with hip-hop, Soul and House' (Gilroy 1993b: 61). This description of bhangra could be contested (it having emerged well before anyone started talking about house, concurrently with hip-hop, and in a complicated relationship with soul) but it is in the capacity of these new styles to 'circulate a new sense of what it means to be British' that Gilroy finds 'these latest hybrid forms will contribute ... and take their place' (Gilroy 1993b: 62).

In 'a system of global communication constituted by flows' (Gilroy 1993a: 80), the list of tele-technological coordinates in this hybrid, diasporic, globalised and postcolonial world seems often to stand in the place of analysis – but what does repetition of this mantra add? Much gee-whiz apocalyptic tone, but little more than lists. This is not more evident than in, for example, James Clifford's surveying of 'diaspora' that recites, on almost every page: the importance of 'a discourse that is travelling or hybridising in new global conditions' (Clifford 1994: 306). This hybridisation travels across 'transnational connections'; telephone circuits; technologies of transport, communication, and labour migration; 'Airplanes, telephones, tape cassettes, camcorders'; 'business circuits and travel trajectories' (Clifford 1994: 304, 305, 306, 309, 311, 328); and then, with Clifford specifically reading Gilroy: 'Gilroy is preoccupied with ships, phonograph records, sound systems, and all technologies that cross' (Clifford 1994: 316) it goes on right up to the very last line of the article where 'global technologies' (Clifford 1994: 328) have still not been unpacked beyond this listing.

One question to be asked is whether or not we are in a position to describe and evaluate, not just list, some of these global technological processes? The telematic mantra – of information flow, new media, travelling culture and the Internet – is construed as a metonymic list which synecdochically signals both progress and change. Theorists of telematics repeatedly tell us that an intensification, abstraction and a speeding up of capitalism, financial flows, media and so on, are the defining characteristics of the current period. Is there really this intensification? A speeding up? How might the relative and abstract speeds of capitalism be evaluated? (Can there be an intensification of abstraction?) There would be much work needed to evaluate the ways tele-technological flows have, or have not, reconfigured capitalist production, cultural or otherwise. Is capitalism hybrid now? My suspicion is that a more useful line of research would examine rather an intensification of the rate of exploitation under capitalism, now reaching what Marx called the stage of the real subsumption, or what Adorno called the 'collectivisation of the world' (Adorno 1951/1974: 139). Would it not be better to attempt to understand this speeding capitalism not simply, and mystically, as a quickening, but as a change in the relations of production appropriate to a given stage of technological development of the forces of production and the logistics of exchange?

Musical Alliances

Does hybridity suggest a political programme? Why is it that the term has achieved such visibility if not through its very tameness? Is cross-over a marketing niche? Does participation in Womad, or on MTV, entail a sell-out, a betrayal of community and roots, a dalliance with destruction? Aren't cultural producers both sometimes far more politically conservative and market-oriented than hybridity-talk would admit? And aren't some cultural activists far more politically focused, and perhaps even more theoretically astute? *What would a radical hybridity look like?*

This final section of this chapter presents a discussion of the early work of Asian Dub Foundation (ADF) as an example, suggesting a way beyond the limits of hybridity-talk as the code for understandings of 'ethnic' popular culture performances. The question to ask here might be something like: does the work of ADF act only as a claim for or defence of a 'cultural' space – in the sense that Gilroy discusses, following Castells, seeing social movements as fragile resistances to domination, not political programmes? Or is there something in their work which builds alliances across the lines marked out by the critiques of essentialism and absolutism and which goes beyond hybrid, diasporic, world music politics towards a more 'stable' (Gilroy's term) transnational anti-capitalist, anti-imperialist and, therefore, anti-racist politics? I think so. The task is to untangle this politics not only from hybridity-talk, but also to explicate this politics in the context of global tele-technological flows.

Questions about the 'hybrid' conditions of production and dissemination/discussion of Asian musics need to interrogate the media and the forums in which the 'message' of Asian music such as that of Bally Sagoo, Apache Indian and ADF are received – video, television, international satellite, technologies of communication – and the ways in which scholarly interest in these technologies rarely moves beyond safe questions about representation. The globalised commercialisation of ethnicity at Womad is an important issue. Is it *post*colonial? The album, video, music recordings, performances and workshops of ADF escape any easy recuperation into world music, hybrid or fusion 'cultural' work, or syncretic postcolonial aesthetics by way of a 'transgressive' assertion of political difference.

In a short video documentary, Smita Malde has shown how ADF emerged from a music technology community workshop in East London. ADF describe their music as neither ethnic, exotic or eclectic (the only E they use is electric – 'Jericho') but, rather, a vehicle for commentary. They are closely involved with anti-racist and self-defence campaigning, especially in East London, and draw on a long tradition of Bengali musical production reaching back to the famous Joi Bangla, Joi, Joi Karma formations of the late 1980s and early 1990s (manifest in diverse projects such as music for computer games and anti-Desert Storm/Gulf War agitations).[3] ADF's inner urban 'dub' consciousness and community activism comes together in brilliant tunes and sharp lyric lines all coded around an agitation politics informed by experience and understanding of the multiple oppressions of racism, colonialism and capitalism. They comment on the South Asian presence in Britain: 'We're only here 'cos you were there. Here in England, A global village. Consequences of your global pillage' ('Debris', *Facts and Fictions* 1995).

But ADF is not only about 'conscious lyrics' ('Tu Meri', *Facts and Fictions*), nor only 'Strong Culture', another track title; their work extends to a political programme that asserts the need for new unities and alliances. ADF is visibly and intentionally 'Asian' in identification and is involved in black political groupings (in ways that might be considered 'out of date' by those who want to write obituaries for black politics). While a focus on hybridity might stop at noting that their first significant 'hit release', 'Rebel Warrior', contains multiple references to, variously, Hindi, Islam, community and the West, the message extends beyond mere multiplicity. The video for the track, filmed in London, featured schoolyard and campaign scenes that underline an upfront political intent: they point out that confrontation with racist groups cannot be shirked and requires forces combined to fight. The track is inspired by, and celebrates in its chorus, the words of Nizrul Islam's 'Bidrohi', but moves from the Ami Bidrohi of the individual faced with oppression, fighting oppression (I am the Rebel Warrior), to combined resistance and a message for all members of the community (A radical fusion ... Unity). This track was considered worthy of a return pressing five years later:

> Repetitive beats
> beating against your skull
> I'll be striking you down
> to the sound of the war drum
> The doum!
> The doum of the dohl
> taking its toll
> ...
> I am the Rebel Warrior
> I have risen alone
> With my head held high
> I will only rest
> When the cries of the oppressed
> No longer reach the sky
> When the sound of the sword of the oppressor
> No longer rings in battle
> Hear my warcry!

A radical Fusion
Strange alliance
The siren and the flute in unison
'Cos that's part of my mission
To break down division
Mental compartments
Psychological prisons

I'll be sowing the seeds of community
Accommodating every colour
every need
So listen to my message
And heed my warning
...
Ami Bidrohi! Ami Bidrohi!
Yes the unity of the Hindu and the Muslim
Will end your tyranny
Ami Bidrohi!
('Rebel Warrior', *Facts and Fictions*, Nation Records 1995, re-released on *Community Music*, London Records, Asian Dub Foundation 2000. Lyrics, Das, Pandit, Zaman, Tailor, Savale, copyright 1997 by kind permission of Universal/MCA Music Ltd)

In this fusion, strange alliance, unity – this combination of the flute and the siren – there is something that would be misrecognised and diminished if called hybrid. Hybridity itself stops short of political action, and ADF are well aware of the dangers of such condensations imposed by academic and mainstream categorisations. Yet they recognise the importance of inserting this message into the media flows of MTV, Star TV, pop shows and talk back. Albeit with some cynicism about the commercial interests of the industry (and its capacity to cannibalise talent), they want to redraw an Asian public culture along explicitly political lines, and in the interests of promoting alliances across differences. This suspicion of the media does not mean cowering before its institutional power, nor merely accepting a proffered space. A similar suspicion of other institutionally authorised make-overs of 'Asian culture' inspires an assertive cultural politics. In another track from *Facts and Fictions*, their most catchy line references just this liberal 'mental prison' that conventional ethnomusicologies, anthro-gazing and social surveillance disciplines operate. In presenting the 'patrons of culture' with 'ethnic' material, they then go further with militant active demands, and they warn the liberals:

An Asian background
That's what's reflected
But this militant vibe
Ain't what you expected
With your liberal minds
You patronise our culture
Scanning the surface like vultures
With your tourist mentality
We're still the natives
You're multicultural
But we're anti-racist.

We ain't ethnic, exotic or eclectic ...
('Jericho', *Facts and Fictions*, Nation Records, Asian Dub Foundation. Lyrics, Das, Pandit, Zaman, Tailor, Savale, copyright 1995 by kind permission of QFM/Warner-Chappell Publishing)

Any suggestion that academic work and the constructs it employs are part and parcel of a wider context which includes exploitation, oppression, racism and cultural chauvinism will not be considered new. Multiple differences are catered for (or are reduced to catering at the food stalls of Womad festival). The danger here is that hybridity and diversity become merely calls for access to the market. Diaspora and transnationalism facilitate circulation and regulation of a global, yet still hierarchical, economy.

Yet within any subsumption of culture into capitalism, the production of escape clauses, nooks and crannies of dissimulation, diversions and dysfunctions offer momentary respites which we should hope to extend, elaborate, valorise – even as so much of this is inevitably absorbed and folded within the factorium (which indeed needs resistances as a kind of motor force). There is in this observation something that goes further than the tainted creativities of hybrid culture studies. Unfixed identities are political; subversion is temporary, alliances are fluid. By new lines of alliance we might refer to those demarcations usually accepted and approved but which might be usefully transgressed – the lines that divide music and politics, the white left and Asian political groups (ADF do this), the lines between bhangra and post-bhangra, or between bhangra and hip-hop, between diaspora and local politics, between technology and tradition, between hybridity and the same. All these are the context in which the politics of 'Rebel Warrior' and 'Jericho' is part of a resistant social formation generating alliances that remake and renew the possibilities for left political practice today and (perhaps) grounding differences and knowledges in a political struggle which fosters those lines of escape, new assemblages, so that these crossed spaces of hybridity and diaspora are open to a politicisation that could blow the complacency of social theory away.

To the extent that bhangra, jungle, Womad, rave, and even house and techno in clubs, and just possibly the 'radical' aspects of rock 'n 'roll, are moments of collective subjectivity resistant or unavailable to commercialisation (and there is nearly always an element, to differing degrees, in each of these forms), then these practices can be valorised as counter-hegemonic. Subsequently these moments suffer the concurrence of entrepreneurialism, industrialisation, bandwagonism, collaboration, opportunism. And the reassertion of hegemonic order is hardly impeded by the almost complete failure on the part of critics and scholars to provide the sort of partisan analysis and vigilance against recuperation to commercialised impoverishment (more or less aided by media filtering and promotion, repressive force, industry priorities and narrow horizons). This is what Adorno called the 'admonitions to be happy voiced in concert by the scientifically epicurean sanatorium-director and the highly-strung propaganda chiefs of the entertainment industry' (Adorno 1951/1974: 38).

In the end it is worth trying to return to Adorno as a way to reconnect capital, hybridity, culture and resistance. Such a return might provide the basis for understanding the cultural politics of hip-hop and the new Asian dance music in the context of the tele-technological formations that Gilroy identifies as important but cannot describe. The key here would be to look at the ways the technological facilitates commodification of culture, and look also to those who may be capable of offering a technologically literate oppositional politics to this. A critique of standardisation, as Adorno presented it 50 years ago, would need to take into account differential production processes and short product runs, just-in-time delivery systems and niche marketing strategies, so that the standardisation of everything that Adorno feared could now be recast in terms of difference and specialisation. Adorno suggests that 'the cult of the new' is 'a rebellion against the fact that there is no longer anything new' (Adorno 1951/1974: 235), since everything is geared towards commodity production.

In a similarly structured 'new' transformation in the sphere of culture, hybridity circulates via tele-technological means (MTV etc.) carrying the markers of aesthetics and authenticity to forums like Womad, while leaving politics and political differences in the local inner-urban (subcontracting?) enclaves. The ways Womad sanitises difference into so many varied examples of a world music culture that is everywhere the same, fits the scenario Adorno described in the 1950s, where he explicitly linked work practices, and work free-time, to the characteristics of commodity culture. Adorno recognises that the culture industry has 'become total – itself a phenomenon of the eversame, from which it promises temporarily to divert people', but this diversion needs to be seen in the context of 'a system where full employment itself has become the ideal' so that 'free time is nothing more than a shadowy continuation of labour' (Adorno 1991: 168–9). Art, for example, becomes only 'one moment of material production' (Adorno 1991: 67), so is abolished along with conflict, though Adorno suggests that a 'secret omnipresence' of resistance can still be found in the 'romantic deception' of imagining culture outside production. The secret task revealed here would then be to fight for a unity of differences which refuses the show-window limits of cultural authenticity in such hybrid spaces as Womad, since these limits are incompatible with expression of political differences except insofar as these limits are transgressed, and to fight for the expression, and organisational extension, of unity within difference in opposition to capital, *even* in the forums of Womad and telematically transmitted culture.

This current from Adorno might correspond to those thoughts on the constitution of ADF (and Asian bands like Fun^da^mental and Hustlers HC) as new assemblages, formations, alliances or – in too neat a musical metaphor – a new 'composition' of forces refusing commodification and working towards a project of social transformation adequate to the contest with capitalism at this time. The task that remains is to look at how the tele-technological resources used by contemporary activists work; to look to the ways these uses constitute a resistance/refusal in the Adorno sense (rather than simply conceeding the 'unwitting' technological facillitation of cultural-political transmission – Gilroy); and to pursue the activist politics of these denizens of 'transl-Asia' (Kaur and Kalra 1996), not in order to find happy-happy world hybrid forms, but to work for that project of redistributive justice advocated by Marx ... [Of course this is just the soundtrack, which is insufficient in itself. Let's dance.]

The duty of the dialectician, as set out here, implies some organisational questions – how an organisational project alongside

Adorno would give this critique some kind of grounding – otherwise this is just a another free-floating intellectual tarot game ready to be re-absorbed – like our concepts of hybridity, postcolonial and diaspora – back into the culture industry, productive circuits of capitalist culture (studies), Womad stalls, and so on ...

In 1967 Adorno wrote that, 'Modern bourgeois cultural criticism ... finds a source of comfort in the divorce between "high" and "popular" culture, art and entertainment, knowledge and non-committal *Weltanschauung*' (Adorno 1983: 27). This view of the world seems very happy to identify differences and celebrate multiplicities, but does little in the way of organising political alliances across these differences. It is all well and good to theorise the diaspora, the postcolony and the hybrid; but where this is never interrupted by the necessity of political work, it remains a vote for the status quo. Adorno would name this as the worst of horrors, even in the hands of the best 'dialecticians' (those tenured Marxists again). To focus on hybridity, and culture, and aesthetic questions, while ignoring (or as an excuse for ignoring) the contextualising conditions in which these phenomena exist (commodity system, political relations, telematics) is to limit rather than extend our project: 'A dialectical theory which is uninterested in culture as a mere epiphenomenon, aids pseudo-culture to run rampant and collaborates in the reproduction of the evil' (Adorno 1983: 28).

Notes

1. UK Apache should be distinguished from Apache Indian discussed in Chapter 5. Only the latter was granted an MTV TV series of his own, *Apache Over India*, 1996. Bally Sagoo is discussed again in Chapter 4.
2. I return to Gilroy, with approval, in Chapters 5 and 6. My view is that his book *The Black Atlantic* (Gilroy 1993a) is the most important text published since Said's *Orientalism* (1978). What does it mean to make such an assessment critically? No doubt there are flaws, but a (sort of) new continent of thought is revealed, and a host of innovative studies are released, by this example.
3. ADF's biography is discussed in more detail in Chapter 7. Of course in a text like this the delays of publication cannot keep pace with the momentum of the culture industry and its constant demand for turnover of the same.

3
'Dog-Tribe'

'Listen conniving *haramzada* ...'
('Dog-Tribe' – Fun^da^mental, Nation Records 1994. Lyrics by
Mushtaq Uddin and Dave Watts. Published by QFM Publishing/
Warner Chappell Music)

Cultural studies approaches to political issues often seem overly eclectic
and so aesthetically obsessed, or absorbed, that the issues get obscured. It
seems to me that academic work in the social sciences has largely and
consistently ignored or misunderstood the more interesting and
important developments in British popular culture. Whether or not this
is true may be a consequence of various discipline-shaping agendas and
protocols, the vagaries of market-driven research interests (the
publishers/research council nexus), and historical-epistemological
particularities. The point is, however, that Asian cultural production,
and especially Asian youth cultural work, has rarely been a favoured
subject, and even when it has managed to find space in the academic
tableau, it has rarely been considered in any sustained political way. At
best such cultural work appears as a footnote to generational, identity
and ethnicity studies, calling for further detailed ethnographic
examination which is rarely pursued in anything but conventional ways.
In those works that do mention 'politics', examples might be cited to
illustrate a consistent avoidance. From the dilettante and neo-orientalist
fascination with cultural difference, exotica, aroma (spices) and ritual, to
ritualised acknowledgement of the couplet 'Black *and* Asian peoples of
Britain' in studies about black British cultures, it seems curious that the
political force of South Asian youth activity goes without much scholarly
attention. It is clearly not the most progressive or disinterested role of
the social sciences, however, to do de facto surveillance work on the

children of diaspora on behalf of the state. Where such work has been attempted it is revealingly difficult to distinguish old-style anthropological report-backs from protestations of 'political engagement'. As a case in point, Gillespie's study of ethnicity and music in Southall (1995), although it is conscious of power differentials between observer and observed, does not at any time break out of the formula of a reporting to the academy on the strange and exotic.

Fun^da^mental, Kaliphz, Punjabi MC, XLNC, ADF and a variety of South Asian musicians (*not* characterised as Asian Kool – the marketing category put out by music industry press like *Select, Melody Maker, New Musical Express*, inc.)[1] are political in a way that suggests an intellectual, commercial and public cultural engagement that addresses contemporary issues and – within the constraints of disciplinary topicality – are still sometimes very close to the proclaimed concerns of anthropology/sociology/cultural studies in Britain. Yet I will argue that more and more the established disciplines have been inadequate to a comprehension of sophisticated and militant social productions such as those, as a specific example, of Fun^da^mental and the controversy around the video 'Dog-Tribe'. The practitioners of the new Asian dance music have long been engaged in a politics of race, identity and cultural production – as well as making important interventions into campaigns against immigration laws, the Criminal Justice Act, anti-militarism, etc. – in a way that demands extended consideration.

The CJA

At the end of 1994 the then Conservative government of Britain passed into law a series of measures designed to curb the 'rising criminal element' in the country. The first arrests occurred in January of 1995, many more over the English summer, and then into election-conscious 1996. The Labour Party were cautious to avoid the issue as they prepared for office and more of the same. Almost without an 'official' whimper then, the Criminal Justice and Public Order Act (CJA) joined the long list of other 'tough on crime' legislation as part of a vote-conscious global crackdown best described as a 'new authoritarianism'. This new authoritarianism was manifest in a wild hotchpotch of legal clauses, and corresponding media scaremongering, and this should be understood in the context of racial and class politics in Britain, as ever.

In very brief summary, the most prominent clauses of the CJA were to ban squatting, to reduce the rights of travellers, to outlaw the activities of hunt saboteurs and to ban raves – especially where youth gather in groups of ten or more to prepare outdoor music festivities and where the music is 'sounds wholly or predominantly characterised by the emission of a succession of repetitive beats' (this is the actual Government definition – Criminal Justice Act 58.1.b).[2]

These aspects of the bill were debated in the alternative press, in the mainstream music press and, very occasionally, in the respectable broadsheets. Throughout 1994 and into 1995, left groups, and the previously ecstasy-besotted rave scene crowd, organised numerous protests and stunts to draw attention to the proposed new laws. These stunts included mass trespass on to the properties of senior government ministers, occupation of the roof of Parliament and huge, by then illegal, raves, as well as marches through the cities of London, Manchester, Leeds, Bristol, etc. The most prominent of these marches came to be known in tabloid sensationalised code as the 'Battle of Park Lane' where the famous monopoly site became host to a three-hour mounted police attack on protesting leftists (on my estimation, the police came off second best). Predictable media clean-up accusations of 'rogue anarcho-provocateurs' followed (including photofit identity pictures in the press culled from snaps taken at Park Lane calling on readers to 'shop' anyone they recognised). Other events included free festivals, occupations, weird propaganda pranks (including an excellent alternative video news service *Small World* circulated throughout various 'pirate' networks) and a wide range of loopy to ultra-left counter-establishment gestures. Important support for the anti-CJA campaigns came from benefit performances by Asian bands Fun^da^mental, the Kaliphz and ADF, as well as the presence of Aki Nawaz from Fun^da^mental on the speakers' platform at CJA rallies.

Despite 'activist' interventions, a classificatory naming system works to diffuse this kind of political work where music industry figures and 'culturally marked' bands are characterised with labels they readily reject – not just Asian Kool, but 'cross-over', world music, Asian rap, world fusion, hybrid, etc. – and much ink and air could be expended on suspect questions about the appropriateness of these terms. The question of why Aki Nawaz cannot be read politically, rather than culturally, is no idle hair-splitting. Racist, essentialist, head-in-sand nostalgias for authenticity and some sort of fidelity to racially inscribed audiences continue to arrive sometimes within academic forums. The point here would be to indicate the nostalgia of those who celebrate traditional forms of music and culture as unchanging, and who assume fixed notions of community and identity, who seem to imagine some notion of already formed 'communities' arriving off the boat as they are, and forever were. This little empire nostalgia offers the only way to talk about 'ethnicity' in Britain. Bands like Fun^da^mental blow this kind of neo-orientalism out of the water. This static survivalist view of the world assigns identities in a wholly modernist and discredited way, and which must be countered by looking to organisational and cultural dynamic and flow, and identifications formed in multiple and changing socio-political contexts.

The CJA was passed through the Parliament despite considerable 'alternative' opposition (100,000 at each of the big London rallies I attended, 25,000 in Manchester). The government ignored vocal public sentiment and pushed the Act through on the strength of its demonisation of rave fans, travellers, gypsies, squatters and other so-called anti-social elements that were considered 'criminal' in 'tolerant and democratic Britain'. Unfortunately the anti-'crusty' agenda of the Act was only a smoke screen to cover still more draconian measures to increase inner-urban authoritarian powers and police control/ surveillance of minority groups (i.e. not just the crusties and other anarchist music fans who like to dance stoned in remote fields, but almost all non-conformist, unwashed, black or working-class 'rabble'). The key *political* initiatives in the Act can be grouped under four headings: (1) *Demonstrations*: assemblies (gathering of 20 or more persons) which may 'disrupt the life of the community' may be banned by a Chief Officer of Police applying to the local Council. Not only raves, but any large-scale demonstration, such as a trade union, left-wing or anti-racist 'assembly' may be banned. Although the government argued that in practice these powers would not be used against most forms of peaceful protest, this law – in practice – relies upon unregulated police 'discretion'. (2) *Trespass*: a new offence of aggravated trespass created where people who are trespassing will be considered to have 'aggravated' their crime if they do anything to disrupt any lawful activity (i.e. hunting foxes, the government said, but this could also apply to all other forms of protest). A further offence was created under which it would be a crime for anyone to disobey a police officer of any rank who has directed that person to leave a particular area of land. A picket outside a workplace protesting against job losses which aims to dissuade people from entering the workplace (by talking to them and encouraging them to support the strike) could attract a charge of aggravated trespass and a prison sentence of up to three months. (3) *Stop and Search*: if a police superintendent or inspector 'believes that incidents involving serious violence may take place in any locality', and it is 'expedient to do so', powers to stop and search people and vehicles for a period of up to 24 hours may be authorised. Even the Home Secretary noted that this was being described as a re-creation of the 'discredited' sus laws which led to the Brixton rebellion in 1981 – an admission on the part of the Conservatives that the Labour Party promptly ignored. (4) *Anti-terrorism*: possession of items like rubber gloves, kitchen scales or fishing line may mean arrest on 'reasonable suspicion' for 'preparing for terrorist activities'. Possession of information likely to be of use to terrorists, whether or not the information is given to 'terrorists', may also attract imprisonment of up to ten years. For example, holding a list of government ministers' addresses, or those of a multinational company, might attract attention under this clause. The offence of 'going equipped for terrorism' reverses the normal burden of proof: here an offence is committed merely on the basis of 'reasonable suspicion'.

Outside black political, and communist circles there were few to challenge the attacks contained in the less publicised parts of the Act. The new authoritarian turn in Britain, in the wake of the end of the Cold War, the dismantling of the welfare state and the abandonment of any other pretence of civic equity, meant that neither of the main capitalist parties felt in a position to do anything but bring down greater repression and coercive force to maintain order and privilege. What also seems worthy of note is the strange silences of intellectuals, both academic and left-wing, in the face of this criminalisation of youth, attack on political rights, expansion of the police state, etc. Why? Most telling was the absence of any discussion of the racist elements of the CJA. It seems particularly remiss for self-appointing advocates of culture – sociologists, anthropologists, cultural studies personnel, journalists – not to have taken a vanguard position in campaigning against these measures. The happy opportunity of these disciplines, surely, is not to acquiesce to any role of compliant approval (for fear of further funding cuts) but to recognise that a role as apologists for state legitimacy is no longer an obligation, and that a critique of everything is (now more than ever) both a necessity and an intellectual requirement. Far worse, however, than the failure of public figures to question the Act is that a corresponding silence on race issues can be found even amongst those who did mobilise. While the inclusion of clauses to increase police powers in the inner-urban areas was of special concern to Asian anti-racist organisations, these aspects were rarely addressed by white middle-class activists more concerned with the attacks on raves and parties. The most political of responses from the white left took up the attacks on demonstrations, the anti-terrorism clauses and the abolition of the right to silence (a jury shall be directed to draw 'inferences that seem proper' from a defendant's silence if that defendant did not provide explanations when arrested), but rarely were the Stop and Search powers taken up as a theme – already in 1995 these powers were used in Police Commissioner Paul Condon's outrageous crack-down on 'black' muggers in London called 'Operation Eagle Eye' (see the ADF track of the same name from the album *Rafi's Revenge*, discussed in Chapter 7).

The remainder of this chapter ventures to rethink the foci of opposition to the CJA, reconsider the role of critics under capitalism, and to move with Asian critics of the CJA towards new configurations, practices and alliances for anti-racists. This will be attempted by way of a discussion of the Fun^da^mental video *Dog-Tribe* and its 'banning', and of music and political mobilisations (Anti Nazi League [ANL] carnival against the Nazis, anti-Criminal Justice Act raves), and of youth mobilisation around anti-racism, anti-government, Parliament, police and the state. A platform for this is to take up the (moral/ethical?) issues of defending defence squads (not the privatised police, but community mobilisations) as presented in the Fun^da^mental video and in the music of similar South Asian groups. A general point is to chart changing configurations of identity and engagement within political struggles in the contemporary period. Examples such as the Revolutionary Internationalist League defence of the Langdale Four and the Kaliphz involvement with Anti-Fascist Action, as well as Fun^da^mental's international media experience, configure new alliances and responses to the hypocrisies of the global factory in which we live and which might thereby offer indications of how this predicament can be reworked, reconfigured and transformed.

In broad terms I am trying to place a specific musical work in its political and cultural context and, although peripheral and anecdotal details are not excluded, the movement of the chapter from Fun^da^mental to leftist self-defence activism by way of discussion of the Criminal Justice Act as it passed through the Parliament is not just a contrivance – I am trying to exploit the contrapuntal effects of placing parliamentary discourses alongside rappers to illustrate Aki Nawaz's observation that anti-racist, anti-capitalist and anti-imperialist politics must be addressed together (at a rally against the CJA, November 1994). This chapter attempts to outline some conjunctions of research on (1) music industry/televisual assemblages; (2) parliamentary and political formations that impinge here; and (3) anti-racist assemblages.

'Dog-Tribe' – The Video

These are not easy problems and not the only ones of course. Writing about video in the language of the cultural salons for which this book is written might also be condemned – and for the same reasons the 'Dog-Tribe' video condemns parliamentary processes. Writing about video sound and image is inherently fraught. Good. This seems all the more reason to bring out contradictions in the ways academic effort has avoided confrontation in this domain – arguably a domain within which it should have significant engagement. Yet a 'banned', and so silenced, video presentation, can despite 'banning' be re-presented in certain institutionally condoned spaces (albeit an already privileged venue and audience – the not quite completely quashed liberties of bourgeois academia), and with the addition of commentaries condoned by an authority accorded in and by this re-presentative space. *Dog-Tribe* is a 5-minute, roughly edited and starkly shot black and white production telling the story of a race attack by white youth/skinheads upon a lone Asian. Its subtext charts the politicisation of the Asian youth (who happens to be Aki Nawaz, the founder of the group). The narrative begins with Nawaz painting a 'Nazis Out' slogan on a wall and he is attacked by three skinheads. They kick into him – the camera lingers too long over the violence. Three passing Asian youth intervene and chase the skinheads off. A close up of Nawaz, bruised and bleeding, spitting teeth, after the attack is also very much in-yer-face-TV. In subsequent scenes Nawaz is observed petitioning a politician – who ignores his statistics – and attending the funeral of another victim of a race attack. The presence of a silent Asian woman mourning in front of the grave passes without comment, but the main point is that a clearly organised self-defence group, who are also attending the graveside, invite Nawaz to join with them – symbolised by the placing of a scarf with Islamic insignia over his face (and over his *keffiyeh* scarf from the Palestinian Liberation Organisation).[3] The lyrics emphasise the message: 'there comes a time when enough is enough ... self-defence is no offence already'. The explicit portrayal of the horrors of racial assault, and several flashbacks stress the point that by joining an organised defence group the supposed passive Asian victim is no longer isolated and becomes an active agent: 'our defence is on attack'. The last scenes of the video show an anarchic and almost carnivalesque destruction and burning of materials and placards of Combat 18 and the BNP. A direct challenge to their activities is made: the signs 'we are waiting' and 'now is the time' are thrust at the camera.

What's the thing that makes a black man insane?
Deranged and wanna give a man pain?
Practicalities, similarities, immoralities of what you call a
racist dream.
Skin-headed warrior fightin' for the country, killing black
children, burning Bengalis. Enough is enough.
Ah ... people say I've gone and lost my mind 'cause I'm not
afraid to die 'ji'.

Chorus
The dog-tribe seeks the skin and puts them in a pound, retaliate
and you'll be six foot underground, pushin' up daisies,
'cause the devil sent you to tame me but you can't face me.
You see I grips mikes, wrex mikes, condition my mind to
finally come to terms,
Anyway wake up, wake up c'c'cos I'm on a self-defence vibe,
never down but always down with the tribe

People wonder why I'm positioned by the window
Ammunition close at hand though,
looking like the man brother Malcolm
If I can't reason, time for some action. You must hear
me though, even though they don't know,
don't ask for violence, just self-defence.
I'm on a Romper Stomper agenda vice versa,
I'm the brown one, my brother Nubian,
Followin' the ways of the days of the Nazis,
Listen conniving *haramzada*

There comes a time when enough is enough,
Afro-Caribbeans, Asians together is tuff,
our defence is on attack, minds are made up,
Bodies are fighting back. Self defence is no offence
And we're ready, ready for a collision with the opposition
It won't be a suicide mission, and one thing about me, I'm
not afraid to die 'ji'.
And after me, there will always be another brother.
('Dog-Tribe' – Fun^da^mental, Nation Records 1994. Lyrics by
Mushtaq Uddin and Dave Watts. Published by QFM Publishing/
Warner Chappell Music)

The clip, and some performances of the band, were discussed, when attention was paid at all, in predictable ways. A focus upon their Islamic symbols dominated attention, and the confrontational style raised anxieties in revealing ways. In the magazine *CARF* (*Campaign Against Racism and Fascism*) the band were described as having a 'no-nonsense anti-racist politics and commitment to Islam' (*CARF* 22: 6). This is contrasted to *Melody Maker*'s early comments on the clip which pointed to the violent nature of the images, recognised some degree of racism in Britain, but ended up repeating opinions that this was a country with 'no history of, or tolerance or capacity for, political extremism' (quoted in *CARF* 22: 6). From comments like these it would seem that the 'banning' of the 'Dog-Tribe' video was understood by the music press as a response to Islamic extremism, and there was little care or concern that political statements could be so readily erased. Powerful symbolism that scarf. Admittedly, later editions of *Melody Maker* articulated the growing youth mobilisation against the CJA, and once provided space for both Nawaz, and Fun^da^mental's Dave Watts to present critical perspectives on racism (the 22 October 1994 edition reported Nawaz's speech against the CJA outside Westminster City Hall on 19 October in a three-page article). Nevertheless, *CARF*'s analysis in this case adequately catalogues a systematic deployment of the music press against the political militancy of the band: they point out that 'articles on Fun^da^mental in the music papers are now peppered with ridiculous diatribes on the threat of Islam, and defences of Western values' (*CARF* 22: 6). Again exceptionally, and obviously responding to criticism, *NME* did manage a discussion of 'Dog-Tribe' in May which explained the track as being 'about members of the community who've had enough beatings, enough of their neighbourhoods being terrorised, and who've decided to fight back' (7 May 1994). This issue also provided a list of names and offences of known BNP identities.

In an interview with *CARF*, Nawaz points out that the politics of Fun^da^mental is not a fashion statement, nor an attempt just to make it big in the music business. The music provides a platform for a statement; in this case a video, 'that should not have been banned' (Nawaz) and should be played on daytime television to raise questions about race violence for young viewers. Nawaz also points out the importance of fighting imperialism and colonialism, which are 'all part of racism' (*CARF* 22: 7). Any suggestion that this is Islamic 'fundamentalism' requires analysis of popular panics about the threat of militant Islam, terrorism and violence that need to be unpacked in the context of media-managed new imperialist demonologies and post-

Khomeini US war-mongering. Rather than an exegesis of the meaning of fundamentalism – a favourite neo-orientalist academic pastime – it would be preferable to develop critiques of media constructions of 'dangerous' others and the way this coincides with new global instances of imperialist aggression and institutionalised racism together (the United Nations in the Gulf and the CJA in the UK both as examples along the same continuum). Such an analysis would need to investigate why a video such as *Dog-Tribe* should be 'banned', and how the mechanisms of the banning (the CJA) relate to new authoritarian turns and ongoing imperialisms.

So *Dog-Tribe appears* to be a dangerous text because of its portrayal of militant Islamic 'fundamentalist' violence. No doubt this could engage scholarly debate in another banal discussion about freedom of speech, although significantly it did not. Academics were quick to jump to Salman Rushdie's defence when it was a matter of an attack on an honoured establishment writer, however progressive, but there is a difference when it is a matter of less literary popular cultural examples of silencing, and examples where it is the British state, not an Islamic foreign power, doing the silencing. Impi D from Fun^da^mental hinted at a wider agenda in an interview: 'You're not going to solve the problem [of racism] by being civil about things. These people [fascists] don't make an attempt at dialogue. We're saying stop whinging about freedom of speech, because these people are not about free speech' (*Guardian*, 17 June 1994).

On paper the 'banning' seems to have been less a government decree than self-censorship in anticipation of such a decree on the part of MTV and ITV, the major television music video distribution outlets (and crucially important for mainstream visibility). It was decided the clip would be likely to attract an 18 certificate from the censor (under the Video Recordings Act of 1985, a supplier can be prosecuted if the video has not received an appropriate British Board of Film Classification certificate), although it is not clear that the BBFC has ever viewed *Dog-Tribe*. ITV's *Chart Show* refused the clip, and MTV chose to show it only after 10 p.m. A showing on Channel 4's *Naked City* (June 1994), also after 10 p.m., made much of the 'banning' and invited Nawaz and Sonya Aurora-Madan from Echobelly to discuss anti-racism issues.[4] The treatment on this show, however did nothing to disrupt panic reactions to televised violence. This was inevitably so even where the clip has a message considerably different from that of most restricted or 18 certificate violent cinema or television, or the widely approved *Terminator* style in which actors like Schwarzenegger or Stallone are seen blowing up buildings full of police without censure, indeed, cheered along. The point is that violent attacks upon Asian youth in Southall, East London, Bradford and other cities is something that affects the whole of the community, including those under 18, so that squeamishness about this violence, or the immediate practical necessity of self-defence, is nonsense.

Nonsense was piled upon nonsense in an escalation of white noise silencing. Instead of a frank discussion of the politics of censorship in the context of racist Britain on *Naked City*, we were treated to simplistic and partial sound bites which offered little. In a letter to *Melody Maker*, Aurora-Madan complained of being 'asked token questions' on the show (*MM*, 23 July 1994) and that the 15-minute interview had been cut to two minutes: 'every valid point that I had made had been edited out and, to make matters worse, they wasted airtime showing *pretty* shots of me ... this sort of censorship is typical of what a lot of female musicians have to put up with' (*MM*, 23 July 1994). At one point Madan refers to the 'fucking BNP' in a way that works also as a token gesture of intentional outrage, calculated to shock, and so inversely confirm, the pretty Asian girl image. In the last sentence of Madan's letter to *MM* she says: 'The media world is full of token questioning by people who don't really give a f*** [*MM* only prints the f and three asterisks]. I am learning that I WILL be misrepresented' (*MM*, 23 July 1994).

This silencing and misrepresentation of Madan (*MM* asterisks), the silencing of Fun^da^mental's message in 'Dog-Tribe' and the historical failure of the white left to hear the political concerns of the South Asian activists or to address the racial aspects of the CJA are not in-consequential parallels. Academic and journalistic protest at this censorship, meanwhile, was nowhere to be seen. Of course, it would be naive to suggest that black musical cultural production is autonomous from an ever-expanding capitalist consumer culture, which increasingly neutralises[5] and sells back 'ethnicity' and cultural difference. But the novelty of banned videos doesn't seem to translate into bumper sales for Asians in the way, perhaps, that notoriety once did aid bands such as the Rolling Stones or the Sex Pistols.[6]

The Criminal Justice Act ('Dog-Tribe' Reprise)

How does something 'cultural' like a music video come to be banned for political reasons? Apart from the 1985 Video Recordings Act, the most relevant parliamentary version of legislation under which a video such as *Dog-Tribe* might be banned is the Criminal Justice Act, specifically clauses added in April 1994 after a cursory 'debate' on racial harassment (House of Commons, Official Report, Parliamentary Debates, *Hansard*, vol. 241 – all references to *Hansard* are from this volume unless otherwise noted). The clauses cite 'publishing etc. material intended or likely to stir up racial hatred' and showing videos which 'present an inappropriate model for children' as grounds for censorship or arrest. Although similar clauses may be found in other legislation (such as the Race Relations, Public Order or Video Recordings Acts), in the context of the Criminal Justice Act these clauses make issues of inequality and prejudicial interpretation and application of the law more explicit.

During the parliamentary discussion of the 150-plus clauses of the CJA there was a symptomatic pseudo-conflict over the inclusion of amendments on racially motivated violence and harassment proposed by Labour member Joan Ruddock (Lewisham, Deptford). Labour members wanted to introduce new clauses into the bill which would increase the power of the courts to impose more severe sentences upon crimes where it could be shown that racial hatred was a motivating factor of the crime. Certain obligations on the part of the police and the courts to investigate and report on racial factors, and a new offence of racial harassment were included. That Labour argued this amendment but abstained from voting on the passage of the bill as a whole, suggests that they were more concerned to be seen to support anti-racist legislative tinkering than to defend the rights of the general population or specific communities. Mark Butler reported this as well as anyone:

> Anti racists have provided the candy coating for proposals to increase police powers. Under these powers the police in places like East London can regularly harass white youths ... and at the same time, they can continue to push around young Asians, this time on the pretext of clamping down on the 'racism' of Asian gangs too. (Butler 1994: 35)

Fine sentiment and rhetorical flair effectively achieved the opposite of what was required.

Conservative MPs were at pains to point out their anti-racist credentials as well, but were on the whole adamant that no support for the Labour bill was possible, and they proposed their own, severely truncated, amendment on the issue of publication of racist literature and increased penalties for race-related murder. Labour members made much of their desire to do 'something' about the increase of race attacks in Britain – the increase was also acknowledged by the Tories – but Labour's proposed legislation (to get the police to do something about it) was voted down 285 to 247.

An ironic summation was provided by Keith Vaz (Leicester East) who said that: 'we can all condemn racial attacks on fellow citizens, but the important thing is what we propose to do about them' (*Hansard*). This insight raises yet again the question of the efficacy of legislative measures of the bourgeois state. Earlier in the debate David Sumberg (Bury South) had railed against the 'evil in society' and the unacceptable rise of the 'hard Right' in Britain (a country he characterised as having 'always been a tolerant, just and humane society – a society that has welcomed immigrants to its shores for many years'). The 'evil', it turns out a paragraph later, is that the existing adequate laws are not being enforced properly, and that there are enforcement loopholes. The evil was to be corrected by the Conservatives' amendment, rather than Labour's new laws.

Why were both parties keen to be seen to 'do something' on the issue of race? A letter sent by the Home Secretary to the Lord Privy Seal provides an answer: there are 'intense public and Parliamentary pressures ... for changes in the law' on racially motivated crimes. The letter goes on to explain the Home Secretary's concern that 'the Government's position is likely to become untenable':

> and at the very least open us to enormous criticism, especially once the urgent measures relating to stop and search powers I intend to introduce in the bill become public [this was before the CJA was tabled in the house]. The proposed new powers are already being described in the minority press as recreating the discredited 'sus' law. (letter tabled by Ms Ruddock)

Why Labour didn't make more of this admission is not clear, but the government's motivation for doing something on racism, albeit only a watered down amendment on powers of arrest for racist publications, was exposed. The Home Secretary continued: 'It is therefore important that the Government take the initiative on racial crimes if it is to counteract the belief amongst ethnic minority communities that we do not take their concerns equally seriously' (*Hansard*). The plan was to get the CJA and its new powers through under cover of an anti-racist smoke screen which would gain multilateral support.

So, for the mainstream political parties, an anti-racist initiative means that the role of the police becomes all important. It seems that the 'evidence of a very senior officer at Scotland Yard' explained police concern that they had little power of immediate arrest to allow them to gather evidence in cases of distribution of racially inflammatory literature. Such increased powers would be of some use to the police. Sir Ivan Lawrence put it this way: 'If there is no power of arrest [in these cases], by the time that the police arrive at the premises from which they think the material is being distributed the birds have fled and all the forensic signs of their culpability have dried up and disappeared' (*Hansard*).[7] When Sir Lawrence talks about forensic evidence drying up we can imagine that he has in mind clauses 45 through 50 of the CJA which give the police additional powers to take bodily samples from persons, detained or not, with consent or not, charged or not.[8]

The debate raged on and on, and it is hardly productive to reproduce much more of its (lack of) substance. Two final curios: the Conservative amendment introduced new powers of arrest and search, without warrant, while the Labour amendment argued for a specific offence of racial harassment where a person, on racial grounds, 'displays any writing, sign or other visible representation which is threatening, abusive or insulting' (up to two years imprisonment). This last reference was to cover things such as the daubing of a swastika on a wall (Barbara Roche, Hornsey and Wood Green) – which perhaps could also be thought of as a form of 'drying forensics'. Whatever, this Labour motion was also voted down, the Conservative amendment was passed and joined to the Criminal Justice Act, and it was sent of to the House of Lords for its next reading.

The final curio from this debate was Sir Lawrence's reference to the powers of the Home Secretary to ban, and of the police to impose conditions upon, 'marches, processions and demonstrations' if it was felt that these 'might result in serious public disorder, disruption to the life of the community and so on'. He went on to note that the Act did not cover marches and processions involving race hatred and 'therefore, the police felt that they were not always able to respond to the community's concerns about marches by right-wing groups which did not, perhaps, result in violence, but which contributed to a climate of fear and hatred among the ethnic minority'. A subsequent amendment to the Public Order Act was proposed so as to cover marches invoking race hatred. Inverting the logic, Minister Lloyd objected that 'it would be difficult to argue ... that a march of Nazi skinheads down Brick Lane would stir the local population to racial hatred, but it may well cause them fear and distress and provoke angry and violent reactions' (*Hansard*). He thought the new clause did not give the police any additional useful powers but would just 'confuse' their 'operational judgement'. Sir Lawrence responded that he had in fact been asked to include the clause by the police, and said that 'if *they* do not understand the present law, what on earth is the likelihood of the ethnic minority communities in Britain understanding it?' The likelihood is that they will understand that here the Houses of Parliament are allowing the police to dictate laws, while all concerned recognise they are horribly confused. It was not a good day for democracy. Here is the Parliament discussing new legislation which will extend the material and physical might of the forces responsible for racist attack upon black peoples and the discussion circles around the painting of slogans and the question of sending videos through the post. A critique that would be adequate to an opposition to such forces – the CS gas, the batons and surveillance cameras, but also the arms factories, the institutions of discipline and correction (prison and school), and the entire ideological apparatus – needs to learn from the self-defence work of those fighting this state. Quietism in the face of such forces is forever inadequate.

The Criminal Justice Act as a whole goes much further than this minor skirmish in the politics of reformism. The incursion of legislative power into more and more aspects of all of our lives – from what we can watch on TV to DNA records – escalates. The new authoritarianism insists that everything is the business of the state. The Act has paved the way for increases in the already over-policed urban areas of Britain, it opens opportunities for a return to the late 1970s provocations of having Police Chiefs and Ministers announce that all blacks are muggers, and introduces and extends the targeting of any groups or social formations that seem set to drift outside the containment of capitalist market economics. It is this last which would explain the hostility of the Act towards otherwise unimportant small fry such as squatters, travellers and ravers. These would need to be understood as examples of public organisation and participation that were to be reclaimed, recuperated and reintegrated – by force if necessary – into everyday commerce. Hardt and Negri note that resistance to capitalism 'is no longer exercised simply in the old forms of trade union defence' in the large factories of industry, but in a period of greater politicisation of all aspects of life, 'new forms of political positioning and attack immediately address social levels of accumulation' (Hardt and Negri 1994: 210). If the commercialisation of rave via house parties, and of squatters via Housing Co-ops, was insufficient to rope in alternative economies, then police repression would be deployed. With an analysis that began with such a viewpoint it would then be possible to understand how the attacks on rave were indeed a part of combating anti-capitalist activity, which unfortunately the conservative forces understood more readily than the ravers themselves. If there had been a more concerted linking up and alliance amongst the different sectors targeted by the Act this might be a different story. In the end reformism has so far been able to prevail over any such formations.

The point of the foregoing legislative discussion is in part to illustrate the bankruptcy of reformism and the contemporary gymnastics of rightist administrations which are the dynamic of both sides of Parliament. It would also be possible to show how the reformist calls of the non-parliamentary fake-left like the Socialist Workers Party (SWP) and Militant are also counter-productive in the face of contemporary capitalism's requirements. The pseudo-management of 'race' in this legislative domain, like other reformist calls, seems always to result in more police powers. It is important to note a separation between anti-racist activity and anti-racist reformism – with this reformism fostered by late capitalism, and even integral to its productive relations (maintenance of an underclass in the Western democracies etc., despite obsolescence of trade-union/welfare state/liberal concessions). There is much more to be said on this – Westminster and democracy discourses should be examined not only for their rhetorical tropes and illusions of meaning, or, yet more tenuous, for active government effects (Parliament as simulacrum), but also as organisational and motivational sites of definition even for those who profess not to believe in, or need to work through, the parliamentary experiment. I am, however, leaving this as an opening in a discussion that moves elsewhere. The point was to illustrate the contrast and contradiction of legislative debate over against the kinds of community activity articulated by certain Asian groups.

Community Defence and Internationalism

What I want to do in this third section is take up the issue of community self-defence as presented by Asian musicians and activists in the context of anti-racism and the Criminal Justice Act. I am equating the silence of academics on the 'banning' of *Dog-Tribe* with silence on the most important parts of the CJA, and suggesting there are echoes of this in regard to the practicalities of combating racist violence today. This section takes up the left press and the explicitly anti-racist work of Asian musicians in an attempt to open and extend a space for political writing about music that doesn't simply avoid these troubles.

At a 1994 Youth against Racism in Europe conference in Germany

(YRE), debates about the relationship of activists to the police, and tactical differences over community-organised defence versus legislative controls, consumed much time. Militant Labour from Britain and their co-thinkers the Voran Group from Germany and the Gauche Révolutionnaires/Jeunesses Communistes Révolutionnaires (JCR) from France argue that the cops are 'workers in uniform' and are a potential ally in the fight against fascism. A Spartacist League (SL) cadre at the conference pointed out – in line with Marxist orientations drawn from the classics – that the police were 'a body of armed men' (Lenin 1917/ 1951) who were 'in the service of the capitalist state'. Trading insults and pamphlets the Militant/Voran group were exposed by the Spartacist League as offering support for social democracy in the guise of an anti-racism that offers nothing to the community except more police. Militant's role in the Tower Hamlets fight against the BNP, where they campaigned for Labour, confirms the SL's position as described in the pamphlet, *Militant Labour's Touching Faith in the Capitalist State* (August 1994). Perhaps calling the cops the 'paid goons of the capitalist rulers' (SL) tends towards rhetorical colour rather than analytical precision, but in the context of immediate struggle against racist attacks by the police, the state and by fascists, this is probably acceptable terminology. A slightly more reasoned presentation of this sentiment can be found in the then Revolutionary Communist Party affiliated Workers Against Racism (WAR): 'In a society like Britain, where racism is woven into the very fabric of the nation, upholding "law and order" means upholding racist institutions and practices' (*WAR News,* 12: 6).

Issues such as this raise questions about organisation in the community and the need to do more than either anti-racist conference-goers or Labour and Conservative legislators. The view of the legislature as completely bankrupt is difficult to refute as all it seems to amount to is variation in the modes of repression available to the state. In the video *Dog-Tribe* it is clear that singular symbolic gestures are considered insufficient – Nawaz is beaten as he puts a 'Nazis Out' slogan on the wall at the beginning of the clip, while in the middle of the narrative a politician is seen to ignore Nawaz's petition (a petition against the CJA was 'left on table' at the final reading). In the parliamentary debate Labour politicians kept on saying the government had to send a message out to the community that it cared. This is a message of reassurance of order – of stability and the status quo, of care, for votes, for individuals, the eternal realpolitik. Mainstream parties will not organise defence, so it is no surprise that practical activity must be taken by the community itself.

In reviewing a Fun^da^mental gig in June, David Stubbs wrote in *MM*: 'I'm at once troubled and inspired by the revelation that it doesn't matter a f*** [*MM*'s asterisks] what good intentions people like me have from now on. What's gonna happen will happen' (*MM*, 16 July 1994). The point is not whether or not audiences, white, black or Asian, think its good or not, the urgent issue is that racial violence against Asian youth happens every day and something is being done ... has been for a long time.[9] What is prominent among the various Asian bands which work closely with anti-racist self-defence groups is an awareness of the everyday complexities of face-to-face racism. There is a difference between making appealing statements in the press, showing placard and poster support for anti-racism on demonstrations through London's main streets or providing mantra-like acknowledgements for the inclusion of anti-racist education in the school curriculum, and the rather different practicalities of estate-based anti-racist defence, support of those subject to police or workplace persecution and the immediate confrontation of active fascist militants in towns like Rochdale. The no-nonsense approach to anti-racism is a far cry from the popular mobilisations for protest marches and festivals that are the preserve of Britain's orthodox anti-racism (see Chapter 6). While there are few youth in Britain today who would express explicit racist propaganda as per the BNP, Combat 18 or other fascists, and while most youth would be happy to say they believe in, and are even happy to campaign for, anti-racism, and especially 'against' institutionalised racism, there is still little that such feel-good reassurances can provide for those subject to fascist and/ or police attack. The blunt solution of the Rochdale band, the Kaliphz, would not find widespread approval from the softer elements of anti-racist badge-wearers. The lyrics of their single 'Hang 'em High' do not rely on subtlety, stating that the 'remedy for white supremacy' is to 'kill the BNP and the Klan in Tennessee':

An eye for an eye, a tooth for a tooth,
a knife for a knife and a life for a life.
Hang 'em high, hang 'em high,
hang 'em by the neck until the mutha-fuckers die
...
I'm no pacifist, I'm a pistol-packing Paki-fist.
('Hang 'em High', Kaliphz, Semtex 1994. London Records, FFRR)

The Kaliphz work to raise political awareness amongst the community and the audiences they attract. Their activism extends from involvement in the Campaign Against Militarism/No More Hiroshimas publicity, to organising community opposition to Combat 18 in Rochdale. (Combat 18 are the declared armed wing of the British Fascist movement). The Kaliphz have gone on record in support of the Anti-Fascist Action (AFA) campaign to make life hard for the Nazis wherever they appear. 'We're not scared of Combat 18. We come from a town where Combat 18 are big and they don't f*** with us. Yeah, Asians have a bad time here, but the way to stop that is by organising themselves and to stop looking for sympathy' (*NME*, 10 September 1994; guess who put in the asterisks). In the Kaliphz own newsletter the band explain that they are not Gandhian pacifists and believe in an 'eye for an eye' (*Slingshot*), but for the *NME* journalist they explain that the 'problem with retaliation is that it has to be organised', and in response to questions about the threat to innocent civilians they say 'you have to do what AFA do: find the Nazis and sort them out. We're not talking about looking for any white person in the street' (*NME*, 10 September 1994).

The Kaliphz often seem caught up in a version of macho Gangsta rapping that is testosterone-fuelled and boyz-in-the-hood aggressive, yet their record in opposition to British fascist groups is considerable. Where militancy and clout are concerned, it seems the Kaliphz have far more sophistication that any of the Blood and Honour fascist bands of the BNP, National Front and Combat 18 circuit. The Kaliphz 1995 album release with a US label had placed them on the verge of international commercial success which would hammer home their tough message. Although this success was not as grand as anticipated, their immediate political rivals from Rochdale branch of Combat 18 remain in disarray.[10]

The anti-racist group who work most closely with the Kaliphz is AFA, and it is AFA who consistently criticise avowed left groups such as the Anti-Nazi League (ANL) for calling upon Labour Councils and the Conservative Party to ban the BNP, to refuse Conservative Party membership to fascists or to reject lease applications for neo-Nazi bookshops. These are criticisms also made by the Revolutionary Communist Party and the Spartacist League under the debate title of 'No Platform?' (the question mark is significant), although resolved in differing ways – with the RCP turning towards a dual critique of institutional racism and imperialism, and offering the powerful slogan 'Ban Nothing – Question Everything' (t-shirts available by direct debit), and the Spartacist League calling for militant action (in joint action with …).[11] The RCP questioning of the SWP focus on Nazis requires them to play down fascist violence in ways that cannot endear them to those who are actually attacked, and yet the ways in which the SWP tactic of lobbying politicians invites further repressive force upon itself is clear. More police power. The major problem with the 'No Platform' stance (with no question mark) of the SWP and like groups was not just the contradiction that had oppositional groups pleading for the government to implement censorship. Although the small clutches of BNP members needed to be dealt with, the repressive apparatus of the state and the conditions that permitted the fascists to exist – such as the effective protection they receive from the police if ever they 'demonstrate' – and the more extensive, legitimised racist violence of the police and the courts, the Home Office, Customs and a variety of other British racisms, were in no way addressed by 'No Platform' calls.

To the question 'Should the BNP be banned?', put by an *i-D Magazine* journalist, Hustlers HC replied: 'To ban the BNP would make martyrs of them and they would play on it massively. Moreover, if they are forced underground, they will become more dangerous. Better the devil you know' (*i-D Magazine*, January 1994 – Asian rappers quoting Kylie Minogue!?). What is evident in interviews with these musicians is a consciousness of a zone of political engagement that cuts across the narrow focus of anti-racist groups to take on a cultural politics that encompasses everything from the names they are called, to international issues or issues of gender. On gender they take up the complicated issue of arranged marriage and argue against jumping to Eurocentric conclusions about it, in terms of names they play against stereotypes and clichés. Hustlers HC worry about acceptance by the hip-hop crowd, evoking a tendency toward forms of cultural cringe which manifest as headlines, as in *Hip-Hop Connection* (September 1994), that play on variations of 'Turban Species' and 'Sikhing to Destroy' (nobody expects the music press to be all that creative, other clever coinages include 'GenerAsian X' and 'Goonda Rap'). Hustlers HC hustle to disrupt expectations. There is an almost standard narrative in live reviews which starts with a question like 'wha? why are these Sikh guys all hanging around on stage?', which then leads into 'then we started playing, everything was quiet', and the dénouement, 'by the time our set was finished the crowd was wild for more, really kicking'. This is a classic breakthrough play, but Hustlers also worry that because of this novelty effect, their message is not getting across. Their attempts at a cultural politics that addresses much more than racism requires a complex series of steps where they say, 'we don't see ourselves as ambassadors for the Asian community' but 'racism is an important subject to tackle because it affects our everyday life' (*Eastern Eye*, 4 October 1994), and their approach to everyday life is also more laid-back than that of Nation

Records labelmates Fun^da^mental, by design: 'we don't talk about racism everyday, we just wanna have fun' (Hustlers, *NME* 15 October 1994, rappers quoting Cyndi Lauper!). Pro-active vigilante style defence activism is given another take in the lyrics of the Hustlers' track 'Vigilante':

> As the night falls its getting scary thinking about
> racist thugs that be moving about
> anger in their eyes and hate in their feet
> as they charge for the Paki or the Blackie in the street
> I live in fear, I wanna see the next day
> but on the other side of London an Asian gets beat
> by a racist jerk, cos he wanted to hurt
> he's a nazi skinhead treating the brown like dirt
> how many more things have to wait to happen
> Don't think of the Police being your protective weapon
> I used to thank god for giving me a life
> now I'm praying for forgiveness for carrying a knife
> My mom she's worried I'm going out she's got the blues
> She doesn't want to see my name headlined in the news
> I'm so vexed why does it have to be
> everywhere I show my head race hate is reality
> we're dodging and diving to avoid the bastards
> but no matter how we run they still come after us
> It's like world war three or the killing season
> Steven Lawrence he died for no damn reason
> Quaddus Ali, he survived, but that doesn't mean nothin
> he and his family went through months of sufferin
> so what do I do, do I run from the country
> or wait for racist Britain to scan me and hunt me down
> Vigilante the peace, the silence the yin,
> the yang is the anger and violence
> Vigilante, You live in fear of me, product of a wall of silence
> conspiracy, they call me an evil thug, indiscriminate
> I've seen the violence, the silence the race-hate
> the beast don't care, they just do the minimal
> comin after me like I'm some kinda criminal
> they'll never understand, what kind of man I am
> I've seen mothers cry, and I cry while little brothers die
> but no more twenty on one, lets turn the numbers around
> no more pretence, defence is from the underground

no more trying implying that I'm weak
I'm the Hindu, the Muslim, and the Sikh
The Asian youth at the end of your street.
Got to get the jackboots stomp from my hood
choose to live in peace if I could
There's a hustler in Chinatown, a 22 goes for fifty pounds
but I wonder when the time will come
when I switch from the knife and go for the gun
I'm not evil, schizo, paranoiac, but I've seen big trouble,
now my anger's overflowing
don't stereotype me, my tactics might be,
defensive not offensive, thoughtful and pensive
patrolling the streets, I'm keeping the peace
tell me what's the point of calling the police
tell me who's going to look after the schoolkids
They are the future they need protection
My direction is anti my target is the racist coward child killer
I am the Vigilante.
Vigilante the peace, the silence the yin,
the yang is the anger and violence
Vigilante the peace, the silence the yin,
the yang is the anger and violence
Now I the accused won't be misused
Stand hard my brother don't take the abuse
crave to live the life of peaceful remedy
But if you mess with me I'll take the role of the Vigilante
Racists be aware I come passing through
but I ain't a thug who takes a human's life
who says a vigilante must carry a knife
it could be enough just for me to be there
the racist is a coward, easy to scare
the attacker automatically gets state defence
video cameras make prosecution sense
so playing the rule doesn't have to mean violence
huh, vigilantes move in silence
but if my cover's blown I could get beat
but it's worth it for the kids on my street
and the moms, the pops, the sisters the brotherman,
need a barrier from the hatred of the other man
so playing this role is a must for me

so you see why we all must be – Vigilante
Vigilante – the peace, the silence the ying,
the yang is the anger of violence
Vigilante – the peace, the silence the ying,
the yang is the anger of violence
'Vigilante' – Hustlers HC, Nation Records 1994. Words by Paul Arora
and Mandeep Walia. Published by QFM/Warner Chappell Music)

Hustlers HC recognise the urgency of the situation. When there are race attacks going on; people must defend themselves; *how to do this* is the question? Hustlers mount a scathing criticism of the police in failing to prevent racial attacks, and more importantly, of the criminalisation of Asian youth who choose to protect themselves. Hustlers advocacy of several forms of self-defence is clear: 'I wonder when the time will come when I switch from the knife and go for the gun ... don't stereotype me'. The music press – which at least provided some sort of a forum for this discussion – raised questions about the militancy of this stance which Hustlers were keen to clarify: 'Some reviewers have said "Hustlers have put up a good defence for violence", and we haven't. We've said vigilantism doesn't necessarily mean violence. There are various options to monitoring and controlling racial attacks. You can drive around with a video camera, you can be ready for a Rodney King' (*NME*, 15 October 1994).

In a similar context ADF are closely involved with East London Bengali youth and their track 'Jericho' expands the priorities of defence to a general political consciousness:

The music, we use it, we're making a stand,
we wouldn't call this a green and pleasant land
a conscious response is what we demand
challenge the system and those in command
express your opinion, it's your domain
if you fail to do this, you're partly to blame
My heart is beating no retreat
the battle continues
we'll suffer no defeat
this war you've been waging
it's time we were raging
in our minds and on the streets
sample this
it's an education

the sounds of the Asian Dub Foundation
('Jericho', Asian Dub Foundation, *Facts and Fictions*, Nation Records
1994. Lyrics, Das, Pandit, Zaman, Tailor, Savale, published by QFM/
Warner Chappell Music)

In tracks such as this (and those discussed in Chapters 2 and 7) ADF
take up the theme of self-defence in the context of a broad political
narrative that combines migrant and anti-colonial sentiments in a
progressive confrontational stance. Here, and in videos like *Dog-Tribe* by
Fun^da^mental, or in the more blunt 'Trotsky's-pavement' squadist
approach of 'Hang 'em High' by the Kaliphz, Asian musicians recognise
that the issue is one of how to organise responses to everyday street and
institutional racist confrontation in local and global contexts, and they
attempt to convey this message to a wider public through their music.
The question remains one of who hears these messages (academics,
leftists, anti-racists, journalists, the 'Asian' community ... ?). An example
of how this work differs from the mainstream anti-racist carnivalism of
the ANL/SWP might be ADF who actively participated in the 3
September 1995 Newham Unity Festival organised by one of the longest-
serving and best known anti-racist local community groupings,
Newham Monitoring Project. In an issue of *CARF*, they explained their
use of music as a mobilising vehicle:

> In the past, Newham Monitoring Project has criticised the 'ANL
> syndrome': passing off anti-racist concerts in black areas, attracting
> thousands of people but leaving little lasting effect, as huge anti-
> racist mobilisations. The Unity festival is different. The venue is in
> the heart of Canning Town, a predominantly white working-class
> area seen by the BNP as fertile ground for recruitment. And the Unity
> festival isn't a one-off, but part of Newham Monitoring Project's
> long-term work in south Newham around issues such as housing and
> employment (Piara Powar in *CARF*, August 1995)

Other featured bands at this event were the Kaliphz and Fun^da^mental,
expressing their commitment to, and support of, local organising
strategies that cut across white–black divisions and which seek to
organise the working classes against the racist provocations of the
fascists and against systematic exploitation in terms of lack of housing
and employment and so on. This sort of engagement combines the best
aspects of carnivalism and hard-edged community self-organisation as
well as cross-sectoral alliance work.

There are left initiatives that also offer more than 'ANL syndrome'. The magazine of the Revolutionary Internationalist League (RIL), *Revolutionary Fighter,* comes out strongly with banner headlines, in huge block sans serif font, declaring the need to 'Organise Defence Now!'. The work of this group also centres mostly around East London and the Bengali community of Tower Hamlets.

> *Revolutionary Fighter* has campaigned for Worker/Community defence over the past year [they are writing this in the summer of 1994] as the only response to make the streets safe. We know the police will do nothing except harass us. We know that all the marches, speeches and protests by themselves can't drive the racist attackers off the streets ... Black and Asian youth have no alternative but to organise and defend themselves.

The argument of RIL is that the youth of these areas are already forced to defend themselves against attacks every day. 'Anti-racists and socialists must help to organise this defence, involving wider forces to prevent the youth from being isolated or criminalised by the racist state':

> The question is not: should young people defend themselves or not? The real point is that defence must be organised. Already school students and youth defend themselves but when it's done in an unorganised way they are more open to attack and the police arrest them for carrying offensive weapons or for some other crime. The youth will not wait for others to agree to defence patrols before defending themselves, but if it is not organised, if structures are not set up to co-ordinate activities, link up different youth, and if there is not a wider political campaign amongst the working class to help organise defence, then the youth will remain isolated, picked up by the police and picked off by the racist thugs. (*Revolutionary Fighter* 3)

Militant Labour's response to this old style rhetoric was not to see that there was a serious and urgent need to act along these lines, but to suggest a council-sponsored conference to discuss. Subsequently RIL have come under attack from the Labour council for their support of the Langdale Four (Bengali students arrested for an alleged attack on a known racist at Poplar High School), and have attracted hostility from Militant and from the SWP in the shape of reformist support for anti-left legal persecutions. The legal apparatus strengthened by the Criminal Justice Act avails itself of anti-left collusions to maintain its racist order.

Workers Power do call for a 'serious approach to organised self-defence' (*Workers Power,* November 1994) when they attend ANL conferences, but it is not clear what practical steps they have made beyond a critique of SWP media campaigns. To the credit of the SL, the *Workers Hammer* came out strongly in support of the RIL, while pointing out that the RIL's Community Defence proposals were inadequate without the support of 'genuine workers' defence guards' (*Workers Hammer,* September 1994). Urgency and immediacy on the one side couched in militant workerist rhetoric, against Militant's cringing bureaucratic surveillance and avoidance on the other. It is the potential role of concerned and equipped critics to provide the required initiatives and explanations for work that will make Community Defence proposals feasible – or at least make them a subject of wider discussion beyond the nether pages of the left press – but most members of the complacent intellectual middle class prefer instead to sit back without even defending their own declining work conditions in the universities, let alone responding to actual everyday violent attacks organised against members of the community. Stop and Search and police anti-crime campaigns at least drew some academic attention first time around in the 1970s, but so much for the sophistication of post-Marxism, when today only the remaining custodians of old rhetorics speak truth to power. It was up to the Spartacist League to draw out the more systematic implications of the reform process that was called the Criminal Justice Act – in September 1995 it named Police Commissioner Condon's Operation Eagle Eye a 'racist dragnet' targeting black youth in London. The SL said:

> Even before Operation Eagle Eye, young black men were ten times more likely to be stopped than their white counterparts. But now backed up by the Criminal Justice Act the cops feel they can go swanning into any place they please, swinging their truncheons with impunity. (*Workers Hammer,* September 1995)

Few others noted the links between the racist elements of the CJA and ongoing Police persecution, despite sufficient evidence to make the connection, and high profile criticism of Eagle Eye in the press. Instead of associating the mobilisation against the CJA with the ANL campaigns and then extending it to Condon's outrageous initiatives, the 'mugging' issue was used as another discrete campaign which could operate only as a party recruitment drive. The cynicism of those who campaigned against the CJA without any long-term strategy was exposed by Nawaz, who noted that not only had the racist elements of the CJA enabled attacks on blacks by police, but that at the very time these attacks came much of the white left had abandoned the campaign, leaving only the committed sound system groups, road protesters, squatters, anarchists and black community groups – with the opportunist groups having picked up a few newly politicised recruits and moved on to the next big thing.

Is it a failure of nerve on the part of middle-class radicals and academics that characterises their piecemeal and short-term contributions to single issues? Or are there other reasons for their refusal to support Asian self-defence? The possible objections of reasonable people must be addressed. The scripted and choreographed academic responses to the issues of defence can be anticipated and side-stepped. The question of violence obviously opens upon the terrain of morality and liberal notions of communal harmony. Enlightenment tolerance is as much the liberalism of academic 'anti-racists' as well. Cohen notes that Rattansi and Gilroy 'have argued the case for new strategies in anti-racist education that avoid ... its "moral symbolic and doctrinaire forms" ' (Cohen 1992: 62). It would be a lesson well learnt by all that certain dearly held positions close down opportunities for action. There are certain protocols of justice, of justifiable force, which come into play when the question of violence is raised (see Benjamin, Derrida, Girard, and so many others) and these are, more often than not, far removed from the questions, evidence and interpretation which are the preserve of law. The question of evidence – also a favourite of academia – is traceable here to Sir Lawrence's dry forensic investigations. Along with evidence come questions of judgement, interpretation and decision – in legalese, of 'ruling'. What kind of violent knowing is it that must investigate all that is sent in the post, and intimate bodily samples? Is there a relation between the samples of the forensic squad and the sampling of *Dog-Tribe*? One authorised by power, the other censored? Engagement with questions of interpretation is demanded when the televisual and justice are conjoined, and vex us as in the LAPD police defence trial where 'samples' of the Rodney King video are 'analysed' and excused frame by frame to exonerate thugs, and we are left as watching couch potatoes while a human being gets smashed. Further questions here would interrogate the media and the forums in which the 'message' of bands such as Fun^da^mental and Hustlers HC are disseminated: the list again is video, television, international satellite, technologies of communication, and the ways in which scholarly interest in these technologies rarely moves beyond safe questions about access. Instead this questioning could explore the role of technologies such as the camcorder and mobile phone in political work and the relation of these forms to institutional structures. For example, does the use of video cameras as the Hustlers HC suggest ('you could drive around with a video camera') imply a 'touching faith' in the court system that experience might suggest was unwarranted? Is the surveillance of the streets such a great idea? Why move to a *Clockwork Orange/Videodrome* world characterised by the idea of Sony-equipped surveillance squads roaming the streets (chanting 'war on drugs, war on drugs' – apologies to Pynchon) while the rest of the population cower in secured suburban bunkers watching live-feed transmissions beamed in from those very same squads (courtesy of the technologies developed by the leisure industry such as Sports-Cam™). Similarly concern about surveillance and dysfunctional aspects of community defence will be raised, and need to be addressed, in terms of gender and conservation – specifically the policing of identity, allegiance and conformity which may arise and include such concerns as the recuperation of runaway daughters and the tar-and-feather approach to collaborators. Such matters are of course a problem for all organisational forms, and are no less prevalent – are indeed more systematic in many ways – on the part of the state. These important concerns should be delegated to discussions on organisational discipline and democratic centralism – on which there is a considerable literature. It should be noted that nobody raises the problems of police violence or the violence of the state and of law in the same ways as is common when moral outrage and tabloid sensation provokes unthinking criticisms.

The possibility of defence groups tending from macho posturing to more aggressive gender and community policing is an issue that raises some psycho-social questions about proposing a militancy which, while linked to organised self-defence groups, will also be taken up and circulated beyond these groups through mass media. The effect of the articulation of a militant refusal of Asian victimologies has political effects that cannot be ignored, least of all within Asian communities themselves, and in terms of relations with Afro-Caribbean communities and white ones. However, what seems significant in the cultural politics of Fun^da^mental as regards Asian identity is that after a period characterised by assertions of Asian specificity in the UK (which can probably be dated from the Rushdie controversy and when commentators like Hall and Gilroy began talking about black *and* Asian), there now seems to be a reassertion of the earlier black politics from a position of greater surety and strength, though there are those who will remind us that this strength was always present, simply unrecognised in the face of media stereotypes about passivity. Rather than consign such developments to old fears about macho militancy or ill-discipline, new alliances can be identified as some writers recognise. The conscious dialectical movement of Asians back to a black politics offers other parallels: talking about the difference between media representations of Asian women (as passive, quiet) and African women (loud, brash), bell hooks argues the necessity of publicly naming solidarities with one another against such stereotypes (hooks 1994: 218). In the 'Dog-Tribe' video another solidarity is displayed (but not named) as the Asian woman sitting quietly by the graveside is later seen actively engaged in the trashing of the BNP office finale of the clip. The participation of women's organisations in anti-racist campaigns will be evident to anyone who has attended any of the rallies for, to mention only a few: Justice for Joy Gardner (a black woman killed by police in her home; police were not prosecuted), the Free Satpal Ram Campaign (imprisoned for defending himself from white racist attack, see Chapter 7), the Brian Douglas campaign (killed by police using the new LAPD-style long truncheons) and the Defence Campaign for Amer Rafiq (injured by police in Manchester after Eid, 1996, see Chapter 6), etc. The presence and work of women organisers and speakers in campaigning is vast and immeasurable compared to their invisibility and apparent 'passivity' in mainstream media representations.

These possible alliances open wide questions that offer a future project only hinted at in 'Dog-Tribe'. The need for the formation of new alliances emerges at a time when some argue the coming of a 'total subsumption' of everything to the production of New World Order Capitalism. Here all social, political and cultural formations are 'subsumed' to the production of value, subsumed to the formation of a coming community, with all its cultural 'differences' in terms of race, class, gender. Within this complex the commercialised production of meaning, identity, spaces, everything, is orchestrated for what Marx called the 'real subsumption' of life to production – a stage that comes after the imposition of an organisational form of capitalism upon 'otherwise non-capitalist' things. Today, all projects tend towards an organisation which produces all life – from leisure to education to formal 'work', and including criticism and analysis, music and sex – in ways that are integral components of a seamless differentiated global factory. Whatever the final assessment of this analysis, and its further elaboration in the work Félix Guattari and Antonio Negri (1990, in *Communists Like Us*) and Michael Hardt and Negri (1994, in *Labour of Dionysus*), it is important to consider the implied programme of

Fun^da^mental's video/lyrical productions in this context. Some wildly general points about this context can be made (very quickly): with the winding back of the welfare state buy-off of the West's workers, racism escalates. White workers were enticed to develop a vested interest in the system – a trick. Racism keeps the working class divided, and the so-called middle classes are also similarly dissuaded from political initiative and alliance against ever more invisible profiteers in a rampant social factory where everything is geared towards global production. Capitalism under crisis relies upon super-profits from a restructuring which designates hi-tech production to the expensive Western labour markets and moves mass production to Third World sites. The necessary costs of development include the education of elite workers in the West (no longer a geographical category), an ever larger service sector and deployment of forces of subjugation (new authoritarian controls) in this new world order. Concomitant requirements of: Fortress Europe and the expulsion or exclusion of immigrant labour no longer needed; martial law/Criminal Justice Act/Operation Eagle Eye; the UN as world police and the moral rearmament of imperialism; First World science development/automation; Third World production/intensive labour; heightened communication, information and transportation flows; competitive state privileges.

Regrettably, most pious academic discussion of racism avoids the practicalities and requirements of everyday anti-racism – beyond attendance at one or two trade union rallies or world music carnivals every few years. Concentrating instead upon neat structural polemics within the tradition, policy initiatives and refinements, and proposals for still more carnivals and conferences is the 'best practice' offered. This is not to say there is not a role for these sophisticated 'interventions'. Of course. But where are the defences of self-defence today? Where was the critique of the Criminal Justice Act? Where was the outcry against the censorship of *Dog-Tribe*? Surely these issues are not the preserve of academics too – what is cultural studies about if not the contest of culture? It is clearly up to intellectual workers to link these issues together in ways that facilitate coordinated actions, is it not? The parameters of academic engagement allow certain kinds of contestation and debate but not others – a more sceptical evaluation of the possibilities of scholarly consideration of racism would note that these parameters were coordinated more by competition for places and advancement than any politics. After all, what can fine words do in practice? Harmonious calls for tolerance and no violence reiterate conservative moralities and the status quo. Academic abstention in the face of this terror ignores the life and death confrontation that simply, bluntly, must be engaged now. As I have said, the list of the names of the dead is not a rhetorical device, but indicates the extent to which passivity and complacency have allowed a retreat from critical engagement on the part of comfortable intellectuals. The task is to wake up from this stupor – this cannot be simply an essay in cultural studies of the left in the UK or some journalistic report from the culture zone. What is at stake, and what small contribution this book might attempt, is to suggest a reconfiguration of the parameters that sustain anti-racist racisms. By anti-racist racism I mean the failure of academics to do anything beyond presentation of feel-good statements that end up fuelling reformist calls for more police. Vigilance is a difficult price to pay to ensure paranoid law-making disguised as good deeds does not enable further attacks. Vigilantes do have a defence, but the place of *Dog-Tribe* has been usurped by the white noise of the censor, the white noise of reformism, and the white noise of complacency. Instead, educational and transformational initiatives within an internationalist framework might counter racist violence, not with isolated and spontaneous fighting but with a defence programme which is anti-racist, anti-capitalist and anti-sectarian and which extends into new lines of alliance against various and multiplying global examples of imperialism, exploitation and persecution. Then, of course, the materials for any organisational coordination of such alliances need to be produced in association with the ready fighters and activists. One of the things this chapter attempts to raise is the question of what to do about the failure of academic and parliamentary anti-racism. It only begins to make a space for elaboration of answers. *Dog-Tribe*, at least in this reading, sounds out that space. Within limited parameters such a discussion can provide possible incentives for movement into practical activity. The trouble is that academic and public intellectual failure to speak about, or even take much interest in, the banning of *Dog-Tribe* or the various new authoritarian powers of the CJA meant that those who did not cower in the face of authority were left without cover. Subject to silencing, exclusion, misappropriation, spin management and media stereotyping by a seemingly anonymous and impersonal corporate machine is possible only if public intellectuals (academics *are* also included here) consent to the narrowing and domesticating agenda of the cultural-industrial complex. To turn this around: informed perhaps by the considerable resources and theoretical arsenal that the institutions' disciplinary academia provide – even post-Marxism and postmodernism, post-structuralism, post-feminism (and post-early-for-Xmas) – there are numerous approaches that have current favour and still might be refashioned and deployed as counterweights here. Is it sufficient to point to the need for this engagement, and to follow the path of some, while encouraging more? To declare the need to provide a defence of defence squads, of anti-racist anti-capitalist organisation, of those cultural and political workers engaged within such struggles? The trick here (in order to end this chapter and leave for other urgent tasks) would be to claim limitations of space ...

Notes

1. I refer to music magazines of numerous stripes within the text. The *New Musical Express* is more commonly referred to as the *NME*. The *NME*'s immediate rival is *Melody Maker* (*MM*), both of these papers being weekly 'inkies', tabloid format news and reviews papers. More glossy versions include *Spin, Select, HHC, Sounds*, while more newsletter/fanzine-style examples include *Sniffin' Glue* and the Kaliphz's *Sling-Shot*. Specifically 'Asian' magazines include *Ghazal and Beat, Eastern Eye, East Magazine* – and in a category of its own devising, *2nd Generation*.

2. Additionally, the Act offered; a return to the discredited sus laws of stop and search, at the discretion of a superintendent or inspector who suspects violence is 'imminent'; abolition of the right to silence; attacks on travellers (unauthorised movement, unauthorised homelessness); increased fines for drug use (class C cannabis, £2,500 fine); privatisation of prisons (entrepreneurial incarcerations); more 'secure training centres', for young offenders, from age twelve; increased police power to take bodily samples, without consent, intimate and non-intimate divisions, saliva, pubic hair, semen (a DNA database came into operation early in 1995); obscene telephone calls surveillance; more police powers; prevention of terrorism (random search without suspicion); prisoner drug tests; scalper crackdown; security for mainstream party political conferences (public purse excise to fund the paranoid wherever they meet); council application for prohibition of trespassory assembly; aggravated trespass in the vicinity of the hunt; impounding vehicles; impounding of virtual space (tekno division); restrictions on bail; offence of research which aids terrorism (Who's Who section); revision of Race Relations Act, no room for Gypsies (Roma family incarceration unit); Stonehenge clause – annual hippie cull; several varieties of anti-party law (in preparation, in attendance, on the way to a rave – repetitive beatings); more police powers; more police.

3. I think it is crucial that the scarf of organisation does not replace the scarf of international political solidarity, but joins it. The *keffiyeh* is not, as some commentators would have it, merely a stage prop or fashion statement in Nawaz's usage.

4. See Chapter 6 for more on this programme in the context of discussion of anti-racism 'carnivals'.

5. Witness the MTV 'ethnic' fashion show *The Pulse* brimming with black

models, and over its closing credits playing the 'Dog-Tribe' track without images, with the refrain 'Primitive ... primitive' repeating.

6. Despite low exposure the Fun^da^mental album *Seize the Time* sold reasonably well in the stores and was reported at number fourteen in the national Independent Music Week chart after five weeks (*Music Week* 30 July 1994). Months after its release, 'Dog-Tribe' was also used as a signature soundtrack for the MTV Europe video awards, without the images (November 1994 and again in July 1995), while segments of the video clip itself were used several times in an MTV/Coca-Cola news item on hip-hop politics.

7. In contrast, just to keep the issue of self-defence in mind, Trotsky recommended dealing with such propagandists through a form of community action which would summarily 'acquaint the fascists with the pavement' – no need to get out the forensic squad here. And no 'by the time they got to the place where they thought the distribution was ...'. The relevant passage reads: 'The tactical, or if you will "technical" task was quite simple – grab every fascist or every isolated group of fascists by their collars, acquaint them with the pavement a few times, strip them of their fascist insignia and documents, and without carrying things any further, leave them with their fright and a few black and blue marks (*Ultraleft Tactics in Fighting the Fascists*, March 1934).

8. For the purposes of the Act an 'intimate sample' means: (a) a sample of blood, semen or any other tissue fluid, urine or pubic hair; (b) a dental impression; (c) a swab taken from a person's body other than the mouth. Non-intimate sample means: (a) a sample of hair other than pubic hair (dreadlock sample); (b) a sample taken from a nail or from under a nail (unwashed sample); (c) a swab taken from any part of a person's body including the mouth, but not from any other body orifice; (d) saliva (punk gobbing sample), etc. Previously the most intimate bodily orifice samples could only be taken in cases of serious offence – murder, rape – now such samples will be allowed for any recordable crime, including offences like fare-dodging, shoplifting or listening to repetitive beats in a field at night with ten friends.

9. I am not going to review the literature on community defence here, nor the legal cases which establish self-defence as a defence in law. The former is only really available in the occasional and small press – although see *Race Today* any issue, but especially 'Charting the Asian Self-defence Movement' (*RT* 10(6): 128–31). In 1990 Paul Gordon wrote a Runnymede Research Report on the legal record on self-defence. This report took up the Bradford 12, Newham 7, Newham 8 and other well-known/not well-enough-known cases also discussed in Kalra et al. (1996).

10. Combat 18, the most prominent fascist militia in the UK, at present seems to be in national decline and confusion, despite occasional outbreaks of violence and their continued cowardly practice of targeting the periphery of left demonstrations to pick off individuals for attention. There is some debate as to their actual numbers, their blustering hype and their organisational coherence – *Dispatches*, Channel 4, 25 October 1994. Yet they have managed considerable intimidation for their small presence. Significantly, C18 feature on the dub version, the instrumental version, and in live performances of 'Dog-Tribe', recorded from an answer-phone message they left on a Youth Against Racism number: 'C18 is watching you, you communists. Nigger-loving Paki cunts. Fucking dickheads, we're gonna hang you for burning the British flag'

('Dog-Tribe – People of the Sun Mix') – note here the conjunction of racism, nationalism and red-baiting hysteria, typical of so many anti-communist, rightist, prejudiced scum.

11. I must note, with emphasis, that I am not attempting a survey of the various positions of the myriad trotocracies and fiefdoms of leftist debate in the UK as this would be exhausting, and possibly very dull for those not transported by the subtleties and nuances involved. It is sufficient to acknowledge the seriousness with which these debates are engaged – the struggle is grim – and to hope that anyone wanting such a survey will read the texts themselves and will, with fingers stained from that black ink specially produced for the socialist press, excuse this clumsy *en passant*.

Part II
Appropriations

4
Magical Mystical Tourism

'White' appropriations of African-American culture, sentimen-
talising images of 'disappearing' Native Americans, condescending
caricatures of 'inscrutable' Asians or 'hot-blooded' Mexicans have a
long and disreputable history ... Their consequences are no less
poisonous when well-intentioned ... identification with otherness
has become an essential element in the construction of 'whiteness'.
(Lipsitz 1994: 53)

Kula Shaker Tourist Tales

In 1997, on MTV Europe, a young white male 'pop star' stood outside a
Hindu temple in India and looked into the camera to say: 'Did you ever
get the feeling you were in a *Star Wars* movie?' His comment on the
project of filming in India: 'What happens here is about what you feel,
you can't necessarily show that on camera.' When filming local
musicians he explains: 'This is the tribal stuff, everyone has a good heart
and they put it into the music ... they are just happy ... them living their
culture just seems completely natural' (Mills, *Kula Shaker in India*, MTV
1997).

If part of the project of progressive social critique is to argue for a
transnational perspective, it is crucially important that it is not one
which becomes the ideology of a new universalist liberalism.[1] The
transnational here cannot be merely some form of touristic culture
appreciation society (slide-shows of the most boring kind imaginable,
sanctified by the new editing facilities of documentary television and
staged authenticity). Instead what must come to attention are the
international networks and interrelations that are the coordinates of
contemporary culture and politics, the integrations and disjunctures of

the inter-state and inter-commercial systems, from the disproportionate distribution of benefit from production, to the concerted global effort to push through a new geo-media satellite hegemony via CNN and the new telecommunications world systems.[2] Within these processes tourism also has a place, since tourists are in large measure engaged in the very processes that bring the transnational to attention, but only as one kind of process amongst others such as migration, media, warfare, liberalisation, etc.[3]

This chapter is a reflection on the politics of music and travel which places theoretical and political concerns alongside the popular culture visibility of 'Asia' in the work of white male 'pop' groups like Kula Shaker. Clearly South Asian musical and cultural forms can be appropriated by global commercial interests even at the point of claims to 'radical alternatives'. Kula Shaker's lead singer and guitarist Crispian Mills makes souvenirs of 'real experiences, man' by meeting sadhus and priests at Indian temples and buying trinket versions of cosmic harmony, singing dirge-like versions of devotional tunes while strumming his six-string guitar ... Of course this souveniring of sound and culture is only possible on the basis of a long history of colonial power and theft (and nostalgia for that idealised exotic India – one that is other and which was resilient despite, or even because of, the British visitors). I also want to tie in the ways in which this nostalgia and souveniring travels now to the UK and Europe. Not just with MTV, but the general population flocking to curry houses to dine out on twisted appropriations of colonialism brought here in new packets; the 'red hot vindaloo' (Banerjea and Banerjea 1996: 111) as national dish; white women wearing *bindi* and nose-rings; world music festivals and the popularity of the 'new' Asian dance music at fashionable nightclubs. All this follows the economic structure of the souvenir – exotica deliciously snapped up at prices cheap because the 'tourists' won't pay full price/the workers and producers of the exotic are underpaid. Synchronously, this underpayment applies also to both the cut-rate club prices and the low remuneration of the curry house workers in England.

In this chapter, tourism is singled out for the very reason that the form exhibits the kinds of reification and appropriations that I would want to examine in other media as well – especially for example, that of the importance of authenticity, the status of representation and the 'authority' to report back (from the local to the transnational, wherever this 'local' might be – after all the local is often a code-word for attribution of unsophisticated or uncivilised status). Is it worth focusing upon the touristic practice of the pop star Crispian Mills? Kula Shaker's orthodox rock singer-guitarist-frontman has considerable opportunity, and resources, to expound his views to the world. Here, music cross-cuts travel and the media in ways that are useful, at least from the transnationalist point of view of the critique I want to make, as illustration of the processes and structures of the current cultural conjuncture of contemporary capitalism. If it is accepted that any adequate transnational cultural studies requires a programmatic agenda that goes beyond all too easy and too often comfortable apathy, this chapter instead attempts to take up hard political questions about culture and feed these into a transformatory project that is interested in changing the world. Some may squirm at the recalcitrant optimism of this, but instead of fashionable ready-to-wear cultural cynicism, I want to extend a reading of tourism, television and music into this domain.

What is political about tourism and music? There is much that can be (and has been) said here: tourism as largest truly transnational industry, massive infrastructural investment, astonishing integration of sectors, from transport and banking, to building industry, guide-book production and suntan-oil manufacture, etc. Music as the soundtrack: satellites float in the sky, strange noises stream through the hotel window, performances travel and tunes dominate the landscape.[4] The entire apparatus encircles the globe. Both tourism's and music's most esoteric aspects are wholly political as well: be it the sun-seeking break from the rigours of bourgeois life to the unabashed romanticism of Western campaigns against Third World poverty – from Concert for Bangladesh to 'Do They Know it's Christmas?' (and why should they care?)[5] – in the former case the leisure industry works as refuelling time for the clapped-out office workers of the First World, serviced by the underpaid service workers of the Third, in the second performative catharsis assuages the guilt born of media intrusions upon complacency as stray images of poverty are transmitted across the international wealth and labour divide. While music exists in a more aural and temporal dimension, the political aspect of tourism is easy to spot. World domination takes monumental forms, as Kaplan writes:

> Imperialism has left its edifices and markers of itself the world over, and tourism seeks these markers out, whether they consist of actual monuments to field marshals or the altered economies of former colonies. Tourism, then, arises out of the economic disasters of other countries that make them 'affordable'. (Kaplan 1996: 63)

Donald Horne's description deserves repeating: he saw tourism as walking among 'monuments to the wreckage of Europe's greatest ambition – to rule the world' (Horne 1984: 211). Today such visits are accompanied by a 'shrunken music' soundtrack (Chow 1993: 142) provided via Sony Walkman.[6] To speak of tourism then is to speak of the politics of those who conquer, and in this context it is important to listen with a critical ear to the travel tales of megalomaniacs. We have long learnt that authentic histories are not clearly audible in the official record.

In the search for authenticity it has become fairly commonplace to acknowledge that authenticity is a sham. Indeed, the more sophisticated poses available in the theory and tourist marketplace, not to mention in the popular music scene, hold that the conscious recognition of the staged character of 'authentic' performance does not compromise, but can in effect enhance, authenticity. It would be enough here to consider the carefully crafted and annually remodelled identities of Bowie, Madonna or even the Spice Girls – in recent times all three took an 'Asian' turn, with the Spice appearing dressed in saris for a performance in Delhi, and both Bowie and Madonna doing Asian-influenced dance tracks on their latest albums – the mercantile girl displacing Asian group Cornershop at the top of the charts with the track 'Frozen' from her album *Ray of Light*. Dean MacCannell, in an early work called simply *The Tourist*, suggested that the search for authenticity is born of an anxiety in the face of the disorienting experience of capitalist modernity (MacCannell 1976: 14). Dis-orienting or not,[7] it has become more common now to note that such anxiety can also be repackaged and sold as touristic manna. John Urry (1990, 1995) is probably among the most prominent commentators on this complexity, with his notion of the 'post-tourist' (for which, deservedly, he has been criticised for succumbing more to the need to coin new terms, than to the presentation of argument or content). Against this post-tourist sham-consciousness, the role of souvenirs – the trinket, the photograph, the jingle, the local sample samba, tabla, rumba and, of course, the travel anecdote – have not lost, but have rather regained, status as markers of authenticity. Seemingly impervious to the onslaught of deconstruction (as if deconstruction was only about destroying so as to find ultimate hidden truths or nothing at all), the souvenir gains, and the holder of the souvenir deploys, authority and cultural credibility. Once again, with a family similarity to the astonishing capacity of the commodity form to manifest in so many endless shapes and sizes, the global reach and interchangeability of the souvenir suggests an imperialist ambition. This, I will argue, is never more so the case as when Crispian goes to India.

Crispian Who?

So there is an important cultural politics at stake in the touristic practice of Crispian Mills, son of Hayley Mills, Hare Krishna devotee and film actress star of Disney's *Pollyanna* and much later *Whistle Down the Wind*. Estranged father Roy Boulting and maternal grandfather Sir John Mills were also film stars in their own right (Grandpa Mills won an Oscar for his role as the village idiot in David Lean's *Ryan's Daughter*). Crispian's travel adventure is another version of the old pop star goes to see the gurus routine. Best of luck to the temple touts who manage to redistribute a few of the pop star's royalty monies, but in terms of influence, media visibility and contribution to international under-standing and/or the flipside of this, prejudice, his pronouncements on India are fundamentally dangerous: for example when he says that 'India is the Ibiza of concepts' (Mills, MTV 1997). Obviously many people who might hear such a comment will laugh, and know that shit still smells like shit when it's dished out undisguised like this. But at the risk of picking on a soft target, there is an element which prides itself on its ethnic cosmopolitanism and will accept such statements with the lack of irony intended. Much more than enthusiasms for temples or for 'India' is required to escape prejudicial patronising and garden-variety orientalism – how many Indologists reading Sanskrit and quoting Vedic verse were also co-conspirators in imperial rule? Slave traders were proto-'Africanists', taking 'native' wives and learning local languages[8] long before anthropologists arrived and realised the practice was good for business. The first arrivees of the British East India Company bought land with silver earned in the slave trade, and they also 'went native' – before the arrival of white wives and 'clubs' and the strict social demarcation that was then enacted (at least in public). Clearly, enthusiasm for 'concepts' is not enough to undermine imperialist incursions however much it may seem preferable to the racisms of hate. Kula Shaker's Crispian may fancy himself as Luke Skywalker in a *Star Wars* adventure, but India is not a fantasy planet and political issues might still be canvassed through the music-travel frame in a way that does not enforce a simplifying stupidity. MTV, however, does not appear inclined to pursue anything other than a science fiction scenario because it still works within a variant of the orientalist paradigm. While Star TV, despite the Murdoch empire controlling stake, can manage a 24-hour election news coverage channel interviewing leaders and candidates of the competing Communist, Congress and right-wing BJP parties, and satellite modernity delivers 43 channels and more to even the TVs of urban *bustee* dwellers and rural *sarpanch* households, MTV Asia still beams only a Lonely Planet kind of India across its screens. MTV's India was pre-programmed by videographic preconceptions ranging from Louis Malle to *Heat and Dust* and seems unable to step aside from these choreographed cinematic old-school conventions. Similarly, in Attenborough's *Gandhi* a mainly Western film score accepted only samples of Ravi Shankar's sitar in a way that was of a continuity with previous trinketising appreciations of even this 'most accessible' of South Asian musicians – it is useful to remember how at the Concert for Bangladesh the audience applauded enthusiastically after Shankar had tuned his sitar, and after thanking them for their appreciation the 'maestro' said he would now play them a raga ... [9]

Let us consider some other possible passages into this adventure. Cool Kula Crispian's search for the alterity of Asia through music, like that trek of George Harrison 30 years ago, means we could also be talking about 'whiteness in crisis' here.[10] I agree there is a crisis to be examined but crucially the discussion needs to avoid a cul-de-sac of apolitical options and self-indulgent brow-beating.[11] Even leaving aside for the moment the anxieties and limited horizons of mainstream commercial actors, the political capability of the white left, and the political role of popular culture, it is too often the case that anti-racism today tends towards conservative introspection that gives an alibi to power. Discussion of such crisis should go on in tandem with recognition of how such a crisis is only possible on the back of the old colonial game, how, in the context of anti-Asian racism, it posits a nostalgic regret for an imaginary India that was not plundered by British imperialism but which cannot ever really admit to that history, and so now warbles on – in song, from the Beatles to Kula Shaker's esoterically named 'Holy River' and 'Golden Avatar' – about cosmic temple tolerance. It is this kind of displacement we do need to examine.

If the desert was the white space inside the dark continent which provided another chance for the heroic European invention of self (Lawrence 'of Arabia' through to Bertolucci's *Sheltering Sky*),[12] then the populated, history-laden, olfactory, sensuous abundance of India for Crispian can be seen as another site of reinvention based on the power to do what you like to the planet – here, the reinvention of self goes by way of a lament and longing for what is missing inside. He has said, in what amounts to a commonplace Western backpacker truism about India, that 'It's a place you go to when you are looking for something, and you will usually find it' and 'that's what it's for, it's a place for changing your life' (*Popview Live* interview 1997). In this routine India becomes the biological/genetic/conceptual repository and archive for values, concepts, styles and 'life-essences' considered absent in the individualistic 'developed' West. As if India were not also subject to development, and as if loss (this feeling of inadequacy, or at best alienation) could be eased by yet another round of plunder and pilfering. This time the theft is spiritual, but yet again by way of gross fetishistic miscomprehension. What seems perhaps at first to be 'something completely different' becomes a comic parody of even whatever degree of counter-establishment sentiment the notion of 'alternative' might once have held. 'Alternative' becomes just one, rather empty, safe and non-threatening, lifestyle choice among others, and ends up affirming only a return to the heyday of commerce and more of the same. MTV programming and Kula Shaker's psychedelic India offer not even a minimal chance for the teenage ritual of rebellion anymore; not the pursuit of experimental mind-expanding chemical experience, nor wild creative forays into communal living, or even the licentious practice of multiple relationships and polyvalently perverse sexualities. What is on sale is a safe rehash of tame Victorian morality glitzed up in gaudy out-of-date fashions and third-rate replays of sounds better done elsewhere. Everything, it seems, can be taken to market a second time around, but the more significant factor might be how this reveals a sense of cultural anxiety and collapse, and an incapacity to do anything much about it, which is Crispian's middle-class affliction. Rehearsing the parable of alienation and failing to see any scope for action to improve his lot at home, such a figure looks towards the (fantasy) horizon jealously. Caught in the self-obsessed dead end of appreciative cultural relativism, he can take no responsibility, has no ambition, no confidence and no capability to do anything but moan about the horrors of self-abuse and the end of the world. Crispian's conspiracy theories and his mysticism are not some form of solidarity with the marginal, the esoteric, or with minority religion, but are instead an opportunist cashing in that steers dangerously close to madness alongside support for a quite pernicious form of Hindutva right-wing cultural politics.[13] Relativism and cultural sensitivity sometimes play with such fire.

Even though urban demographics – and therefore many from MTV's audience – provided much of the Bharatiya Janata Party's electoral base, there is not a great danger of the BJP's fortunes being furthered by the support they get from bands like Kula Shaker. Yet the effect of the 'anthropological' gesture of relativist understanding without judgement is somewhat similar to the role played by ethnographers in revitalising Brahmanical ritual traditions without consideration of the context of a resurgent Hindu chauvinism and the contemporary ascendancy of such politics. The self-ish project of temple tourism played out by Crispian on the influential media circuits of satellite imperialism cannot be wholly separated from this context.

Crispian's musical search for the alterity of Asia celebrates an 'India' that is almost entirely in his mind. Supreme irony then that Madonna's sanskritised single lyric repeats: 'You only see what your eyes want to see' ('Frozen' 1998, discussed in the next chapter). Crispian and the MTV film crew went to India to explore the 'Eastern influences' of the band. Embarrassing travelogue this: in one scene the singer faces up to a Brahmin priest who mixes and applies red paste to Crispian's brow. Crispian says he doesn't know why it's done or why the Brahmin says he needs it, but afterwards – well, after an edit cut away to Crispian on his own outside the temple – he explains it is a 'third eye' and that it is the sun, just set, on his forehead. This process of moving from incomprehension to explanation, from letting something happen to explaining it to camera, from participation to observation (and later dissemination to the MTV audience worldwide) is the typical structure of ethnographic storytelling and the way exotica is always coded and consumed, irrespective of local significance. Collecting cultural experiences and displaying them provides the pattern for intercultural engagement that relentlessly produces meaning and text (and videotape) in the global tourism apparatus.

The violence of this appropriation is that an already violently marked scene becomes an object for consumption in a traffic of ideas barely understood: be it of the imperialist history which allows Crispian to be there in the first place, the authority of the roving camera eye which can go everywhere – without even stopping to remove shoes – or the sinister echoes of communalism and the unacknowledged project of the Hindu far right. The *bindi* becomes a free-floating universal fashion item, and is recruited as an icon of display signifying experience, otherness and understanding at the very moment when it is none of these things (is it ever just a fashion item?). The spiritual souvenir here is just another example of the flexibility of market appropriation and the ongoing subsumption of all things in all corners of the globe – the capacity to find in even the most esoteric aural or spiritual realms, material to enhance the sale of commodities. The plunder of such realms for profit means that the simple *bindi* is rarely innocent of some play of power, whatever its originary significances.

But fashion saves: according to Crispian, it is by paying attention to the supposedly 'timeless' spiritual message in the music that the contemporary ills of the planet can be cured. To a journalist who asked him if all this India pose wasn't just a bit 'out of fashion' and kitsch, he insists that it is not some:

> incense burning, talking philosophy bollocks. It is always relevant, it always means something. India is the source of all, they hold a lot of secrets ... We are in a civilisation about to destroy the planet. Everything is destroying itself ... and so where is the rescue mission gonna come from ... we have something to learn from India ... it's just about keeping a door open in the back of your head ... for some people it's just a fashion, but for others it is timeless. (*Popview Live* interview 1997)

The moral certainty is presented as instruction, the music is the message, the planet must be liberated (this missionary zeal). Indeed, most of Kula Shaker's public relations repertoire is moral and ethical (why, for example, does Crispian need to tell us he isn't into drugs any more? How does he cope?). To understand the marketing of the band in this register it is important to remember that cure-alls for alienation and moral-epistemological crisis have long been sold in mystic bottles. Call this the snake-oil medicine man gambit of the cultural frontier.

Pothead Pixie Jaya Jaya

Too many *bhang lassis* Crispian? Could it really be that he thinks mumbling conspiracy theories about an imminent apocalypse out of Asia is funny? Important by self-decree and MTV/Sony publicity, such amusing speculations from the youthful oracle of things-mystic are too sorry for words. The accusation that Kula Shaker are racists and 'racist by ignorance' (*Time Out*, various issues 1996–7) was always going to be controversial, however substantiated by actually and really offensive comments (Crispian says rap isn't music, it's attitude; and so buys into the view that it is just a form of complaint rock – the favoured explanation/dismissal routine of the right-wing reactionaries). No matter how well intentioned and multicultural the lead singer might claim to be with his studies of Eastern scripture, the consequences of commercial appropriation and decontextualised decorative aesthetics were always going to offend. Gross ignorance is confirmed in slide-shows at live gigs which superimpose Lord Horatio Kitchener (the butcher of the Transvaal) over Radha (Krishna's consort), as well as in the imperious arrogance of planning a concert at the Great Pyramid of Cheops on Millennium Eve. This big gig would have gone ahead presumably only if the promised armageddon, which Crispian believed would begin with conflict in Pakistan, India and China, could be averted by the saviour St George arriving from a place of spiritualism destined to free the world – that is, from England. As we now know, Crispian's fears of the world's end were unfounded, but the Cheops concert did not proceed in any case.

Further evidence for the unacknowledged but ever up-front persistence of colonial nostalgia is the reproductions on the first Kula Shaker album cover. Imitating the Fab Four and Sgt Pepper's Lonely Hearts with a collage, including Rudyard Kipling, Kitchener again (this time towering imperiously over the image of Jomo Kenyatta) and Ben Kingsley (Attenborough's import-substitute Gandhi), with also JFK (perhaps this particular arch-imperialist balanced by Martin Luther King), as well as Clark Kent and Captain Kirk to remind us of contemporary US fantasy imperialisms in the sky (all K's, but tactfully no Ku-Klux-Klan, yet no KC and the Sunshine Band either. Karl Marx is included as fashion statement, alongside Khrushchev). Finally, among others such as Boris Karloff and Katherine Hepburn, an image of Kali and the centre-piece of Krishna and Radha (the only three non-Western representations of things Indian) which confirms that orientalism also thrives in the days of desktop publishing.[14]

That Crispian is covertly rehearsing a grand epic nostalgia for the days of the British Raj must be taken seriously. Although for many of his generation, consciousness of family participation in the imperialist venture of England would not be prominent, when forced to consider the variety of likely connections, most can recall some immediate family link to the implementation of global political, economic and ideological power. For example, a grandfather who taught at a mission school on the Zambezi, a great-grandmother tending to the administration of a club in Simla, a father or uncle in the forces during the war, and not demobbed in 1945, perhaps even participating in the pre- and post-war anti-communist police actions in South and South-East Asia ... [15] Or, in Crispian's case, his thespian relatives worked in the ideological division, grandfather John portraying the heroic deeds of such as that same slide-show Lord Kitchener (in the film *Young Winston*).

Salman Rushdie famously commented that the trouble with the British is that their history happened overseas and they remain unaware of it (Rushdie 1981). I would argue that they are well aware, only that they are in severe denial born of the continuing project, and this denial has been repackaged for commercial gain by Kula Shaker and bands of their ilk, circulating through the new international circuits of satellite television, international distribution and mediatised tourism. Given that the project of capitalist development and restructuring is, on the face of it, incompatible with the tranquil temple romance of Crispian's dreams, perhaps his representations of Indian mysticism can be read as a kind of guilty rehearsal, parallel to the paradoxical – or hypocritical – structure of imperialist nostalgia recognised by Rosaldo: 'A person kills somebody, and then mourns the victim.'[16] Rosaldo goes on with contemporary resonances:

> In a more attenuated form, somebody deliberately alters a form of life, and then regrets that things have not remained as they were prior to intervention. At one remove, people destroy their environment, and then they worship nature. In any of its versions, imperialist nostalgia uses a pose of 'innocent yearning' both to capture people's imaginations and to conceal its complicity with often brutal domination. (Rosaldo 1989: 69–70)

Kaplan, following Rosaldo, and indeed quoting the same passage, adds that: 'Imperialist nostalgia erases collective or personal responsibility, replacing accountability with powerful discursive practices [or in Crispian's case, tripped out ones]: the vanquished or vanished ones are eulogised (thereby represented) by the victor'. Kaplan includes 'the recent rash of "Raj" nostalgia' as an example in narrations of the Euro-American past as 'another country' (Kaplan 1996: 34), although her focus on history does not necessarily mean that the history that is denied here is so long past. Indeed, India does still exist, if never in the benign forms, beloved of orientalist desire, fantasised by the Raj and by the likes of Kula Shaker. This India is subject to ongoing participation in capitalist production, structural adjustment programmes, tourist and service industry expansion, satellite installation, and so on. Neither vanquished nor yet vanished, except in Crispian's complicated psychosexual pathology.

  In some ways the notion of imperialist nostalgia requires flexible adaptation to the practice of those present-day 'mystics' who find that through the mechanisms of the tourism industry and tele-communications, that which is feared lost in the West (spiritualism, meaning, harmony), can be sought out in the temple trails of the subcontinent and broadcast again. Another parallel denial process is necessary for this nostalgia to work – contemporary India must be completely ignored, kept off-screen. The extent of this process is profound and codified into budget travellers' experience of India from the word go – even the Lonely Planet set find Delhi only to be a starting point for travels to 'real' India.[17] In the MTV special, Crispian repeats this denial of Delhi, adapting half-understood snippets of Vedic philosophy to sweep industrial development and urban culture aside as an illusion – if only it were true that years of imperial plunder were just so much *maya*. There is another dimension to this temple tourism that can be read in the code of anxiety. The crisis of guilt for the brutality of colonialism alongside the lost honour and glory of strong empire is resolved by Crispian's visit. On MTV, as global witness and tribunal, the white boy-knight can demonstrate that the temple was not desecrated, the traditional remains intact, the contemporary sensitivities of a caring sharing world sighs with relief that the violence of the past can now be safely ignored along with any recognition of current political contexts – for example, structural adjustment and ascendant *hindutva*. If the temple was not desecrated, as evidenced by the presence of Crispian in the temple, then by extension this opens the possibility of temple visits for all other Western tourists, and horror stories of imperialisms now past can be reassuringly erased from the current guidebooks. This kind of fantasy nostalgia fits India up again as a site for more than simple touristic consumption, a nostalgia directed at, and intrinsically part of, the politics of the present.

Kula Shaker plays at a struggling re-run of the psychedelic late 1960s because that was the last moment of excitement before the post-imperial crisis really hit home (yet even the 1960s UK music scene fascination with an 'other-worldly' India of peace and good vibes was in large part in denial of, and even counter to, a sharp and strident worldwide political movement – eclectic and disorganised in some ways, but with serious student politics and worker alliances in Chicago, Paris, Algeria, Japan, and, in different ways, China). Today's tamed psychedelics operate without the counter-establishment threat – neither Crispian nor Clinton inhale these days. In retro 1960s nostalgia, opportunities to extend the parallels to political issues are never taken. Whatever the tactical incoherence of the Situationist International at the Sorbonne in 1968 or of Abbie Hoffman and Jerry Rubin's exuberant Youth International Party (Yippies) in Chicago, it was at least possible for the vehicle of music to convey concerns about Western imperialist aggression in Vietnam and racist exclusion and white supremacy at home. This is not matched in the rerun of the 1960s sold to us today (what is Crispian's view on direct foreign investment in India? On the bombing of Baghdad or Sudan? On anti-Muslim sentiment in the media? On racist violence and murder on the streets of Britain? On import/export quotas? Or must we remain in trivial fanzine-land and only ask him about Rajasthani mirror-work vests, the Knights of the Round Table, his horoscope and his star-sign?).

Asian Sounds, Sounds Asian?[18]

The Kula Shaker (KS) sound is blind to the circumstances of its own production even at the point where it tries to claim some sort of heritage. That KS sitarism can place itself on the Eastern end of British pop, in full knowing ignorance of the presence of myriad Asian musics in the UK is not only naive. The wilful failure is of the Sony Music-signed stars to recognise the full heritage of Asian musics in their own country at the very time when Sony were attempting to market those musics (through a temporary alliance with Birmingham turntable stalwart Bally Sagoo, and the release of a double LP sampler of other 'new' Asian artists).[19]

What does Kula Shaker know of how Asian musics have travelled to Britain? They trace their interest in 'Eastern' sounds to white 'innovators' in the West. The Byrds, the Incredible String Band, Donovan and later Quintessence (Shiva Jones), Gong (Daevid Allen), Magic Carpet (Clem Alford) and the Teardrop Explodes, right on up to Paul Weller's Parisian sitar experiments on *Wild Wood* are the examples. Yet theirs is only the white Britpop side of British Asia (are Kula Shaker Britpop like Oasis? – What does Oasis signify if not T.E. Lawrence's mirage desire for a green and pleasant island in an inhospitable desert?).[20]

There is, of course, much more going on in British music than the market hype of guitar bands. It is plausible to think of groups like Fun^da^mental and ADF as the avant-garde of a well-pedigreed sound that was saccharinised for commercial purposes in the Sony production sampler and in popular mixed club nights like Anokha in London. This does not mean that outfits like Fun^da^mental and ADF have not also sought commercial success, nor were the efforts of bhangra, Qawwal and playback singers before them without commercial desire. But as much as the publicity machine was cranked up around the Fun^da^mental videos produced for MTV, financial success was secondary and in any case not readily forthcoming[21] – the Nation posse directed their efforts to using the media space, and all their time and energy, on projects like bringing Pakistani Qawaal Aziz Mian to British audiences, and, as discussed in the previous chapter, on the CJA and issues such as campaigning against the removal of Asylum rights from British law.

The political aspects of these antecedents of the so-called 'Asian Underground' are in danger of being lost in the attempt by Sony to claim mainstream sales through High Street marketing of artists such as Bally Sagoo. Sony have woken up to the size of the Asian market, but failed thus far to find a way to capture the sales, with Sagoo and Sony parting company after a year, citing 'mutual agreement' but also with rumours of bootleg sales controversy and 'artistic differences'. Sony's next attempt to break into the Asian dance arena was *Eastern Uprising: Dance Music from the Asian Underground*, a sampler which included tracks by some of the best Asian dance music practitioners, including ADF, Black Star Liner and respected Bengali outfit Joi, but the album's four sides failed to deliver a coherent sense of the diversity and sophistication of the 'underground' sounds, or of the political context out of which Asian dance music comes. Instead, the liner notes read like the script of one of those awful package curry dinner advertisements from the telly: 'Cor blimey! Strike a light. By 'eck ... What the f**k is going on' (Sony's asterisks). 'The embers of the empire shimmer like a distant blood-soaked sunset as the urban subtopias of downtown blighty rumble to the rhythms of a brand new internationalism.' The cover mocks a serious politics and instead proposes that the listener 'take a stroll' (good old English pastime this) 'through inner-city Britain and you will be bombarded ... The cab drivers are all clued up and glued down to bhangra FM ... BMW nightriders cruise the streets issuing menace with bruising drum'n'bass and the cornershops echo to the shrill syncopation of the Bollywood thriller.' This language is in fear of muggers and drug addicts; the respective code-words are menace and BMW nightriders (at one point the text refers to 'safe European streets'), while it is also orient-alist romanticism; 'the lustre, melodrama and breathless panorama of Asiatic culture and tradition ... Top! Wicked! Safe! Who? Where? Why?' (*Eastern Uprising*, Sony Corp 1997). A reader who mistook this mockery as a report 'from the streets' would be seriously misled.

So What Does Karl Marx Think about the New Asian Dance Music?[22]

The Sony text waxes lyrical and corny in ways only cheap advertising can. But perhaps every word is not a total loss. Written most likely by more than one hand, it would be plausible to distinguish the 'cor blimey' and 'safe' citations from knowledgeable sentences about the scene in Brick Lane and the pernicious effects of boom and decline in British manufacturing and its ravenous need to chew up and then spit out the 'legions of Norjawan'. However, the unintended irony of a sentence that describes the music as the sound of a new breed of urban Asianite, 'Freed from the dead end of industrial employment, liberated from convention and able to juggle duality and pluralism with more skill than a pre-coke Maradona' is striking. Leaving aside the overdetermined designations that Asians are dextrous and hybrid ('juggling' between two cultures yet again),[23] I would like to take this contradiction – 'freed' from employment – into another, quite different, level of analysis. The point here is to establish the basis for arguing that cultural appropriations such as those by Kula Shaker in regard to 'India' are not innocent, but rather do ideological work for a basically exploitative frame – the inexorable logic of value misappropriation, prejudicial division of labour, inequitable distribution of resources and a homogenisation of social relations throughout the world. The homogenisation of the world under capitalist relations proceeds by bringing all differences to the HMV bargain bin and it indeed 'thrives' on 'cultural' content where differences can be equated through abstract equivalences. All this so well foreseen by Marx, not Madonna.

Can the Sony copywriters have intentionally been quoting Marx's famous passage about the transition from feudalism to capitalism as a sly commentary on the consequences of post-industrial Britain in decline? Since 'freedom' did not come to India/Pakistan at 'decolonisation',[24] perhaps Sony are repackaging it today with a deeply subtle play? The allegory at least deserves a closer reading. In the Economic Notebooks of 1857–8 (*The Grundrisse*), Marx sets out his moment in a vivid, if abstracted, passage:

> when the great English landowners dismissed their retainers, who had consumed with them the surplus produce of their land; when their tenant farmers drove out the small cottagers, etc., then a mass of living labour power was thrown on to the labour market, a mass which was *free in a double sense*: free from the old client or bondage relationships and any obligatory services, and free also from all goods and chattels, from every objective and material form of being, free of all property [*eine Masse, die in doppeltem Sinn frei war*]. It was reduced either to the sale of its labour capacity or to begging, vagabondage or robbery as its only source of income. History records that it tried the latter first, but was driven off this road and on to the narrow path which led to the labour market, by means of gallows, pillory and whip. (Marx 1857/1986: 431 my italics, trans. from 1857/1974: 406)

The goods that had previously been consumed by the feudal lords and their retainers, and the released produce of the land, are thrown on to the exchange market, as are those who would be known henceforth as labourers. That sale of labour power must be instilled by discipline – the gallows, the workhouse, the prison – and becomes the only choice.[25] Even the poorhouses and their charity instil the discipline of work (only Dickens's Oliver dares ask for 'more' it seems). That this was conceived by Marx as part and parcel of capitalist development can be confirmed from other (re)writings of almost the same paragraph.

In *Capital* Marx returns more than once[26] to this scene:

> Thus were the agricultural people, first forcibly expropriated from the soil, driven from their homes, turned into vagabonds, and then whipped, branded, tortured by laws grotesquely terrible, into the discipline necessary for the wage system. (Marx 1867/1967: 737)

Over and over Sony and Marx 'free us from employment'.[27] One ironic, the other obscene: the obscenity is from Sony, because here the way out of the ghetto is the old often repeated trick/panacea of pop stardom or forced wage slavery. That MTV and the music industry can market this lottery dream as a vehicle for selling ever more records is no longer a surprising point ('you can't actually be the popstar with the escape clause, but buy the album and you feel like it could be you'). The trick is that we are free to endure this, we volunteer to be retold the improbable tale over and over, we walk willingly into the record store:

> For the conversion of his money into capital, therefore, the owner of money must meet in the market with the free labourer, *free in the double sense*, that as a free man he can dispose of his labour-power as his own commodity, and that on the other hand he has no other commodity for sale, is short of everything necessary for the realisation of his labour-power. (Marx 1867/1967: 169 my italics, Marx's gendered language)

That this too is no equal exchange is of course the biggest trick of capitalist appropriation. Though it would seem that in the marketplace the capitalist offers a 'fair' price – money for labour, wages – and that the entire history of reformist unions has been to ensure the 'fair trade' of this exchange, the capitalist does not in fact pay for every hour that the labourer works (nor for every cost of reproducing labour power). Here, at the crucial point of the labour theory of value, the expansion of the trick of the market is played out. This moment is exported universally. It would be worth reading the history of Asian labour in Britain as a variation on the dynamics of this market trick. Here it is helpful to draw again upon the work of Virinder Kalra (1997).[28] Disciplined by the inequities of the international division of labour, workers from the colonies are brought to the UK to work the mills in shifts. Irregular employment means they do not benefit from the welfare net of superannuation and pensions and, with the decline of the mills, they are 'freed' into unemployment, taxi-driving (the Sony text again) and service work (kebab shops and the like).

Again towards the end of *Capital* labourers are 'free workers in a double sense':

> The capitalist system presupposes the complete separation of the labourers from all property in the means by which they can realise their labour. As soon as capitalist production is once on its own legs, it not only maintains this separation, but reproduces it on a continually extending scale. (Marx 1867/1967: 714)

The extending scale of this process as we see it today seems well anticipated, but this was only a 'sketch'. In a letter to the editors of the paper *Otechestvennye Zapiski* in the last years of his life, Marx warned that the chapter of *Capital* which set this out in the most detail – Chapter 27 – should not be 'transformed' from a historical sketch of the genesis of capitalism in Western Europe to a 'theory of the general course fatally imposed upon all peoples, whatever the historical circumstances in which they find themselves placed' (correspondence of Marx in 1878 reproduced in Shanin 1983: 136). Far too often the technical abstractions necessary in setting out Marx's *Capital*, which begins with commodities and expands in complexity to encompass trade, circulation of capital, rent, etc., lead to orthodox fixities and dogma. Nevertheless, the general point of the expansion of the logic of market exchange and the creation of 'a "free" and outlawed proletariat' (Marx 1867/1967: 731) can be illustrated thus and it makes sense to use it to understand the circumstances in which the politics of the Asian dance musics might be elided by a commercial outfit like Sony Corp. The history of this expropriation is written 'in letters of blood and fire' (Marx 1867/1967: 715).

There is little need to go further into the hagiographic mode of repeating Marx as oracle, particularly when we have Crispian. There are sufficient other examples too – Félix Guattari: 'it is clear that the third world does not really "exchange" its labour and its riches for crates of Coca-Cola ... It is aggressed and bled to death by the intrusion of dominant economies' (Guattari 1996: 238). Harry Cleaver, summarising, quotes Marx pointing out that 'the veiled slavery of the wage-workers in Europe needed, for its pedestal, slavery pure and simple in the new world' (in Cleaver 1979: 76). Marx there adds a footnote to make it clear that he is talking about the global cotton trade (Marx 1867/1967: 759–60) which again makes it relevant now to link this section to Asian workers in British mills. Cleaver continues: in any study of the ways colonialism 'had to use force to make the indigenous populations accept the commodity form at all' the various examples would range from slavery and death to persuasion (Cleaver 1979: 77) and, especially today, co-options of all kinds. Though it might not have been their (worthy) intention, and though the outcome is not guaranteed, the ambition of Kula Shaker belongs to the wider propensity of capital to always insist on being *free* to take whatever it chooses to market. This trick is nowadays articulated through the rhetoric of the 'open market', the 'level playing field' and 'a fair day's work for a fair day's pay' (and equal access to the pop star dream for all) necessarily subservient to the master trope of the direct equivalence of exchange values mediated through the universal standard money form. Not everyone has the same resources to bring things to market, so what is it that enables Crispian to appropriate India as the 'Ibiza of concepts' and take this booty to Sony for a multi-million deal, while the sadhu and Brahmin custodians of the concepts barter *bindi* for rupees?[29] The rough discipline of inequality and colonial (white) supremacy. Why is it that the trick of the market is not ready to pay out in the same ways for those South Asian practitioners in the UK such as Fun^da^mental, ADF or MC Mushtaq, who have been working with the community for many years without corporate support? Why does culture defer to Crispian's grasp? Cleaver lists 'massacre, money taxes, or displacement to poor land' as the ways that capital dealt with resistance and refusal to be put to work. We could add cultural appropriations and the repetitive drone of a Britpop monoculture that absorbs all into its pre-packaged grip. On the basis of this comes the 'civilising' mission of the West, that would teach 'backward' peoples the values of thrift, discipline, saving and a snappy melody (see Dube 1999). In a contemporary extension of this, we could read Sony's wayward attempt to capture the Asian music market from the cornershops and the bootleggers as an institutional instance of pretty much the same missionary zeal run aground once again on the rocks of the foreign.

Freedom in the double sense can also refer to the double bind of this trickery. Some are free of chattels and possessions, and may ever so freely choose when to sell their labour if they ever want to eat. Some, though, are free to travel the world in search of trinkets. The old colonial adventure is performed with Lord Kitchener as overseer. Capital drives hard to subsume pre-capitalist, non-capitalist (and even post-capitalist retro reruns) into its cannibalising orifice.[30] The 'free flow of ideas', the free operation of the market, the freedom train. In a mercifully brief psychedelic moment of their career the Rolling Stones sang, in an ironic lament: 'I'm free, to do what I want, any old time'. This (always) arrogant freedom is (always) now in crisis, but Britpop wants to defend it as it is. 'Cor blimey'. The posturing moralism, holier-than-thou spiritualism, and good-ethics-guide preachery of Mills is a still more zealous example of the same righteous sermon.

So when Sony and Kula Shaker present themselves as a 'rediscovery' of the Asian sound and its cross-over into popular music they ignore the significance of political and musical histories that paradoxically they must also acknowledge, if only to appropriate and convert. This is nothing more than the operation of a business-as-usual colonial project. It is still about wanting to rule the world.

Travellers' Souvenir India for Show and Display

The 1996 single 'Govinda' is a dirge which has Crispian singing semi-obscure *bhajans* in Sanskrit. The accompanying video deploys a clichéd narrative of fire and brimstone followed by redemption, placing the band in the symbolic space of a monotheised Krishna. The versions of Krishna often deployed in Western tourist renditions of India rely on the translation of three major Hindu deities – Shiva, Vishnu, Krishna – into a Christian-style triumvirate, which then allocates Krishna a Jesus-like position. The popularity of cartoon versions of this part of the Mahabharata among travellers is especially appealing to those of the banana-pancake-trail-backpacker-*bhang-lassi* set just where Krishna seems to bestow a psychedelic experience on his follower Arjuna. This popularity was reinvested on a Kula Shaker CD release ('Hey Dude') which featured the dulcet tones of Crispian reading from the Mahabharata.

How such 'translations' and associations appeal to backpackers can be clearly heard in the Kula Shaker repackaging of souvenired knick-knack mysticism in tracks like 'Tattva' and 'Govinda'. When, in the MTV travelogue, Crispian was faced with a unscheduled performance at a conveniently 'found' Hindu 'party' at a Roadside Hotel stop, the most uncomfortable and awkward moment of 'intercultural relations' is shown in full glorious colour. The mix of pop star prima donna and nervous pre-stage appearance tension, the embarrassing, halting, jangling, acoustic and discordant – though mercifully short – performance, and the attempt to authorise this difficult moment as the culmination of Crispian's India pilgrimage illuminates the hypocrisy. The disturbing spectacle of consumable India presented to audiences in this version at least has the merit of being too transparent for most viewers and fans to swallow whole – though it may be feared that even this could sometimes be taken as representative of a real and available India. The only image that conveys the possibility that there is also a political domain in India is a split-second still of a red protest banner declaring 'Coke-Pepsi Quit India' – but you need a dextrous hand on the pause button to read it. Music industry reception of the band has in large measure been sceptical,[31] but tourist-package promotionals on MTV travel far. Sales suggest something big is going on in the marketplace, and, in any case, any degree of scepticism and cynicism from the music press (or academic commentators) is insufficient to undo the ideological stereotyping achieved by the new media orientalisms that Kula Shaker, Madonna, Bowie and Sony Corp are able to deploy. The post-tourist, post-guru, post-psychedelic revival has the air of sanctimonious and righteous truth.

Trinkets and Tablas

In the end we are left with an apocalyptic vision of a scary alternative universe: what should we make of Crispian's interest in Arthurian legends, his St George English flag pasted onto his guitar (ironically?) alongside the Sanskrit Om? His eulogy for empire in his display of both Kitchener and that flag evokes a nostalgia for the East (nostalgia as a career? to paraphrase Disraeli)[32] that omits the oppression, violence and struggle of history, as if a different outcome to the Raj can be imagined into being through Crispian's mystical trip. The high visibility of trinket Asian sound-bites on the media circuits of popular culture are souvenired baubles in an ongoing Raj powerplay. A sitar-strumming, tabla-thumping, temple-touring knick-knack grab-bag philosophy of distortion and remix of the past.

Can the Subaltern Dance?[33] I know this is a conceit; Crispian is no subaltern, but in the 'post' empire the struggle to retain a faded glory now appears as a parody of the old psychedelic appropriations. Of course the serious side of this is the Sony Empire that finds contingent convenience in marketing this nostalgia (since it can't yet find the code to market Asian musics to Asians). But can Crispian keep to a different beat, or will the Mosley and Thatcher anxiety of swamping require a return to orthodox Fortress Oasis Britpop? So much of cultural life in the UK today is marked by South Asian influences that further incursions into South Asian cultural production for general sale is the almost inevitable outcome of Sony's initial forays into the zone. Hegemonic and institutional, and remaining dominant in all significant class, gender, race and socio-economic categories, Anglo-Saxon culture increasingly trades only on the basis of nostalgia (both Britpop and Kula Shaker trade on the 1960s revival, white flight glosses urban abandon as a return to old rural values). Dining out still on the benefits of Empire, dining out in the curry corridor of urban England as the last feast of colonial power: as I will show in Chapter 7, it comes as no surprise that Brick Lane in London has been designated an 'Official Tourist Zone'.[34]

Rather than the global jukebox which Kula Shaker and so many others seem to imagine as the perfect multicultural soundtrack to the feast of Eastern dining, an engagement with political issues, exclusions and the co-constitution of racism and imperialism would be a far better project.[35] Indigestion in the face of deportations, police attack and repressive force may seem unsavoury, but an injunction to 'Shut up and dance' to the *bhajans* of Crispian or the sitars of Sony is just not an adequate response to the expansive gluttony of the capitalist project today.

Notes

1. The project of a transnational cultural studies correlates dangerously closely with the market-niche agendas of the media empires of Murdoch, Time/ Warner and MTV. The notion of a shared 'electronic community' celebrated by audience studies 'ethnographers' like Ien Ang (1996) fits all too neatly with the target audiences of specialised satellite television provision and the theoretical arabesques of 'diasporic' cultural studies in eloquent personnel such as Clifford (1997) and Gilroy (1993a) (as discussed in Chapter 2). The transnational does not mean the economics of the capitalist nation has gone away, rather, insofar as it may have been displaced to some degree by new cross-border markets, the nation-like economic and demographic scope of these markets remains the same. No, the nation has not disappeared, it's just sometimes a cross-border frequency and a corporate-sponsored timeslot. As Saurabh Dube reminds me, the IMF and World Bank still seem to think (discourse, ideology, practice, police) in terms of nation and flag/logo.
2. In this the work of Armand Mattelart and Michelle Mattelart is exemplary (1986/1992 and Mattelart 1996). It would be possible to question Mattelart's claim that the 'historic turning point of the deregulation of communication networks' is responsible for 'the move to worldwide economic integration' (Mattelart 1996: 303), but it is certainly the case that, 'The integration of

everyone into the material benefits of modernity reserved up to now for the few has become more and more problematic' (Mattelart 1996: 305).

3. Appadurai's famous essay gives a useful code already (Appadurai 1990), but see also Mattelart who begins his *Mapping World Communication: War, Progress, Culture* with the sentence: 'The nineteenth century saw the slow emergence of a new mode of exchange and circulation of goods, messages and persons, as well as a new mode of organising production' (1991/1994: 3).

4. A rare self-reflexive bit: the first two or three times I visited the Indian countryside it seemed strangely empty until I realised the soundtrack I'd been pre-programmed to expect from so many films and documentaries wasn't playing the same tracks 'in the real'. Of course this critique of Kula Shaker is also autobiographical, but I'd contend that this confessional is relevant only in a minor register (see note 16).

5. At a Kula Shaker performance in 1996 I found graffiti, obviously written on the venue walls on an earlier occasion, which captured the sentiment of the point I want to make here with wit and economy: 'Christmas Teaches Kids to Love Capitalism'.

6. See du Gay et al. (1997) for a very accessible introduction to cultural studies via the famous personal music system of Sony.

7. In *Dis-Orienting Rhythms: The Politics of the New Asian Dance Music*, we began by noting how the voracious appetite of the market had turned all manner of 'Asian' markings into exotic objects of value – saris, vindaloo and Ravi Shankar being the least offensive items – but we also noted that this was concurrent with increased racist violence and murder on the streets, police persecution and deportation by the government, and a purulent voyeuristic interest in 'culture' on the part of much of academia (see Sharma et al. 1996).

8. See the film *Ill-Gotten Gains* 1997 (directed by Joel Marsden, Spat Films 1997) for a recent uncompromising take on this theme, far and away better than any moment of Spielberg's *Amistad*.

9. This is a paraphrase of a comment by Philip Hayward at the Globalisation and Music conference, Centre for the Studies in Social Science, Calcutta, 1998, and I thank him for the reminder. See his *Music at the Borders: Not Drowning Waving and their Engagement with Papua New Guinean Culture* for a very different version of cultural engagement on the part of white rock (Hayward 1997).

10. This formulation was originally written in discussion with Ashwani Sharma.

11. I would share Liz Fekete's (1998: 77–82) critique of a therapy model for anti-racism which would approach white masculinity looking for latent causes and reified oedipal complexes within 'identity' formation rather than pursuing racisms politically.

12. See Banerjea (1999) for another take on this heroism.

13. *Hindutva*, especially in its Mumbai Shiv Sena form under Bal Thackeray, has been explained as a consequence of Hindu nationalism mixed with 'casino capitalist' black market speculation and Green Revolution pay-offs enjoyed by the landed elites. There may be resources within Hinduisms that would not lead to support for the far right, but ignorant participation in the 'natural' celebration of Brahminical and fascist *hindutva* populism by white pop stars cannot pass unacknowledged.

14. It might be a little hard-line to claim that the repressive nostalgia of this

imperialism is structured into every cup of tea drunk in the British Isles, but the teapot also features on the Kula Shaker cover, K is for kettle – here, on K's, I'd also add *Khatam*, the war word of the Naxalites from the foothills of Darjeeling. As I will discuss in Chapter 7, the Naxalite movement has recently been celebrated by Asian Dub Foundation and *Khatam* was also the name of a Manchester South Asian club night. The possibility of underlining so many of these congruous links does seem overwhelming, although it must be left for the later chapter to address the ways these kinds of politics are left out of even the growing recognition and international travel of South Asian dance musics.

15. British (as well as US and Australian) soldiers in the South-East Asian theatre were kept on after the Second (imperialist) World War to fight various communist insurrections. In Malaysia many communists were slaughtered, and this is just a part of what was a concerted effort to 'cleanse' the world of the 'Red' threat. A useful, if harrowing, documentation of the millions killed for the crime of wanting the best possible world for all is Kovel (1994).

16. Nostalgia and guilt operate in travel and in ethnography (see Phipps 1999). The doyen of ethnographic fieldwork himself is complicit, and arrives with the cops: Malinowski admits, in a revealing confession: 'The discipline of Ethnology finds itself in a ludicrous situation ... For ethnology to live, its object must die.' Malinowski arrives in his South Sea Island village in the company of the police, with the begrudging support of the District Governor and the approval – for the reason that his research might help in native affairs – of the Australian Government (Atlee Hunt in Mulvaney and Calaby 1985: 453n). The opening words of the premier text of the fieldworkers' method, *Argonauts of the Western Pacific* (Malinowski 1922) begins with a confession, and indeed this is the house style of the discipline. Today, more than ever, the confessional tone characterises the reflexive turn, the postmodern fashion, the postcolonial angst, and this has now been universalised and exported as prerequisite for all. A pale mimicry of criticism/self-criticism continues even into the recent family resemblances which can be traced into cultural studies and, for example, the work of Jean Baudrillard, who in similar words, even 'the same' words as Malinowski (without citation), writes about the discovery of the Tasaday people in the Philippines: 'For ethnology to live, its object must die. But the latter revenges itself by dying for having been "discovered", and defies by its death the science that wants to take hold of it' (Baudrillard 1983: 13). (Curiouser and curiouser, the Tasaday seem to have been an invented 'lost tribe' set up as a touristic publicity stunt – a simulation that would not disturb Baudrillard's schema much at all. Who were these people? Who were they fronting for? Who 'disappeared' them? Who took the cut?)

17. Credit for directing travellers first into the pit of the Pahar Ganj tourist strip, and thence on to trains and buses out of Delhi in the direction of Rajasthani forts, the Taj Mahal or Varanasi's burning *ghats* is due to Tony Wheeler, publisher of the Lonely Planet 'survival' guides. It was Wheeler who wrote that 'real India is on the trains' (*Lonely Planet* 1984, 1991, 1997, etc.; see Phipps 1999; Hutnyk 1996a).

18. This heading is an adaptation of Sanjay Sharma's chapter title 'Noisy Asians, Asian Noise' (Sharma et al. 1996). In that chapter Sanjay carefully catalogues the emergence of South Asian dance musics in the UK, from bhangra to the present.

19. It could be objected that Sony Corp is after all an 'Asian' company – but I think in this case the reification of Japanese business practices tends towards another mode of exoticisation – I would argue that the capitalist 'identity' of Sony overrides any corporate 'ethnicity' which might be deployed. Elsewhere I will discuss the question of Sony TV's South Asian satellite channel offerings. In the context of the subcontinent itself, things are slightly different. The company's effort in India seemed equally opportunist, if considerably more successful, in its deployment of nationalist sentiment in releasing A.R Rahman's version of the nationalist song 'Vande Mataram' on an album that commemorated the fiftieth anniversary of India on 15 August 1997 (and which included tracks featuring Nusrat Fatah Ali Khan, thus complicating the nationalist reference somewhat). However, Sony's success in this case has not translated to all that deft handling of the 'same' sort of material subsequently. For discussion of 'Vande Mataram' see Rangan Chakravarty's excellent dissertation (Chakravarty 1999).

20. Of course the Gallagher brothers cannot be blamed for getting it while they can. Thankfully they don't really go in for identity therapy, except maybe in relation to the uneven fortunes of their Maine Road football team, Manchester City.

21. In 1998 Nation Records released a double CD compilation of the label's most well-known and memorable tracks, entitled *And Still No Hits* ... .

22. Since many won't recognise this, the question in this subtitle follows the format of a series of articles on the history of left critique published in the mid-1990s in *Rabelais*, the newspaper of the La Trobe University Students Representative Council.

23. For an incisive critique of the social scientific and social work deployment of this culture clash trope see McLoughlin and Kalra (1999).

24. For one specific and detailed examination of the uneven play across this difficult 'postcolonial' border which raises questions of differential 'freedoms' see Kalra and Purewal (1999).

25. Michel Foucault's somewhat reluctant Marxist inheritance in his inspiring and influential work on asylums, clinics, punishments, etc., emerges from these insights, although it is important to remember that labour itself is a major mode of disciplinary formation.

26. Also:

> They were turned *en masse* into beggars, robbers, vagabonds, partly from inclination, in most cases from stress of circumstances. Hence at the end of the 15th and during the whole of the 16th century, throughout Western Europe a bloody legislation against vagabondage. The fathers of the present working-class were chastised for their enforced transformation into vagabonds and paupers. Legislation treated them as 'voluntary' criminals, and assumed that it depended on their own good will to go on working under the old conditions that no longer existed. (Marx 1867/1967: 734)

27. There is, of course, an extensive literature on freedom in this context. For a beginning see Marx's famed 'Paris Manuscripts of 1844' (1844/1979). Marcuse spoke of freedom in the 1960s in ways that would require Crispian to do more than sing about revolutions of the mind: 'Marxism must risk

defining freedom in such a way that people become conscious of and recognise it as something that is nowhere already in existence' (Marcuse 1970: 32). Another reworking which draws upon Luxemburg, the existentialists, Mao Zedong and Hegel is found in the writings of Raya Dunayevskaya: *Rosa Luxemburg: Women's Liberation, and Marx's Philosophy of Revolution* (1981/1991) as well as her *Philosophy and Revolution* (1973). Today we might want to ask how the struggle for freedom seems to have turned into the struggle for the extension of free trade (the freedom of a free fox among free chickens as Rosa Luxemburg might have said). In general terms, freedom from employment would perhaps be fine if this freed us *for* creativity, but the distribution of resources and the fact that the trick ensures that only some are 'free' to make a viable living in the cultural industries and others are 'free' to work in even less pleasurable ways – even at its best, in the service sector of the cultural zones, remuneration in music, tourism or food is rather less than that afforded to, say, the Spice Girls.

28. It should be work like Kalra's that Featherstone has in mind when he writes: 'One could envisage a ... book on cotton which would focus upon the relations between Manchester capitalism and imperialist presence in the Indian and other colonies.' He interestingly continues: 'we should add that this and similar topics (chocolate, tea, etc.) are being addressed as student projects on cultural studies and communications courses' (Featherstone 1995: 156). Indeed, as it is non-tenured and sessional Asian researchers who have been teaching such courses, the absence of full-time employment and adequate teaching release for black academics ensures the citation remains anonymous (see Kalra 1997, 2000b).

29. This is not to forget that there are other (internal?) hierarchies and appropriations at play here in sectors complex as well as profound – the discussion of these, however, is engaged elsewhere (see Kalra and Hutnyk 1998).

30. Of course subsumption arguments cannot simply be stated and left as self-explanatory guardians of what goes down. Complicated processes of co-option, recruitment of comprador classes, hegemonic cultural and political struggle and the myriad local variations that anthropologists love to point out would need to be accounted for in any comprehensive study. It is sufficient here to note that good, worthy, zealous dim Crispian has been sequestered by the ideological division of such processes, aware of it or not (indeed, if he were 'taking the piss' it would be less offensive, but unfortunately the 'seriousness' with which Kula Shaker take themselves is never ever shaken).

31. Especially over Crispian's comments about the swastika being a great image, as reported by Stephen Dalto in the *New Musical Express* from a March 1997 interview (but see *NME* 4 April 1998 for analysis of Crispian's recantation, and his unconvincing excuse, as implied by the *NME,* that he himself is Jewish – he has a Jewish grandmother). Photographs and stories reporting his involvement with the National Front have not been mitigated by his claims that the band, Objects of Desire, which included former NF member Marcus McLaine (Crispian's mother's ex-lover), was 'a teenage thing' and that now Crispian 'loathes' the far right (*Vox,* May 1988). In an amazing response to one journalist's reporting of the original controversy, Crispian offered a

long letter, subsequently posted on the Sony www page, which in part
reads:

> I have travelled to India many times and have been influenced greatly by
> its people and philosophy, especially that of Bhakti or devotional love. It
> is my love of Indian culture, and its artistry, music, rich iconography and
> symbols that prompted my comments in the *NME* [about the legitimacy
> of the swastika and its ancient Indian origins]. My comments were not in
> any way a support of the crimes that are symbolised by the Nazis use of
> the swastika ... I apologize to those who have been offended by my
> comment and humbly ask that they accept that I am completely against
> the Nazis ... Lately I have considered how confusing some of the things I
> have said appear, especially when they are taken as sound bites, and on
> occasion, out of context. Communication seems challenging at the best
> of times, and I now appreciate that my bundling of themes like the Grail,
> Knights Templars and Hinduism has not done much in the way of helping
> deep understanding. You are correct when you comment on my
> 'complicated and intriguing mystical worldview' saying that you, 'find it
> hard to understand in simple terms' the co-mingling of all these ideas. I
> think the only way one can reconcile their relationship (if indeed one
> accepts that there is one), is if one looks at them from a mystical or
> spiritual point of view. There are of course lines of thought that suggest
> how eastern ideas made their way to the West, especially via the Crusades,
> but it is true that for the most part they do not have a currency in modern
> thought. Thus in essence, the co-mingling is largely a personal expression
> of a desire to know and understand the deeper secrets of a spiritual or
> inner life. From the little that I know or understand, I see that somehow
> similar themes appear in different cultures and settings ... I appreciate that
> my own special mix of themes is at best eccentric. (Crispian Mills, letter to
> Mr Kalman, *Independent*, 17 April 1997. For the full text consult:
> <www.music.sony.com/Music/ArtistInfo/KulaShaker/reviews/
> inde_fax.html>)

32. The oft-quoted phrase 'The East is a career' appears in Disraeli (1871: 141). I
take the citation from Chow (1993: 185), for whom it was located by
Prabhakara Jha. There is, however, something disturbing in Chow's use of
this phrase to make a point about students 'of the East'. She writes:

> The difficulty facing us, it seems to me, is no longer simply the 'first
> world' Orientalist who mourns the rusting away of his treasures, but also
> students from privileged backgrounds Western *and* non-Western who
> conform behaviorally in every respect with the elitism of their social
> origin ... but who nonetheless *proclaim* dedication to 'vindicating the
> subalterns' ... they choose to see in other's powerlessness an idealised
> image of themselves and refuse to hear in the dissonance between the
> content and manner of their speech their own complicity with violence ...
> even though ... [they] may be quick to point out the exploitativeness of
> Benjamin Disraeli's 'The East is a career', they remain blind to their own
> exploitativeness as they make 'the East' *their* career. (Chow 1993: 14–15)

Chow then asks how we might intervene in the productivity of this
overdetermined circuit, and I hope some of the answer is illustrated in this
book.

33. My reference here is to Gayatri Spivak's famous essay, 'Can the Subaltern Speak?' (Spivak 1988). I would point out that not only is Crispian Mills not at all subaltern, those that do 'speak' but are not heard here because of Crispian's verbosity – and so are the ones who thus take the place of the subaltern who 'can' dance – are also, keeping in mind the previous footnote, hardly subaltern at all. While I want to register the ways exotic versions of 'India' muffle the political articulations of bands like ADF and Fun^da^mental, they are themselves able to access media avenues with extraordinary reach (again see Chapter 7 for a discussion of the incongruity of ADF's single 'Naxalite', referencing the history of peasant struggle in West Bengal, being beamed by satellite to receivers simultaneously in London and Calcutta). Nevertheless, here I play with the mode of address, and wonder not what matter who is speaking, but that it matters what is said and with what purpose. Once more Adorno might be evoked – there is a big difference between the anger of writing poetry *about* Auschwitz, and the aesthetics of reading poetry *after* Auschwitz – no matter whose poetry it may be. Music or ham?

34. 'What Brick Lane needs is more investment in housing, jobs and new local businesses – not just the curry houses' (*Eastern Eye*, 19 September 1997). Debate over changing the name Spitalfields to Banglatown rages in the local press (see *East London Community News*, August 1998)

35. Against the saccharine multiculturalism of the Global Jukebox, Nation Records inaugurated their Global Sweatbox club night in London, March 1998.

5
Authenticity or Cultural Politics?

> Who the fuck wants purity? ... the idea of hybridity, of intermixture,
> presupposes two anterior purities ... I think there isn't any purity;
> there isn't any anterior purity ... that's why I try not to use the word
> hybrid ... Cultural production is not like mixing cocktails. (Gilroy
> 1994: 54–5)

'Cultural politics' as a popular charm has come to carry the hopes and
aspirations of politically minded academic commentators making
'interventions' in the public sphere for the good of us all. The designated
code-phrase, avoided by almost everyone else, appears along with a
range of associated magical terms used not only to sell texts (buzzwords)
but also to demarcate certain authorial innovations from an 'older'
politics and writing, mired, so goes the routine, in 'orthodox' questions
and perspectives. However, despite the enthusiasms of the revamping
cultural politics lobby, the actually specified culture and politics, and the
content of the various circumscribed buzzword terms, remains quite
obscure. It is time to take stock of a wider range of commentary in the
cultural studies marketplace. In this chapter, writings by Rey Chow, Lisa
Lowe, Iain Chambers and Timothy Taylor are examined under the sign
of the material girl's Asian turn. This makes it possible to re-evaluate
buzzwords like multiculturalism and hybridity, to rethink the politics of
visibility and authenticity, and to argue the case for a cultural politics
that must go beyond mere appreciation of the soundtrack of difference.

As argued earlier in this book, hybridity is now such a contested word
that its referent has decomposed into mulch. Biological and botanical
histories contest with creativity and adventure, complicated by puri-
fications and blends. The criticisms of hybridity can be collected into
several categories: the heritage of hybridity's botanical roots (see Young

1995); the sterility of the hybrid mule, and its extension to mulatto, mixed race, half-breed and other obscene racisms; the reclamation of the term reconfigured as creativity at the margins and as advent of vibrant intersections that cannot be otherwise incorporated; the hegemony of the pure that co-constitutes the hybrid; the inconsequence of hybridity in the recognition that everyone is hybrid, everyone is 'different'; the commercial co-option of multiplicities; and that if everyone is hybrid, then the old problems of race, class, gender, sex, money and power still apply. All of this is the terrain of hybridity-talk made fashionable in the salons of culture commentary.

Nowadays, culture is valorised as a site of struggle, where, in the accounting processes of the public domain, the mere fact of appearance counts as a politics. In this chapter I want to carefully acknowledge that visibility does matter in a context where exclusion from resources and opportunities is much more than an absent-minded and myopic blindness of the dominant cultural groups, to be repaired by policy. But it is also my argument that visibility here is only part one of a struggle, as state-sponsored celebration of increased visibilities for hitherto 'marginal' groups can readily be turned to market opportunism. There are many ways in which the cultural industries select privileged brokers as the commissars of multiplicity and the shop-floor traders of difference. At the same time, criticism of both opportunism and co-option as the dual traps of authenticity has a flip-side in the appropriation observable as favoured 'marginals' become the resource material of iconic style kings and queens, strutting wares of dubious patrimony.

In a provocative volume, *Ethics after Idealism,* Rey Chow suggests that the popularised concepts hybridity, diversity and pluralism may be grouped with others such as heteroglossia, dialogism, heterogeneity and multiplicity, as well as with notions of the postcolonial and cosmopolitan, as serving to 'obliterate' 'the legacy of colonialism understood from the viewpoint of the colonized' and to 'ignore the experiences of poverty, dependency, subalterneity that persist well beyond the achievement of national independence' (Chow 1998: 155). This is quite a claim, but one with which I concur. That some can imagine that the 'whole world is postcolonial today' is a kind of thinking which offers a smooth 'either/or' as if it were 'a matter of choice between being a colonizer and being colonized'. Chow continues: 'The enormous seductiveness of the postmodern hybridite's discourse lies ... in its invitation to join the power of global capitalism by flattening out past injustices' in a way that accepts the extant relations of power and where 'the recitation of past injustices seems tedious and unnecessary' (Chow

1998: 156). Forget colonial violence, white supremacy and systematic exploitation and oppression: hybridity saves.

This suggestion that hybridity-talk smoothes over historical violence is not simply a call for a return to studies of the 'Third World' or the poor and excluded. It matters everywhere. Thus I have been asking how useful the term hybridity is in the 'advanced' North Atlantic zones, especially as it is deployed in discussions of South Asian popular culture and music performance made in these zones – the now also overly codified cultural industry's 'Asian' turn. The difficult fact is that those who are well connected and globally mobile can plunder the cultural resources of the world without restrictions – presently it is Asian dance music that provides the merchandise for resale in the elite salons. Shorn of political roots, toned down and sweetly packaged as exotic magical mystery tourist fare, these transnational flavours do not burn the tender tongues of middle-class liberalism. Examples abound: chameleon groover Boy George has been working in Mumbai with Bappi Lahiri on a Hindi film soundtrack *Love Story '98* (*Eastern Eye*, 3 January 1998); Talvin Singh's Anokha night-club in London has spawned imitations across the planet (New York, Frankfurt, Tokyo); Oasis regularly seek out Asian-ish support for their US tours. Thus, 'Asians' are visible in the cultural marketplace. The 'coolie has become cool', in Sanjay Sharma's deeply ironic phrase.[1]

Pointing out the contradictions of both South Asian public culture visibility and the hybridity-theory talk which pretends to explain it does not excuse writing which only collects anecdotes. Accumulating wondrous ironies, displaying jaded culture industry fascination with co-option, compromise and hypocrisy, and revelling in reflexive celebration of the problems and epistemic dilemmas of study does not promise much. The 'postcolonial' appearance of that seductive reflexivity, which wins 'hearts and minds',[2] is only the flip-side of orientalism 'at home'. Reflexivity is often an excuse for business-as-usual, the export trick of postmodernism which displaces both intimate enemies and inter-nationales across the known worlds. This mode of orientalism develops by importing caste-, tribe- and village-obsessed ethnographic habits to initiate contemporary 'back-to-the-field' renderings of ethnicity and culture where politics might more readily explain. South Asia 'itself' disappears as it is consigned to the documentary zone of disaster, poverty, religion, music and food. This Third World is transposed to become a 'colourful' backdrop tableau for the visits of presidents, first ladies, Foreign Secretaries and Special Negotiators (read IMF/World Bank hacks). 'Culture' here provides material for ever similar photo-opportunities, and so it is clear that a growing subsection of the market is allocated to esoterica as a lifestyle choice. Similarly, as the new university is restructured into a mass teaching/instruction facility, cultural performance is designed in large part – especially in the cultural studies, sociology, anthropology sector – to perform an identificatory function, preparing the way for ready insertion of producers and consumers into a global service economy. The production of 'content' (culture) to fit the bandwidth of the new technological revolution in transportation (tourism), representation (niche 'identity' markets, music, food, fashion, etc.) and communications (satellite television/MTV, Internet, radio) is subcontracted to the avant-garde and otherwise visible but silenced 'minorities'. In this context reflexivity is often the paradigm that facilitates only a change of the guard within the institutional apparatus.

Appropriation

In the serious culture salon discussions, a more immediate malaise seems to prevail. Hybridity-talk serves as a cloaking device, not of cultural authenticity (for what is that if not a strategic construct?) but of political, social and economic differentials. Perhaps there are just too many celebrants of the East, like Madonna in this chapter, with their transparently naïve but mass media resourced pantomime, as well as too many celebrants of 'more authentic' *desi* sounds, such as bhangra purists or strict Qawwali devotees, or even too many enthusiastic sociology department fans of Apache Indian. All these, however, participate in a 'cultural' exchange that assumes a level of equivalence – a terrain of multiculti creativity – which occludes the underlying structural inequalities of the contemporary field. The visibility of Apache, for example, in both the USA and UK, is held up as a paradigmatic instance of hybridity as an interventionist politics. But while Apache is much discussed, this is more often as an iconic hybridity rather than a politics to be analysed. What politics in any case? Arranged marriages and anti-drugs social messages, but not so much more (as discussed earlier). Apache becomes the exemplary example of hybridity cross-over, but the circumstances, and even the specificities, of his work are not systematic-ally engaged: dining out on the cultural cachet gathered from the mix of Jamaican patois, Indian stylee and Birmingham English (see Back 1996). Conversely, silencings can be imposed on some modes of mixing, making invisible how a certain upper elite fraction have the resources to operate the system and others are less well placed. This can be seen most explicitly in Paul Simon's refusal to grant Fun^da^mental clearance for a song sample from 'The Sound of Silence' (also discussed below) – this from Mr World Music himself, happily trading on recycled sounds and borrowings from afar. It is not the borrowing that is offensive here, but the differential operation in the mix: hybridity never threatens Mr Simon's identity or security as it supposedly does for 'non-traditional', devalued, marginal, cross-cultural beings (it is always cross-cultural for some, and entrepreneurial for others).

In a not unrelated way, hybridity-talk drags theorists into authenticity denials and the binary logic of difference, which leaves them unable to posit a politics that does more than acknowledge complexity. For me it is much more interesting and useful to note the political eruptions that may still be discerned amidst the 'hybrid creativities' allocated to the postcolonial. I believe these cannot be understood only as hybrid, they imply a critique of the projects of hybridity, identity and simplistic notions of (commercialised) difference. I'd more readily celebrate groups like ADF or Fun^da^mental for their 'political' identity than their ethnic flavour (even as that offers a context for the political struggle at the present time), however much Fun^da^mental are considered by some critics to be 'too militant' and not yet wholly digestible (even as scholarly commentary chews them up, masticates and domesticates the sounds).

Reassertions of bhangra purism, condemnation of cross-over styles, uneasiness at the co-option and compromises entailed by high profile 'mixed' mixers, – all this has heightened the authenticity and appropriation debate, and made hybridity contested terrain and newsworthy copy. By the middle of 1996 even the *New York Times* was announcing that Hindi pop had met hip-hop 'as a New Generation of South Asians finds its groove' (*NYT*, 30 June 1996), and no, this was not an ad for Pepsi but a feature article written by Somini Sengupta, reporting the Asian dance scene at Planet 28 – though focused somewhat voyeuristically on the gang rivalries of groups like Punjabi By Nature (PBN) and Madina, a Pakistani crew. Nevertheless, the celebration of an ascendant Asian-America advances by way of new television channels presenting Hindi films and music (for example, ITV, the local cable station), new clubs in Manhattan, Jackson Heights, Queens, and an 'explosion' in the Gujarati party scene – all featured as examples of that cultural diversity which makes New York proud (see Maira 1998). Of course, this congratulatory multiculti activity ignores any detailed analysis of the race politics of Asian America and, as Chow suggests, 'obliterates' experiences of colonialism, poverty, dependency, etc., even in the US context, and especially with regard to US imperialism. What, for example, does Asian-America really mean? Is it relatively privileged 'second generationers' clubbing in the cool night-spots of NYC, or even white kids with *bindis* smoking *charas* and down with the *ganj* (hood)?, or is it Madonna doing easternised dance tracks, learning to meditate (MTV Special May 1998), and dressing up exotic for the cover of *Rolling Stone* (August 1998),[3] or for the Grammy Awards (February 1999)? Fragmenting the notions of where America actually operates, is 'Asian-America' more visible in Coca-Cola versus Pepsi in Panjab; or in policy initiatives and sanction threats over the Indian or Pakistani bomb; structural adjustment and financial transfer; outsourcing of micro-computing and secretarial work to Bangalore; or the establishment of Microsoft Corporation's second headquarters in Hyderabad, Andhara Pradesh? The questions to ask here between politics in the world and performance in the clubs would be: why is it that cultural celebration rarely translates into political transformation? Does sanctioned visibility in the centre occlude secret agendas and invisibility for the rest? Can high profile be traded for redress?

Is it not good news that North Atlantic Asian culture has a new degree of recognition? There is obviously more complicated stuff going on here than a new craze for dance parties. What, for example, does the celebration of visibility and creativity mean in this context? At a time when politics has become 'identity' and the 'right' to be different, how needful is an analysis which questions the terms in which the new debates proceed? At a time when explicit class politics in the West seems blocked, does the shift to identity, hybridity and the postcolonial express a decline in aspirations (to transform the entire system) and an accommodation to things as they seem now and forever to be? Importing culturally 'hybrid' styles via the mass media that sanitises and decontextualises the political context of those styles – explicitly in the case of the self-defence and spatial politics of much South Asian music from Britain[4] – might be recognised as a danger. Similarly the dilemmas of accepting a performative 'place in the sun' as hybrid or exotic novelties in order to claim space and pay rent while day-to-day racism and exploitation prevails is not without its necessities. The contradictions here are clear where the 'melting pot' may mean participation at the feast of culture, but not always as a diner – there are cooks, service staff and guests, and perhaps even some who give speeches among those who deserve to be theorised. Yet all of these subject positions may be recruited to the equation of visibility with equality which serves to perpetuate the economic system that profits from racism, colonialism and the trick of surplus labour extraction (see Lowe 1996: 26).

What is there that is common to Madonna dressed in a sari for *Rolling Stone* on the one hand, and the sociology of identity (and diaspora) on the other? Madonna is a privileged site for discussion of music video. Probably more ink has been shed over her work than over any other single theme in cultural studies. This is somewhat tragic then, and an indictment of the discipline, but there need be no apology for adding to the carnage by addressing her work in the context of Asian America. Promotional videos for the album *Ray of Light* include decontextualised symbols of Hinduism floating in ethereal new age mush with embarrassingly clunky *bharatanatyam* dance imitations. The album includes sanskrit lyric passages – 'Shanti-Ashtangi' – and in interviews Madonna has professed her great interest in the Kabbala, Buddhism and Tibet (the smorgasbord of the East doesn't require geographical coherence here). Kitted out in a new stylee, Madonna takes the old imperial frock (of Edwina Mountbatten as readily as that of Eva Peron[5]) and gets herself up like a twentieth-century version of the colonial memsahib, lording it over the plantation workers (see bell hooks on Madonna as plantation mistress, appropriating gay exotica that time round).[6] With the same well-resourced and grasping opportunism that enables international interests to exploit the opium trade where local producers cannot,[7] Madonna capitalises on the popularity of the new Asian dance music because she (or rather her corporate organisational existence) has the global resources to represent the localised creativities of those who devised the forms (allegedly equally creative performers with whom she loves to work). Tea plantations and cotton farms had their own material girls up at the big house, even as the fields were full of those engaged in back-breaking toil. We could refer here to break-dancers back at the Cotton Club, or bhangra gigs in reconditioned Manchester cotton-mills (such as the ironically named Hacienda). These are examples of the way the plantation structure has now been transposed (recomposited) on to the information-entertainment economy (CD production plants in Malaysia and China replace the old sweated labour with clinically air-conditioned ones).

Madonna revels in identification of the 'esoteric' other in the USA, while in Britain – after also supporting Oasis on their US visit – Kula Shaker's singer Crispian Mills declares we can learn so much from the 'timeless spirit of Indian philosophy' (and by timeless he means well and truly past – totally unconcerned with contemporary Indian philosophy, let alone politics … or 'reality'). Across Europe, courses on alternative healing, shamanism (even inside the university) and world music festivals are thriving, and circulated in hyper-text, wide-band, multicolour cult-layout, crazy-pixel new-Britannia Kool. The role of Asians in Britain and the USA is convoluted: admitted for economic reasons, distanced from national citizenship (the Tebbit test in England, exclusions in the USA), they now participate in the emergence of an alternative cultural space which enacts the dialectic between that which cannot be contained within national imageries and the creeping subsumption or assimilation of aspects of that culture which can be so contained, repackaged by the material girl to then be sold in the millions.[8]

Culture-ism

What role for talk of 'culture' in this domain? In her book *Immigration Acts: On Asian American Cultural Politics*, Lisa Lowe argues that it is 'only through culture that we conceive and enact new subjects and practices' which question the modes of government that suppress dissent and reproduce capitalist relations of production. Lowe suggests that it is 'because culture is the contemporary repository of memory, of history' that, through culture, 'alternative forms of subjectivity, collectivity and public life are imagined' (Lowe 1996: 22). It is, however, unclear exactly what is meant by culture here, and Lowe seems to locate oppositional practice – action and theory – outside the realm of material and political struggle. True, she says this is 'not to argue that cultural struggle can be the exclusive site for practice' (Lowe 1996: 22), but it seems that her analysis overdetermines the cultural in ways that are possibly reactionary responses to a rigid economism inherited from the more overtly 'orthodox' reifications of Marxism. If this bogey were not considered so threatening – I believe it is a shibboleth adopted from Stuart Hall's work[9] – then the privilege of culture may be less absolute. What, in any case, does cultural politics signify in a market relations context?

What do we make of the process by which once unassimilated aspects of culture – say body piercings, *bindis* or spicy food – have been integrated within mass commercial culture? Is the aestheticisation of cultural 'quirks' according to a capitalist rationality (that all differences can be equated at the market) something that can be fought and won at the level of 'cultural struggle'? Surely all that is fought for at this level is authenticity – and not material redress and transformation.

It is Lowe's argument that the new conditions of flexible production demand a new conception of culture and generate a 'need for an alternative understanding of cultural production' (Lowe 1996: 33). But contrary to her assertion that Marxism 'cannot account for the current global restructuring of capitalism' (Lowe 1996: 25), or flexible transnational accumulation, undermining of citizenship or racialisation and feminisation of labour, I think the notions of real and formal subsumption, and the evident extension of capitalist relations to the entire planet, are the coordinates of Marxism that today make the most sense, and make sense of the place of cultural production within global restructuring (see Hardt and Negri 1994).

Elsewhere, however, Lowe is critical of liberals who remain 'wedded to a culturalist paradigm, however "multiculturalist", that still tends to isolate culture from material relations' (Lowe 1996: 39). Here her critique is of the function of university education which 'serves to socialize and incorporate students from other backgrounds into the capitalist market economy' (Lowe 1996: 40). This is exactly where I think the celebration of cultural struggle as a potential site of disruption begins to falter, since co-option into the assimilation project of the multiculture of capital is all too readily always on offer – with attendant material benefits for a few, the forlorn promise of their always postponed delivery for the rest (only some elite staff of colour in the institutions, only some gangstas making it out of the ghetto alive). That Lowe points to the efficacy of interdisciplinary studies as a potential disruption of 'the narratives of traditional disciplines that have historically subordinated the concerns of non-Western, racial and ethnic minority peoples' (Lowe 1996: 40), does not yet make for the basis of a transformation of that system, nor defend against the co-option and assimilation that facilitates generational change within the institutional structure. Critique of disciplinarity, even where it refuses to set up a counter-disciplinarity, does not yet distinguish this move from, say in anthropology, the reflexive critique of the 1970s and 1980s that enabled a (partial) personnel transfer (at a time of shrinking job opportunities), nor from the countercultural movements that elevated baby-boomers to the establishment, or further back, the ways movements in art like Cubism or Surrealism inaugurated generational change in the galleries. What remains absent here is the politics of an organisation capable of actual disruption not only of the university or of individual institutions, but of the market system in entirety. Lowe does note this danger, writing that:

> institutionalizing such fields as Ethnic Studies still contains an inevitable paradox: institutionalization provides a material base within the university for a transformatory critique of traditional disciplines and their traditional separations, and yet the institution-

alization of any field or curriculum that establishes orthodox objects and methods submits in part to the demands of the university and its educative function of socializing subjects into the state. (Lowe 1996: 41)

Lowe, however, would risk institutionalisation and appropriation into the system because of the possibility that the interdisciplinary institution may remain 'a site from which to educate students to be actively critical' of the traditional function of the university (Lowe 1996: 41). I have a lot of sympathy for this position, yet think that more is possible.

Hybrid cultural practice is assigned to the ethnicised zones of the margin from the very outset. That the most rigid versions of the centre-and-margin model operate a hegemonic white supremacist vision has often been pointed out. That its more sympathetic renderings also carry a perniciously homogenising 'future' vision of an integrated Western culture-in-multiplicity is the grand trick of capitalist 'difference'. The critique of the notion of hybridity can be tracked between these poles ...

Hybridity-talk entails a contradiction even in its own postmodern terms – as a name for heterogeneity it essentialises. Differences are grouped again under the one name – 'hybrid'. This contradiction seems to sit happily alongside another – that contemporary capitalism thrives on an internationalisation of differences at the same time that it requires a system of discrete and coherent administrative units (hitherto called nation-states, henceforth cultural Disneylands) which will fuel the international difference machine.

This begins with a reification of the 'homeland' that is often used to fix identity and culture. This is the God-ego trick of elevating a continuist 'identity' over and above all moments of identity: 'I am now' and 'I was then' joined in the reified 'I am' and thus 'I will be'. This process performed first by 'ego' is then projected on to all other possible 'identities' in a diminutive mode – you are what you were and will always be. Culture gets stuck here in the anthropological brochure. As I argued in Chapter 2, for many 'South Asia' remains a site of mystery, aroma, colour and exotica, and then even in its most hybridly creative manifestations, the fixed image prevails over all other possibilities. The highlighting of this – the routine of spice-trade thinking – obscures the aporias of sanctioned multicultural discourse (Spivak 1995), and through a kind of paralysis, in effect, ensures continued exploitations and inequalities arraigned across both 'cultural' boundaries and explicit national ones – be these the immediate borders of the geographical USA or Europe (immigration controls) or across the foreign 'diplomacy' demarcations of US/UN imperial hegemony (sanctions, IMF controls, etc.). At the same time and through the same process, continued maintenance of white privilege in education, the marketplace and the public sphere is left unchallenged by the self-congratulatory mutual fascination with fantasy versions of cultural pluralism – the diversity of culture is the happy narrative that hides the structural socioeconomic disjunctions of the world.

Would the sign of hybridity attached to the demarcations of Asian American studies extend to analyses of, say, the influence of the Black Panther Party on the Dalit Panthers of Bombay, or perhaps to the formation of the first Communist Party of India in Tashkent, Uzbekistan, by M.N. Roy, who had honed his organising skills in court trials (the Hindu Conspiracy case) in California and then Mexico as secretary of the Mexican Socialist Party? (See Chapter 7). Would hybridity, post-coloniality or transnational studies as conceived in various popular journals now finding favour amongst the cultural studies glitterati be able to comprehend the internationalist political hybridity of Peruvian shipment of Kalashnikovs to rural peasants in Andhara Pradesh? Is a rice-farmer with a machine gun hybrid? It is always important to ask these questions in a double movement – what about America in South Asia? – from imperialism to subversion, from US support for Pakistan in Cold War times, through NRI remittance support for *hindutva*, to the mixed (but large) fortunes of the Coca-Cola corporation in the subcontinent? Again: is Coca-Cola in Kovalam hybrid? Why would *dal bhat* in Detroit be considered exotic, but Levi's in Lahore not? These examples could be replicated.

Authenticity

There could be two different narratives played out on this stage. One celebrates a phantasmagoric fascination with the East: George Harrison, Gong, Teardrop Explodes, Paul Weller, Kula Shaker, Madonna; the other follows a cultural authenticity showcase: Ravi Shanker, Qawwali, Hindi film songs, bhangra and some of the Asian Underground. Of course there will be overlaps between the competing narratives, and ways in which they partake of the same principles may sometimes seem more evident than others (the duet between Nusrat Fateh Ali Khan and Eddie Vedder in the film *Dead Man Walking*, for example, complicates the neat list). Neither alone is authentic, the second no less than the first, since both would require turning away from the complexity of social, economic and political relationships by elevating cultural practices to an autonomous and self-sufficient realm. To do so is again that master trick of the capitalist system – pretending that all exchanges take place on an equal plane. Advocates of cultural 'roots' who do not acknowledge this – at the very moment when they affirm the authenticity of their culture – have succumbed to discursive co-option as readily as Madonna with a *bindi* appropriates it.

Authenticity is bound up here as the unavoidable secret nemesis of hybridity theorists – caught in a dialogue which separates, they must then posit difference and its bridge, and offer an understanding of this process as the crucial site of cultural politics. Important and interesting issues are raised, but ultimately the secret comes to undermine any political possibility. The binary logic that they would have us refuse, and in understanding of difference and through dialogue, would have us resist, serves the same operating logic of the capitalist market – all differences in exchange – and still the underlying exploitation of the system remains. Does the critique of purity and the 'ethic of difference' which sustains positive evaluations of hybridity – as a descriptive word – not fall prey to the logic of capital it would want to escape? The step to an organisational politics that would really challenge the commercialisation of differences – and the exploitation of people of which it is the effect – cannot be taken unless deconstruction moves beyond discussion.

In order to challenge Madonna's efforts to include 'authentic' Asian styles in her music, or to condemn Kula Shaker's trinketising versions of temple harmony and Hindu spiritualism, there is no need to posit a fixed and authenticated Asian 'Culture' as the benchmark for critique. Madonna and Kula Shaker patently get it wrong as they play into the hands of Hindu fundamentalism and essentialising fantasy. But what is offensive is that they have the industry backing to circulate their fictions worldwide in ways that have consequences in other spheres – for example in perpetuating notions of India as the land of timeless spirituality, not as a location of modernity, nuclear tests, IMF restructuring, elite exploitation and social struggles, etc. To question this does not require a fundamentalist notion of true or traditional roots (contra Chambers 1994: 73), nor even a strictly agreed 'imagined community'.

Chambers suggests that the 'notion of the pure, uncontaminated "other", as individual and as culture, has been crucial to anti-capitalist critique and condemnation of the cultural economy of the West in the modern world', and he argues that the 'privileged occidental observer' defined authenticity in terms that suited occidental desire (desire for what should 'constitute the native's genuine culture and authenticity') and prevented the 'other' from speaking (Chambers 1994: 81–2). But anti-capitalist critique was perhaps not in every case beset with this limit that reinforced the logic of definitions, even as verbose Western critics did so often accept 'the Other [as] authentic without a problem' while the 'only the dominant self [could] be problematic' (Spivak 1990: 66 cited in Chambers 1994: 82). This is indeed 'very frightening', as Gayatri Spivak suggests. But what a number of anti-capitalist critiques of inauthenticity and appropriation pointed to was not simply that there shouldn't be appropriation – and so authenticity should remain the preserve of timeless authentics – but that the logic of this system required organised resistance leading to its overthrow. If the 'Other' were 'allowed' – Chambers's word – to speak within capitalism there would still need to be other Others. Talk of tradition displaced by 'traffic' in the 'sights, sounds and languages of hybridity' (Chambers 1994: 82)[10] might rather be the latest resource of a cannibalising capitalism that now sells us difference, inauthenticity, irony and reflexive (self-indulgent) critique as its most privileged market strategy.

Chambers wants to remember that there are 'real differences' as well as 'brutal defeats and dead ends'. But in this 'Broken World' he also wonders if it is not possible to:

> glimpse in recent musical contaminations, hybrid languages and cultural mixtures and opening on to other worlds, experiences, histories, in which not only does the 'Empire write back to the centre', as Salman Rushdie puts it, but also 'sounds off' against it? Is there not here, apart from the obvious economic power of the Western world to distribute and market these sounds, that novel, these words, those stories, a poetic twisting and turning of language against itself that constantly undercuts hegemonic pretensions on reality[?] (Chambers 1994: 84)

The obvious power of marketing and distribution is the key. So obvious, it seems, that there shall be no need to account for it, no mode in which something more than accommodation is considered, it is the fixed backdrop – there is no alternative. Or is there? Perhaps Chambers does catch a glimpse here – his hybrid gaze – as he seeks out another location:

> The result is a hybrid art that confounds and confuses earlier

categorizations through a vernacular mixing of languages that were previously separated ... In this deconstruction of both language and its technologies, in these gaps, in the holes in prose, the breaks in sound, there emerge further means and meanings: those differences that permit the process of deferring, and the dispersal and redistribution of powers, of authority, of centre and periphery ... an opening to another place. (Chambers 1994: 85)

This cultural activity in the domain of world musics, has parallels with the imaginative cultural struggle celebrated by Lowe, and elsewhere championed, in different ways, by both Kobena Mercer and Homi Bhabha. In the end we can applaud, and certainly enjoy the new means and meanings, but there remains much work to be done before the holes in prose and breaks in sound – in which the screams of the millions stomped into the dirt by rampant, even hybridising, capital – may be not only heard, but redressed, liberated, freed.

Chambers ends his 'Broken World' chapter with a scene from Gurinder Chadha's film *I'm British But ...* (1988) in which a bhangra band perform on a rooftop in Southall, mimicking and displacing (Chambers's words) the Beatles on the roof of the Apple studios nearly 20 years before. That this scene offers a 'very different sense of history, of identity, of centre' (Chambers 1994: 87), may indeed be an example of a 'dialogue of difference' in which 'our sense of each other is displaced' and 'both of us emerge modified' (Chambers 1994: 86), but what would be required for the 'our' and 'each other' binarisms of Chambers's subject positions to be displaced yet further? What changes to the global socioeconomic coordinates of the music industry would be necessary so that the white musicians who were singing 'Get Back' (to that land where you once belonged) in 1969 were not simply the ones who had the power and resources to make a hit, 'Norwegian Wood', with an 'Eastern' sitar melody, while today, some 30 years of 'dialogue' on, a South Asian version of that same track, in Panjabi by Cornershop, is bumped off the charts by the likes of Madonna because of her superior marketing organisation?

More 'thoughtful' folks than those who expect to find their 'world' musicians to be untainted, premodern 'natives', writes Timothy Taylor, also cannot 'escape the old binaries and expectations' when 'authenticity is jettisoned and hybridity is celebrated'. Taylor does note that it is always the 'natives' who make hybrid music, while 'Musicians at the metropoles rarely make musics that are heard as hybrids (even if they are every bit as hybridised as musics from the peripheries)'. White mainstream artists 'instead are placed in more prestigious categories and praised, as was Paul Simon for *Graceland*: Simon reinvented himself artistically and successfully engineered a "creative rebirth"' (Taylor 1997: 21). The point that the 'native' or marginal person, or culture, is more often hybrid than the centre or dominant one repeats an old pattern. The flip side of this is the reservation of high status for the hybridiser-king in the centre. Simon says. The more prestigious categories here are those of auteur, entrepreneur and 'creative' genius. Elsewhere in the book, Taylor (who has it in for Simon, planning a work specifically devoted to the *Graceland* controversy)[11] refers to reports that Simon's next album after *Graceland*, called *The Rhythm of the Saints*, used recordings of a town square performance by the percussion ensemble Olodum, which were taken back to New York where Simon 'improvised music and words over them and added other layers of music' (interview with Bob Edwards, National Public Radio *Morning Edition*, 18 October 1990, quoted in Taylor 1997: 64n). The hybrid nature of these tracks may readily be recognised, but it is clearly not the case that the Olodum performers gain as much credit for their foundational drums as Simon does for his later orchestration. The album is remembered and known to be 'in' Simon's name (as opposed, one presumes, to that of Paul Simon and the Olodum ensemble), and no doubt the publishing rights to the music remained with the 'creative' genius. Towards the end of the book Taylor writes: 'it is Simon who profits – his position in a powerful economic centre – the United States, a major corporation – means that he cannot escape his centrality, despite his assertion that he works "outside the mainstream"' (Taylor 1997: 203).[12]

Taylor also notes that Womad impresario Peter Gabriel is known to 'treat borrowed music' in the same manner, by 'recording over it' (Taylor 1997: 41), and, rather spitefully, writes that 'he sings over everybody, and he owns the copyrights' (Taylor 1997: 43). Whether or not 'Third World' or 'indigenous' musicians owning copyrights would amount to any substantial transformation in the unequal power relations which saturate this sector of the music industry (and of course the other parts of the culture industry), it is clear that such accusations have a special resonance when it comes to evaluating the seemingly convoluted intricacies of authenticity, cross-over, mixture and entrepreneurship. Unfortunately the power dynamic seems quite straightforward when looked at through particular case studies. As mentioned at the beginning of this chapter, Paul Simon occupies an important place of privilege – when Fun^da^mental recorded their version of Simon's song 'The Sound of Silence' for inclusion on their 1998 album *Erotic Terrorism*, their request to clear the sample was refused. Asking for permission once again, Simon was offered the publishing rights for the new version, which included an additional backing vocal, but Simon again said 'no' (interview with Aki Nawaz, May 1998). Did the Olodum percussionists have any say as to use, recording and ownership of their sound, or even a forum for expression of either any opinion or, more unlikely still, any control of their sounds in the way that Paul Simon so clearly and insistently has? No. For the album, Fun^da^mental re-recorded the 'Sounds' track and renamed it 'Deathening Silence'.

Apache

> Hybridisation and its meanings don't work equally well in all the places the diaspora has reached … Lipsitz's interpretation of Apache Indian's texts as political and liberatory must also be understood in conjunction with Apache's own admission that he injects his music with political concerns and signs of his ethnicity based on his reception on MTV in England and that his popularity among Indians outside the UK is quite contested. (Taylor 1997: 168)

It was still possible, in 1996, for editors and surveyors of the internationalisation of hip-hop to refer to Apache Indian as the only example of a South Asian genre related to rap. South Asian? Important details, such as that Apache Indian hails from Birmingham in the UK, are often overlooked. And it gets worse. In his acknowledgements for the book *Droppin' Science*, William Eric Perkins thanks Anu Rao for introducing him 'to the "bhangra" music of South India' (Perkins 1996: preface, 269). Clearly someone such as Rao should have known that bhangra is, in India, a northern form, from the Panjab, and in Apache's version, it's something that comes out of England considerably transformed from the harvest music of that region. Internationalism here sticks to rather strict, limited and misleading national demarcations. Nevertheless, Perkins's narrative is insightful, especially where he discusses the influence that 'one segment of African American culture plays in the global interdependence shaping the post-industrial … world' (Perkins 1996: 259).

But if this influence is considered in the context of the extension of US-derived cultural forms across the planet, then the 'affirmative' spatial politics claimed, through what Tricia Rose elsewhere calls the politics of rap, begins to look rather complicated. Rap claims space at the expense of other cultural forms struggling in the face of cultural imperialisms, transnational jeans, and sports shoe or tracksuit manufacture. It is certainly not the progressive side of hybridity that has everyone doing flips and twists to get into a pair of American blue jeans, and bouncy Nike trainers.

Is South Asian dance a vehicle of global homogenisation? Taylor's discussion of Apache Indian focuses in exhaustive detail on the track 'Arranged Marriage'. For him it is a 'fascinating ... remarkable' (Taylor 1997: 159), 'ultimately ambivalent' (Taylor 1997: 162), 'interesting' piece, which, however, South Asian listeners find 'too clever', or offering little, and which 'juggles and juxtaposes identity conceptions, with India sometimes far, sometimes near' (Taylor 1997: 163). The identification of the UK as a 'former colonial power with many of its colonised now living in the UK' (Taylor 1997: 157)[13] does raise important points about how Apache's identity 'self-fashioning' proceeds. Recognition of the importance of MTV as a vehicle for his experiments is well and good, but it is not clear how much stress should be placed on the 'former' status of Britain as a colonial power. Perhaps a reconsideration is required when we consider the subsumption of world music to the market, and the role of identity self-fashioning as a mode of accommodating differences to that market and the way that modes of consuming difference are rehearsed, displayed and reinforced by artists such as Apache Indian. That the exotic product (fascinating, remarkable, ambivalent, interesting, clever and many other terms such as hybrid, pastiche and chaotic seem ready to fit here ...) of an artist like Apache works to translate culture for the marketplace is not an insignificant function.

This role can take several forms, sometimes self-declared 'subversive' ones, but as with so many other pop-politics performances, so long as, in the end, the product gets to market, subsumption prevails. Apache Indian has participated in various anti-racist campaigns, such as when he recorded a track, 'Movin' On', critical of the ultra-rightist British National Party in Tower Hamlets (see Back 1996 for another discussion of this), and he has produced tracks, indeed, such as 'Arranged Marriage', which comment on matters of relevance to his community. However, it is not clear what Taylor is trying to do when, writing in the context of the anti-racist track rather than the one about marriages, he says: 'Whereas an Indian might not be able to find the distance necessary to critique his or her own culture, a geographical outsider with an insider's interest might get the job done' (Taylor 1997: 158). The here and there demarcations in this case are simplistic and locate Apache Indian as a kind of displaced person – Apache as 'outsider' to his 'ancestral' land, in the 'seat of the erstwhile Empire' (Taylor 1997: 158). This formulation is in danger of buying in to the very white British xenophobia which fuels the BNP rhetoric in the first place. It is difficult to understand why this characterisation is then followed by a quotation from Apache, which Taylor offers to complete the paragraph, making a totally different point about underestimating Asians as artists and attempts to 'put India on the map' of pop stardom.

Taylor quotes with approval, agreeing 'thoroughly' with Dick Hebdige's comment on 'second-generation British Asians' (note the hyphen in Hebdige is not between British and Asian, but between second and generation), where bhangra is a 'vibrant trademark':

> played across the gaps and tensions not just between 'home' and 'host culture', with their different language, behaviour norms, belief systems, and cuisines, not just between *two* cultures (the 'traditional' East, the 'permissive' or 'progressive' West), but between many *different* south Asian cultures, between the multiple boundaries which for centuries have marked off different religions, castes, ethnic traditions with a 'community' which appears homogeneous only when viewed from the outside. (Hebdige 1996: 139)

The trouble with Hebdige's now standard point against the homogenising of 'objects' like the East or the West, is that here the East as a place of difference feeds, equally as well as the old homogenised and essentialised entity, into the carnivorous machine of capital. Not only is the culture of the 'second-generation' already stamped with a trademark (in a way that inevitably anticipates Cool Britannia marketing), but the East as site of difference is reified again in the anthropological mode where strange tongues, other beliefs, centuries-old (read unchanging) religions, (intractable) caste divisions and the staple trope of spicy food mark out the other community. The pattern of reportage which runs: look at these different people, look closely and I, as expert witness, will show they are even more different than it seems, does not undermine exoticisation. Rather, this reflex action gives an alibi for business as usual marketing and consumption of difference.

Does visibility confer benefits on the appropriated culture? When we consider the way that tea, coffee, tobacco, the potato, chocolate, *Neighbours* and so on, have been absorbed into British culture, there has been little corresponding benefit to those whose culture first provided the 'content' (indeed, in so many cases with disastrous consequences, plantation work, slavery, bonded labour and death). Why would anyone expect that the market for various world musics should suggest any different pattern of subsumption?

Cultural Politics

Exclusive identity affiliation and separatism poses an obstacle for alliance and solidarity, but it is possible to imagine affiliations across identifications (see Sharma and Housee 1999). In an interview with Lowe, Angela Davis offered the formula of 'basing identity on politics rather than the politics on identity' (Davis 1997). Since groupings like Asian, South Asian, and even Indian or Pakistani, as well as British Asian, Asian-American, etc., can only be usefully thought of as socially constructed entities and never in the natural or static ways that are deployed by racists, nationalists and dullards, any strategic deployment of these terms in a 'positive essentialism' should maintain a watch over the ways terms may be reified and become counter-productive even within the politics for which they are deployed. The 'scrupulously visible political interest' proposed by Spivak (1987: 205) must do serious duty in the context of alliance formation with other groups in colour, class, sexuality and gender-based struggles.

Lowe cites Fanon's recognition that any movement to dismantle colonialism faces the challenge of providing a 'new order' that does not reproduce 'the social structure of the old system' nor any assimilation to the 'dominant culture's roles and positions by the emergent group, which would merely caricature the old colonialism' (Lowe 1996: 72). Fanon's text about anti-colonial nationalism proves instructive in the context of the so-called postcolonial, as elite and comprador classes seem to have failed exactly this challenge, and have done so, it would seem, by way of abandoning the Leninist project which required of revolutionaries that they first of all smash the state apparatus.

Schools, communications media, the legal system, etc., work to assimilate diverse differences in a melting pot public domain[14] which operates a rhetoric of equality or rights but consistently forgets and occludes the material inequalities that persist – for clear historical and political reasons – within that domain.[15] This is yet again the same trick which suggests that the sale of labour power by the worker to the capitalist is a fair and free exchange. In the culture industry's fascination with curry and cornershop, hip-hop and dreadlocks, and so on, it is possible to witness the cultural operation of this rhetoric of equality which appreciates difference on the basis of an oblique blindness to inequality and material opportunity. The recognition of this contradiction, in which fetishised and celebrated 'objects' of culture come to do duty for obscured social relations between really existing people, is a first, but insufficient, step towards a cultural politics.

While it is certainly necessary to take part in the fight against the ways inequalities are obscured by pluralist multiculturalism and its restricted notions of identity, we also need to take up a more militant and organised project which goes beyond this first step of learning to 'think through the ways in which culture may be rearticulated ... as a site for alternative histories and memories that provide the grounds to imagine subject, community, and practice in new ways' (Lowe 1996: 96). It is also possible that the isolated announcement that culturalism enacts an exclusion of material reality is itself in danger of reinforcing that very exclusion, especially where the prescribed action is also culturalist, however strategic. What is missing here is how a culturalist politics cannot just recognise real material issues but must actually attempt to do something about them. Lowe groups together 'testimony, personal narrative, oral history, literature, film, visual arts, and other cultural forms as sites through which subject, community, and struggle are stratified and mediated' as 'oppositional narratives'. These 'are crucial to the imagination and rearticulation of new forms of political subjectivity, collectivity, and practice' (Lowe 1996: 158). Very good. But this 'alternative politicization', on its own, is in danger of operating only an administrative change at the helm of the institutions of cultural management (dusky brethren curating the new museums, a few postcolonial superstars on the conference circuit, feted rap and sports personalities, but between these examples and the material reality of cultural operation exists the same difference between the service personnel of a five star hotel and the international jet-setting guests). Lowe's occasional references to the formation of a 'new' workforce 'within the global reorganization of capitalism' which is 'linked to an emergent political formation, organizing across race, class, and national boundaries' are offered in programmatic terms only at the end of the book and not in detail. The call remains for 'alternative forms of cultural practice that integrate yet move beyond those of cultural nationalism' (Lowe 1996: 171); for 'oppositional and contestatory' immigrant cultures, provoking contradictions which may be 'critically politicized in cultural forms and practices' so as to be 'utilized in the formation of alternative social practices'; as part of a 'process based on strategic alliances between different sectors, not on their abstract identity' (Lowe 1996: 172); and to 'propose, enact, and embody subjects and practices not contained by the narrative of American citizenship' (Lowe 1996: 176).

While the 'explicit dimension' of 'Rap's cultural politics lie in its lyrical expression', Tricia Rose reminds us that alongside this, there are other important factors. It is the struggle over public space, meanings and interpretations that is critical in 'contemporary cultural politics' (Rose 1994: 124). It is crucial to add that the struggle of black Americans to claim public space is not one – however large a percentage of the *Billboard* top 40 chart may be claimed by Def Jam, and however much rap provides the soundtrack for urban lives – that is easily won. The key problem here, as in – to use Rose's own formulation – the case with cultural production in general, is that there is more than one context, more than one public, more than one interpretation and more than one struggle, many reactions, many things to say. This is the contradictory nature of the cultural industry – at the very same time as a struggle for meaning and space opens possibilities of articulation that were previously closed, the extension of 'saying' into public space in a larger context can risk closing off other possibilities, or engaging a ventriloquy which speaks on behalf of others. That Apache Indian becomes the sole representative of bhangra is a case in point: bhangra, South Asian musics, even Apache himself, are much too complex to be glossed in this, albeit understandable in the context, fashion. The contradiction which is to be kept in mind is that progressive sounds in one space may become the agents of imperialism (and sales projections for Nike) in another.

The nature of commodity fetishism and the ever multiplying fragmentation of 'culture' and social relations into a million products in the market is what requires critical analysis. Difference is selling well on the display tables of tourism, technology, television and tele-marketing. Difference is in style. Yet if we recall the ways these commodities (souvenirs, identities, band width, melody – anything that can appear in the culture-vulture tradehouse hall) are, as Marx explained, congealed social relations between people in, however refracted, communication with each other, we can begin to reconsider difference as something to be reclaimed, not as identity-product, but as a grounding for solidarity and unity and a possible way beyond the culture industry.

The abundance and wealth of the capitalist world has been distributed, segmented, fragmented, hierarchised and stratified dysfunctionally in ways that favour some at the expense of all. A few much more than some, some much more than the rest. The impediments to an immediate redistribution of productive powers and pleasures across the entire social spectrum is not a matter of limited resources, or insufficient capacity, but rather of division of will, of opportunist power-mongering, of marketing division for gain. The ways in which culture is theorised today as hybrid, diverse, full of differences, multicultural, polyversely plethoric, etc., must be immediately reappropriated from the abstract and fetishised marketised/mediatised reification of social relations.

The envelope within which 'identity politics' operates may certainly be pushed and widened by all the advocates of multiplicity and difference, but the flip side of this development is the socialising of new accommodations to multifarious capitalism. We learn new ways to coexist with the operation, rather than work for its overthrow. Multiculturalism is 'business in drag', as one wit called it with characteristic disconcern for the PC-ness of analogy. This critique of hybridity is not one which rejects the creativity of bringing cultures together, mixing resources and sharing, exchanging, cooperating with ideas. The effervescence of creativity is premised – always – on such trading. That is not the point. To think that a celebration of the trade is sufficient is the problem. Celebration of multicultural diversity and fragmentation is exactly the logic of the mass market. A twisted version of unity in diversity where the unity is alienated and abstracted away from real relations between people and becomes relations between things. It has been thus for a very long time under capitalism. Indeed, this is its framing presence.

For all the good words and great 'critical' books, articles, newspaper op-ed columns, right through to Asian-American visibility in literature and business, or to the cross-cultural alliance of South Asian musics with the 'Black CNN' of rap and its message, through all this, the world socioeconomic situation remains in large part unchanged. If anything, conditions for those excluded from bourgeois welfare are worse than they were. The mixture of multicultural good news and mixed lives lived under the wire – as seen for example in Mira Nair's film *Mississippi Masala* (see Chambers 1994) – is not to be condemned in itself, but its articulation is insufficient and pointing out a few escapees from the exclusion machine does not make a politics. Just as hybrid creativity does not by itself pose a challenge to the brutalisation of human life entailed in capitalist society, neither does an individual escape offer more than a partial fantastic exit. Much more is necessary. Visibility is not the marker of arrival. Opportunist space in the sun does not disrupt enough. What kinds of organisations are needed to build on the creativity of the hybrid challenges to capital? To what degree does the opportunity to rest comfortably minimise or undermine political engagement? How must organisation combat this? When?

Notes

1. In the intro for *Dis-Orienting Rhythms* (Sharma et al. 1996: 1).
2. There is a considerable literature in anthropology on reflexivity, see Hutnyk (1987, 1998), but the seduction I have in mind here is that pointed out by Koushik Banerjea (1999) as discussed in the next chapter.
3. In 'Kalkutta Calling: Madonna's *Neue Kleider*', August 1998, German-language edition.
4. See Kalra et al. (1996), and Chapter 3 of this book.
5. During the Madonna special on MTV to promote the album *Ray of Light*, she explained her interest in the Kabbala, Zen Buddhism and Tibet: 'all religions are saying the same thing'. To which the interviewer responded: 'You mean in the beginning was the word?' Madonna: 'Yes' and 'I still have a soft spot for Catholicism you know, but all those other religions, um, like Judaism, Buddhism and, um, others, they are more adaptable to modern life ... I never expected to be called the Material Girl for ever ... though I still have a soft spot for that person, whoever she was, she's a million miles away from me now'. When did Madonna have this insight? It was 'just after filming the role in Evita Peron' (MTV Interview May 1998, several screenings).
6. Of the earlier incarnation of the pre-Spice feminist icon, hooks has written:
   Madonna's image usurps, takes over, subordinates ... Mirroring the image of a plantation overseer in a slave-based economy, Madonna surveys the landscape of sexual hedonism, her 'gay' freedom, her territory of the other, her jungle. No break with stereotypes here. And more importantly, no critical interrogation of the way in which these images perpetuate and maintain institutionalized homophobic domination. In the context of *Sex* [the book], gay culture remains irrevocably linked to a system of patriarchal control framed by a heterosexist pornographic gaze. (hooks 1994: 17)
7. I discuss this in relation to Marx and Clifford in Hutnyk (1998).
8. On the other side of the Atlantic, the British Prime Minister, Tony Blair, commends South Asian businessmen for developing cash and carry, catering and so on, and for having made Britain 'richer as a result' (Blair speaking at a dinner for Britain's 200 Richest Asians, sponsored by the *Eastern Eye* magazine). Cherie Blair wore a vote-winning sari. The year before she had borrowed one, improving in 1998 with a specially designed number from a respected fashion house (for more on this see Kalra and Hutnyk 1998).
9. Some other time I want to show that Hall's 'Marxism without guarantees' relies upon the rejection of an 'orthodox' Marxism most prominently displayed in the UK context by pseudo-Trotskyite sects (middle-class self-declared vanguards whose patronisingly simplistic exhortations to the working class must embarrass most workers). It is not the case that Marxism was ever so guaranteed, though it is not difficult to see why Hall was provoked to the position he took.
10. Chambers says that 'to talk of authenticity has invariably involved referring to tradition as an element of closure and conservation, as though peoples and cultures existed outside the languages and time'. He prefers to 'move in the traffic between ... worlds [of cultures, arts and individuals], caught in the sights sounds and languages of hybridity' (Chambers 1994: 82).

11. To be called *Paul Simon, Graceland, and the Continuation of Colonialist Ideologies* (in preparation, see Taylor 1997: 35n).

12. Taylor notes that it is Paul Simon's access to 'copyrights, agents, lawyers, publishers, record company executives' that allows his 'voracious aesthetic' to 'appropriate anything and do anything with it' (Taylor 1997: 22). Remembering 'The Sound of Silence', it should not be surprising that the tariff and protectionism advantages that accrue to capitalist business in manufacturing are also evident in the culture industries – this was noted long ago, even as the catchy tunes of *Graceland* tend too often to make us forget.

13. This is unintentionally amusing – the idea that 'many' of the billions subject under Empire might turn up in Britain would certainly swamp the small percentage there at present (India's population 900 million, Asians in Britain, under 2 million). Of course the free movement of people would be a good thing – forcing a serious rethink of 'race relations', for the moment Fortress Europe conditions prevail.

14. 'Multiculturalism is central to the maintenance of a consensus that permits the present hegemony, a hegemony that relies on a premature reconciliation of contradiction and persistent distractions from the historically established incommensurability of the economic, political and cultural spheres' (Lowe 1996: 86).

15. 'In the United States, pluralism admits the existence of differences, yet it requires conformity to a public culture that tends to subordinate alternative cultures ... hence, the important antagonisms of racial and ethnic immigrant cultures to the state in counterhegemonic critiques that do not exclusively reproduce pluralist arguments of inclusion and rights' (Lowe 1996: 144).

Part III
Internationalisms

6
Critique of Postcolonial Marxisms

As far as I can understand it, my agenda remains an old-fashioned Marxist one. Marx attempted to make the factory workers rethink themselves as agents of production, not as victims of capitalism. They advanced their labour, the capitalist repaid them only partially. Their claim to the rest was their claim to socialism (tone it down: the welfare state; dress it up: civil society). Today in the old metropolitan countries, the capitalist is the benefactor 'creating jobs,' and the worker is systematically deprived of welfare because it is a 'free' gift. (Spivak 1999: 357)

Indy-pop

In *A Critique of Postcolonial Reason*, Gayatri Chakravorty Spivak attempts to 'construct (im)possible practices' by impertinently re-reading 'classic' texts such as Kant, Marx, histories, cultural commentary and so forth, 'for the sake of disciplinary critique' (Spivak 1999: 336). But not just this. Along the way she applauds 'gestures that could not lead to a model for action' and takes an 'obtuse angling, if never irrational, distanced perspective from the principle of reason from within' (Spivak 1999: 336).[1] These are telegraphed formulas in a bigger project focusing on the postcolonial subject in the process of recoding the colonial subject. Here she increasingly turns disciplinary critique into a diagnostic vigilance that would address the violence of globalising capitalism, refracted through telecommunicative informatics, across the bodies of the peoples of the planet, with special attention reserved – a word I add with intended grim irony – for those indigenous peoples most grievously impacted upon, but forgotten, at the very moment the 'disciplinary' forms babble so much about them.

I am not at all sure that my reading of Spivak's book can be extracted from a bias that would demand a more rigorous at the same time as flagrantly unorthodox politics – an obtusely angular Marxism. Nor am I sure that my take on anthropology – a disciplinary structure I find myself working against/within – can be matched up with this critique. That I want to do this in the midst of a further defence of the necessary politics of self-defence activism and a critique of white left anti-racism complicates the matter. Affiliations with a broad spectrum of those who are labelled 'self-ethnicising', nostalgic and implicated in a transnational cultural studies – in the pay of evil empires – and interests honed and no doubt distorted in subjective embrace, might also incapacitate this reading. But I have found this book inspirational and of use. In this regard, I will recklessly assume that my few extrapolations might be worth sharing. That the book is centrally relevant to the theme of evaluating the 'critical practice' of 'anthropology', its relation to 'native informants' as construed in metropolitan postcolonial diaspora, and to the continued usefulness of Marxism and music as a 'political' force, will become clear.

What strikes me first is a tiny aside that evokes the music discussed here in my other chapters. The aside is in fact to 'the new Asian dance music' (Sharma 1994), but which Spivak renames a little clumsily as 'Indy-pop' (Spivak 1999: 346). There is much more that could be said about this phenomenon than we actually get in Spivak (the book is, after all, not 'about' music), but I think it is not too unreasonable to link this particular aside to the more often explicit discussions in her work of those 'new diaspora' and 'hyphenated' types now so prominent in the moment of globalisation, transnationality and 'postcoloniality'. The reference to 'Indy-pop' comes in the midst of a discussion of difference where Spivak has been working through Roland Barthes's book on Japan, *The Empire of Signs* (Barthes 1982), and has denounced the 'clear-headed assumption that claims the other as grounds for difference' (Spivak 1999: 345). In the course of reinforcing her case she alludes to a French fashion catalogue where 'the faces and the clothes in the catalogue are recognisably "Japanese" without "real" Japanese specificity' and continues by making the point – here it comes – that this is 'comparable, let us say, to the "India" in that by now mythical art-object, George Harrison's "My Sweet Lord," or contemporary "Indy-pop" in Britain' (Spivak 1999: 346). There is then a footnote: 'Under the auspices of the New World Order, the production of such authoritative hybrids as representations and representatives of an unmarked origin is the name of the game, especially in the field of ideology as culture in the service of the political calculus that manages the abstract economic machine' (Spivak 1999: 346n).

I want to use this, I think, but need to unpack it a lot. It is interesting because I recognise that the hybrid fantasy 'India' of 'My Sweet Lord' is directly implicated as doing ideological culture-representation work in support of the abstract economic machine in the same way that Kula Shaker's versions of magical mystical tourism give an alibi to structural adjustment interventions into an 'East' that is deemed in need of liberal tolerant care (this appears as humanitarian bombing in other theatres). But I do want to suggest that there is also a myopia here, and the danger is that it can misrecognise 'Indy-pop' in a way that perhaps has an inverse symmetry with the blindness of Harrison/Kula Shaker to an industrialised autonomous capitalist India. That 'Indy-pop' may be, if it includes both bhangra and Cornershop, say, more than accommodation to the requirements of a 'postcolonial elite' differentiating itself from a state of underclass migrancy, seems worth considering. This, I'm afraid, is not a question of disciplinary critique so much as one that can lead to questions of discipline, of the organised political activism variety. Thus, wanting to disaggregate 'Indy-pop' and its uses a little, I'll ask: are all proponents of such pop so bland? Are all differences recouped in the Empire of Signs? Is the political work of ADF or Fun^da^mental, for example, or that of the politicised bhangra bands discussed in Kalra (2000a), to be reduced to this complicit and in-denial 'hybrid' post-colonial diasporic scene?

Are the cultural workers of the new Asian dance music of a type – symbiotically related – with the white fantasy Asianism of George Harrison's 'My Sweet Lord'? Where Spivak demands that the 'hyphenated' might 'think themselves as *possible* agents of exploitation, not its victims' (Spivak 1999: 357), this possibility has to be taken seriously. Of course there is a reverse proviso here – Spivak is not saying that all those who are 'hyphenated' (aren't we all?) are *necessarily* agents of exploitation. I just want to insist on the disaggragation, while keeping the 'possible' firmly in view.

Let us expand the citation a little: Spivak is critical of the ways new transnationality potentially restructures the world for capitalism. She counsels:

the hyphenated Americans belonging loosely to the first and the fourth groups [we can take it she means diasporic First Worlders, formerly Fourth Worlders] might think of themselves as possible agents of exploitation, not its victims; then the idea that the nation

state that they now call home gives 'aid' to the nation-state that they
still call culture, in order to consolidate the new unification for
international capital, might lead to [what she calls] 'transnational
literacy'. (Spivak 1999: 357)

Much here. Even if we do have to calculate the differences between the
USA as nation-state giving aid and Britain's similar, but lesser (not super-
power) role. The point, here, is not to give up desire, but rather than play
out the performed exoticism of 'culture' for others, to claim a different
agency, to shift the position a little away from 'only the desire to be the
agent of a developed civil society' (Spivak 1999: 358). I think it is exactly
where this sentiment applies to Britain that an important distinction is
to be made between the work of ADF, educational, not exotic or eclectic,
etc., and the more eager marketeers of exotica, tablas, joss-sticks or self-
declared hybridity that emerges in the Sony-sponsored culture industry
fascination with Asia.

But it would not do to rush into affirmations of political credibility for
favourite tune-smiths, especially in the very site of writing that is
identified as most complicit. It is necessary to ask why such a distinction
might need to be made in a cultural studies text. Consider.

Spivak writes that:

> culturalist moral imperialism finds ... self-ethnicized nostalgia
> altogether useful. An unexamined cultural studies internationally,
> joins hands with an unexamined ethnic studies ... to oil the wheels of
> what can only be called the ideological state apparatus ...
> triumphalist hybridism as well as nostalgic nativism. Business as
> usual. (Spivak 1999: 319n)

The comment above this note discusses architecture and the US context,
and the ellipses leave much out, but I think it useful to take these words
as also providing a reminder that the unexamined enthusiasm for an
international cultural studies that makes the hybrid diasporic its core
object, and leaves this a largely undifferentiated concept, is of course
tolerated within the higher education institutions for a reason. How to
work within this apparatus against, rather than co-opted into, its
ideological function, requires the vigilance of examining, not
invigilation of exams. Derrida's work also often proceeds by setting an
impossible metaphoric comparison to work and showing how it is a
repetition of the same which is not the same, a difference which is not
one. The graphematic code that already structures writing and speech

like 'writing' cannot be read off as code as writing can (see Spivak 1999: 321).

So with cultural studies, more so with anthropology. In an essay discussing the interest of hip-hop exponents Wu-Tang Clan's fascination with kung fu cinema from Hong Kong and other exoticisms for the East, Koushik Banerjea identifies the anthropological project as part of a wider 'map-making and fact-faking' that is the orientation of Enlightenment social science and observes that 'self-professed methodological absolution' from stigmatised disciplinary affiliation remains an 'unseemly spectacle' (Banerjea 1999: 18). Reflexivity is no guarantee that ethnography can escape the 'enclave' of knowing science, the compound security of what was already identified as 'propertied whiteness' (Banerjea 1999: 19, see introduction). Surely this has to be, however difficult, dis-owned, reclaimed and detourned in a moment that moves past mere recognition of complicity to reconfiguration of more than just mapping. Spivak writes that the 'domestication of the dialectic in a desire to map the world' (1999: 326) is an academicist gesture that would see the political movement of radical thought and practice as merely documentation of contradictory reality. The role of the ethnographic as descriptive code, and even as imaginative subjective narrativisation, is clearly ideological in this light. This is not to be against all ethnography perhaps, since everything codes, but to require that it be brought into productive engagement in a more examined way than its domesticating forms allow. I am tempted to suggest that Mao's report from Hunan might provide an ethnographic model because the next step is programmatic activism. To return to Spivak, far from Mao in so many ways, she points out that Marx is showing us 'not how to think well and ill of capitalism at the same time, but that one must work to sublate the good things in capitalism out of capitalism' (Spivak 1999: 327). In the same way the work of cultural politics in diaspora can claim either ethno or politico modes, and centrally. Or at least these options are there to be explored.

On responsibility? Can the persistent effort of 'disclosing responsibility towards the other-as-beneficiary by effacing radical alterity' (Spivak 1999: 355n) found a, however micrologial, political programme? There may be a place for this. It is certainly better than muddling through with no rules at all, yet the dynamics of this requires a subtle two-step. Spivak writes, in a rejoinder to Benita Parry:

> Postcolonial persons from formerly colonised countries are able to communicate with each other (and to metropolitans), to exchange,

to establish sociality, because we have had access to the so-called culture of imperialism. Shall we assign to that culture a measure of 'moral luck'? I think there is no doubt that the answer is no. This impossible 'no' to a structure that one critiques yet inhabits intimately is the deconstructive position. (Spivak 1999: 191)

Arguing a line that would endorse ethnographic voice, Parry has suggested that Spivak, among others enamoured with deconstruction, will not let the native speak (Parry 1987: 27–58). Spivak's response also seems to serve as a rebuff to the criticisms of Aijaz Ahmad in his article in *Race and Class* which questioned the location and styles of writing of the metropolitan-based 'postcolonial critic', specifically taking to task a position in which 'postcoloniality equals the "heritage of imperialism"' (Ahmad 1995: 3). This goes right to the heart of what the postcolonial intellectual, or postcolonial critique may be – though it is Ahmad who removes several key words from his quotation of Spivak on this, where she refers to the legacy of imperialism in nationhood, citizenship, democracy, socialism, etc., and says these concepts are 'written elsewhere', but 'effectively reclaimed' (Spivak 1993: 60, 280–1).[2] The legacy is rewritten, actively; there is speaking, however ambivalent – and this restores agency and notices activity in a way that less alert analyses would bypass. This does not mean these concepts are simply taken up as is, and it is a gross misrepresentation to say that Spivak implies that imperialism is 'a matter of the past' (Ahmad 1995: 3). Keeping with anthropology, it is worth noting another aside here where Spivak observes the continuing desire for the 'object of conscientious ethnography' on the part of the neo-colonial anti-colonist – these are celebrations of the voice of the 'other' in nationalism perhaps? If there will be such ethnography let it come with the proviso of a forewarning about its relationship to the (compromised) history of the discipline of anthropology (Spivak 1999: 191). Written elsewhere, to be reclaimed?

A risky generalisation is offered as a formula: 'Elite "postcolonialism" seems to be as much a strategy of differentiating oneself from the racial underclass as it is to speak in its name' (Spivak 1999: 358). And if that separation-ventriloquy act is the lot of 'postcolonials', what then of the self-reflexive posturings of anthropologists and cultural studies entrepreneurs? The differentiation comes with a claim to righteousness, benevolence and liberalism that would be praised as radical, not just workaday political common-sense required to effect solidarity with, for example, the gender and economic inflected trials of women such as the Burnsalls strikers in Birmingham (Kalra and Hutnyk 1998 and below).

These women, who could not be called subaltern but suffer an 'underclass diasporic women's exilic predicament' (Spivak 1999: 104), should be a site of solidarity and alliance-building public activity by intellectual-activists within the metropole, yet Birmingham today seems also too far from London, and concern for such predicaments now devolves only into polite dinner conversation amongst those who troop into the East End curry enclave of Brick Lane for a late night meal – a meal served by the often undocumented and underpaid curry shift workers who can only dream of a cultural industries Asian Kool star trek path out of the 'ghetto'. Banerjea (2000) offers more on Shoreditch and the interface of cultural industry restructuring and Brick Lane. But witness also the post-curry procession to Aldgate East just before the last tube draws the curtain on another day of cultural hybridity in the thriving multicultural city. Mind the Gap. Despite the fervour of new info industry resiting in the cultural quarter, late night shouting of 'Hey Sabu, where's mi' fuckin' vindaloo' is obviously not the high point of sophisticated diological exchange (see Banerjea and Banerjea 1996: 111 and the next chapter).

Let us not leave Birmingham so quickly. Lynne Segal, in a 1997 review article on differences in feminism in Britain since the 1970s, noted that 'Twenty years ago it would have been hard to find a single self-respecting feminist who had not trekked out to the Grunwick factory in West London in support of the predominantly Asian women on strike' (Segal 1997: 11). Today, however, the situation appears different as, in the 1990s, 'it would be hard to find a self-respecting feminist who had even *heard* of the predominantly Asian women on strike at Burnsalls in Birmingham over an almost identical set of issues: refusal of union recognition, low pay, and the use of dangerous chemicals'; and she adds that even if this struggle had been noted, few if any would have 'contemplated supportive action' (Segal 1997: 11, citing Melissa Benn 1993). Considerable numbers of self-respecting feminists, however, *have* heard of Burnsalls and have engaged in support action – it is 'just' that they are not registering on the grid of white feminist theory since they are mostly South Asian themselves.[3] They have been joined, in addition, by exactly those *possible* diasporic agents of exploitation that many would dismiss as 'self-ethnicised' cultural workers or lumpen bhangra 'entertainers', as Virinder Kalra's collected 'ethnographic fragment' shows:

> Music is politically engaged not solely because of its ability to make a space or because of its lyrical content, but both because it affirms

community and because it tells histories. A case in point in terms of Panjabi music was the way in which music came to be a source of strength and inspiration to a set of workers at Burnsalls. The relationship between folk music with local struggles is seen in the example of the Burnsalls strike. On 15 June 1992, 19 predominantly Asian women workers went on strike challenging the appalling factory conditions and low pay they were receiving from their employers Burnsalls Limited. This company produced metal furnishing and was based in Smethwick in the West Midlands. The strike attracted national media coverage only after six months of the strike when the union, the Birmingham branch of the GMB, expressed its lack of support and enthusiasm for the strikers. The picket line on the doorstep of Burnsalls Limited – whose address is coincidentally 10 Downing Street – was a rallying point for supporters from the local community, particularly upon the withdrawal of union support. Rallies organised by the strikers' support group reflected not only solidarity from trade union activists, anti-racist organisations and other left-wing organisations, but also became a focal point for the local working-class Panjabi community.

This is best reflected in two ways. In July 1993 a benefit was held, only half a mile from the picket line in which 'stars' of the bhangra music industry, such as Safri and T.S. Bilga, performed to a minimum accompaniment and for no fee. This stands in contrast to the antics that normally accompany musicians of repute, where egos often outsize performances. Tejinder Singh, one of the strikers, also performed at the event and was instrumental throughout the strike in providing uplift to the strikers through the singing of popular songs. A second show of solidarity came from the adaptation of a classical Panjabi love song, *kehnde ne naine* ('My Eyes are Saying'), as an anthem for the strike. The haunting tune and poetic style of the love song voiced the angry and militant feelings of the striking workers.

We proclaim
We are here to stay
You who have ruined our lives,
What more can you want ?
I am tired of bowing down
The time has come to rise up and stand tall
From today, I vow to have no fear

In life only unity brings victory
Without struggle
There's no fulfilment
By fighting for our rights
We find peace of mind
What more can I say?[4]

This is merely a reminder that not everything in the 'metropolitan postcolonial' register should be thought to comply with undifferentiated (indy-pop) theoretical generalisation. Some feminists did support the Burnsalls strikers, some cultural workers are further from complicity. The cultural trajectory of those who migrated to Britain from the 'colonies' refracts in complicated ways across class, but can be seen to include elite, upwardly mobile lower and middle classes, and an entrenched underclass. The indigenous elites in the former dominions became the object of 'a benevolent third-worldist cultural studies' in the 1970s (Spivak 1999: 360), but it could be argued that this was in large part only a displaced and still marginal anthropological movement. In the metropolitan scene migrancy studies did make an object of first migrants, in the 1970s, and then the renamed diasporic population, especially in the late 1980s and 1990s, but with certain occlusions even here. Increasingly the beleaguered position of those subject to the knowledge industry management of difference becomes one where, as Spivak warns, there is much room for misunderstanding. She carefully demarcates a critique which will try to:

> account for the sudden prominence of the postcolonial informant on the stage of U.S. English studies ... [who has] ... rather little to say about the oppressed minorities in the decolonised nation as such, except, at best, as especially well-prepared investigator. Yet the aura of identification with those distant objects of oppression clings to these informants as, again at best, they identify with the other racial and ethnic minorities in metropolitan space. At worst, they take advantage of the aura and play the native informant uncontaminated by disavowed involvement with the machinery of the production of knowledge (Spivak 1999: 360)

Kalra's ethnographic work, or Sanjay Sharma and Shirin Housee's article on the category of black political identification in diasporic Britain, might suggest what turns out to be the 'at best' scenario (see Sharma and Housee 1999). Perhaps better would be the international work of the Indian Workers Association and its cultural activism which continues in an 'orthodox' party form. But even in debating these migrancy issues, is there a tendency here to understand all 'ex-migrants' as having just arrived? As always diasporic? And always fodder for ethnography? The two at worst scenarios are cultural authenticity-continuity claims and/or upward class-mobility claimed as resistance, 'confining the destabilisation of the metropole merely to the changes in the ethnic composition of the population' (Spivak 1999: 361). The self-declared hybrid haunts all these forms unevenly, but actual postcolonials are accessed and controlled only through the upper echelon of these types – information sector and telematically enriched workers of left and right stripes – the Burnsalls women are more often ignored. In terms of visible diasporics, it is a matter of historical record that the right is in the ascendant in this regard – left solidarity decline and *hindutva*/Islamist mobilisation, forced competition between sweated labour in metro and postcolony. Adequate analysis of this requires vigilance and textual fidelity such as that inscribed by Kalra, and 'the obstinate amongst us might want a broader perspective that does not merely refer to the international division of labour, but also takes the trouble to acquire transnational literacy in the New World Order that has come into being in the last decade of the second millennium' (Spivak 1999: 398).

Marxisms-Activisms

Spivak can teach us about the project of an 'early' Marx in a way that may help clarify positions on responsibility and difference, transition and its advocates, and the politics that might be appropriate to the 'postcolonial' (note, it is not 'the' early Marx here, not the 'one true' early Marx, though continuist versions are also up for grabs). She writes of a Marx who wants to 'annul' the difference that history has imposed on the subject (us?). I guess this might also be read as alienation, or the difference between the 'is' and the 'ought', which would be useful to what Marx takes from Feuerbach when he, Marx as 'activist philosopher', perceives that, 'given social inequality, it is not possible for each human being to take himself [Spivak adds herself] as the *correct* case of being-human as such'. Instructing us to look to the origins of thought and action, Spivak then notes that 'action as creative performance of a given script is learned in a responsibility-based rather than a rights-based system, and Marx's intuition is towards the former from within convictions spawned by the latter' (Spivak 1999: 78, italics in original).

The rights-based system requires structure and law, the (ethics of) justice works a different politics through responsibility (to the other).

One version of representing this task to ourselves might be to forge a new transnational cultural politics without producing entrepreneurial self-promoting identity and pop star ego maniacs acting out the guilty conscience of a liberal capitalism wilfully blind and actively forgetting exploitation 'hidden' in adjacent theatres. Thus, a cultural politics would wish to work as an adjunct to organisational and structural productive formations (rapprochement and solidarity plus more) and would actively and vigilantly work against mere culture-vultures. Safri and TS Bilga not 'Live Aid', ADF not the *NME*, Fun^da^mental not the SWP, Lisa Lowe not Mary Gillespie, Ravi Shankar tuning up at the 'Concert for Bangladesh'.

Marx himself was not writing away from events nor writing any abstract analysis, even where his mode of exposition, as he called it, proceeded through abstraction (the long march from the commodity form to the total circuit of capital). His attention to the specificity of events modified his efforts: 'the failure of 1848 moved him away from confidence in the inevitable outcome' (Spivak 1999: 75) of the class struggle waged between bourgeoisie and proletariat as presented in *The Communist Manifesto* written over the November–January period of 1847–8. Subsequently, Marx's work took the form of researching then writing a 'textbook' to train the proletariat to read the tricks of capital, and again after the failure of the Paris Commune in 1871, to reread the 'differential relationship between capitalist and socialist modes of production of capital' (Spivak 1999: 76) – and along the way, not incidentally, to write reams and reams on ethnology in the last ten years of his life (see *The Ethnological Notebooks of Karl Marx* [Marx 1974]).

In the context of discussions of difference and interest in those who work within capitalism for its sublation, it would be relevant to acknowledge how the debate over the Asiatic Mode of Production spirals away from a brief appearance as an 'imaginary fleshing out of a difference in terms that are consonant with the development of capitalism and the resistance *appropriate* to it as "the same"' (Spivak 1999: 79). Remembering that Marx's setting out of the development of capitalism was a 'sketch' and not prescriptive, it is worth considering what happens to this sketch when codified by later accountings. This 'Asiatic mode' is granted greater importance where those who are 'different' want to become 'the same' (the reference would be to Stalin's speeches on nationalism and multiculturalism [Spivak 1999: 79]), and its significance when considered as the movement towards developed capitalism is greater than its appearance in the sketch. On difference, Marx is more interested in 'a system that will remove difference *after* taking it into account' (Spivak 1999: 79). The difference between the is and the ought is recognised, then overcome in the heterogeneity of species-being.

This is perhaps where Mao Zedong's development of Marxism as in need of a permanent cultural revolutionary vigilance and struggle even after 'the' revolution comes into its own, since the restitution of capitalism within the Party – as seen in actually existing China today – requires continued work at the fold of the is and the ought. In the absence of a strong world communist movement, this still offers a lesson that can draw upon the resources of Marx's textbook on capital in the 'ruthless critique of everything' (Marx) and on what Spivak calls his 'speculative morphology' (Spivak 1999: 84) (though this occurs at the moment when she seems to give up on the Party organisation modes of Marxism):

> There is no state on the globe today that is not part of the capitalist economic system or can want to eschew it fully. In fact, within the economic sphere, Marxism – at its best a speculative morphology, devised by an activist-philosopher who had taught himself con- temporary economics enough to see it as a human (because social) science, and through this perception launched a thoroughgoing critique of political economy – can operate in today's world *only* as a persistent critique of a system – micro-electronic post-industrial world capitalism – that a polity cannot want to inhabit, for that is the 'real' of the situation. (Spivak 1999: 84, my italics)

Persistent critique here is the appealing and necessary formulation, and one which I will happily recommend. But thinking of the context in which cultural politics and lyrical opposition hits the airwaves in counterpoint to rigidly fixed organisational forms in no way reflexive, responsive or subtle at all, I wonder at the strength of the 'only' in the last sentence of this quote. In her next move Spivak warns that to take Marx's 'speculative' (sketch) studies as 'predictive social engineering' – 'assuming a fully rational human subject conscious of rights as well as impersonal responsibility' – can, and again the word seems somewhat prescriptive, '*only* have violent and violating consequences' (Spivak 1999: 84, my italics).

It is clear that the bourgeois Enlightenment notion of rights cannot deliver social redress, but is it ordained that the Party formation must operate this predictive framework of orthodoxy? Surely there can and must be an organisational form that deploys the persistent critique and does not codify and violate to that degree of excess? The whole point of Mao's cultural revolution and the squeamishness that vested interests have attached to its history (its violence) would need to be evaluated here. The silencing of those who would write their own script, and know it, is what prevails if the organisational necessity of coordination – since capital is big, global, has tanks, etc. – is abandoned. The 'right' to form trade unions, or the right to be different, multicultural, queer, etc., is not enough, and I would particularly include here the debates over necessary self-defence vigilantism as championed by Fun^da^mental in 'Dog-Tribe', or by Hustlers HC in 'Vigilante' (see Chapter 3).

My departure from Spivak is minor at this point. The dialectical movement that critically thinks rights, difference, modes of production and systems in relation and movement cannot be dismissed, even though Spivak would not excuse it from association with:

> the violent consequences of the first wave of global Marxisms which, under the myriad overdeterminations of military and political pressure, read the paradigm shift [of Marx's work] within the realist assumption that a speculative morphology was an adequate blueprint for social justice. (Spivak 1999: 91)

The violence that forces actually existing communism into quick-fix searching for such justice was however not 'there' in the text of Marx, or all those who would struggle with him, so much as a violence of anti-communism that will necessarily have to be dealt with in any future liberation project as well. Perhaps this was a violence underestimated in the past – an adequate response today would require stronger defences. Then, the violence was that of the Western armies that surrounded the Soviets in the early years after 1917, later it was the violence that facilitated attacks by Hitler against Russia (appeasement etc.) and the delayed establishment of a second front by the USA–UK alliance. This sort of distorting anti-communist violence continues throughout the 'Cold War' with persecutions and slaughter of any small explorations of alternatives to capitalism – 3 million dead in Korea, 3 million in Vietnam, half a million in Indonesia, etc. Today this sort of violence arrays itself across the planet as structural adjustment programmes forcing cuts to services, abolition of workplace securities, health and welfare where present, as well as with humanitarian interventions for 'peace and democracy' and the 'logics' of the market which punishes with unseen brutality those who are not in charge. This is a process that can today be called immiseration without risk of overstatement, and indeed with some irony at the level at which this underplays the horror of capital's contemporary effects.

To speak then of excuses for the slippage of speculative analysis into predictive social engineering is a call for a more vigilant and dextrous critical Marxism. The requirement of adequacy would also mean a potential to respond to the violence with which any alternative will be met. For me, however, this requires more than persistent critique. The attacks are under way, and so without organisation of the fighting back that is already taking place, the danger is one of being picked off by the cops or the thugs, by the system or its exclusions. We are all already in the thick of it.

The White Left's Interest in Musical Anti-Racism

It is worth interrupting theory discussions – learnt this from Spivak – with lessons learnt in struggle. Some history of anti-racism might be appropriate as it is not only the diasporic who are the 'possible agents of exploitation'. I want to move on to a discussion of organisation and structure via a three-part look at the place of music in white liberal anti-racist politics in Britain, returning to some of the issues that belong to the relation between community self-defence and popular anti-racism, but focusing on the late 1970s, the early 1990s and 1999.

In the 1970s Rock Against Racism (RAR) 'carnivals' were the organisational form in which the British left, especially the Socialist Workers Party (SWP) and the Anti-Nazi League (ANL), mobilised against racism. Focusing upon the relations between organisers of RAR (who were mostly white) and black musicians (who were often ignored) reveals important slippages. Metropolitan-based 'diasporic' musicians, and their politics, were subsumed within the 'Anti-Nazi' focus of the ANL/SWP, or used in 'token' ways to provide credibility to the white left. In terms of active audience, Rock Against Racism was a largely white mobilisation which did not often intersect with Asian organisations like the supporters of the Burnsalls strikers or larger organisations such as the Indian Workers Association or Asian Youth Movement groups.[5] Despite the musical and political possibilities that might have made such an alliance fruitful, RAR carnivalism did not result in any significant change in racist Britain. Many suggest this was a feel-good exercise for the white left. Critiques of Rock Against Racism called for alliances between Asian defence groups and the RAR/ANL formations – these came from both the white *far* Left such as the Spartacist League (SL), and from black commentators who were suspicious of the white left practice of parachuting in on local self-defence and anti-racist campaigns to do publicity for their rock carnivals.

Way back in 1976, on stage in Birmingham, befuddled rock star and prime candidate for exploitation agent status, Eric Clapton announced that he supported ultra-racist Enoch Powell and thought Britain was 'overcrowded'.[6] In the south of London punky anarcho-poseur Johnny Rotten snarled at such dinosaur rocksters to 'fuck off' and said he 'despised' the National Front, that 'no-one should have the right to tell anyone they can't live here because of the colour of their skin' (*Zigzag* 1977, no. 77: 4) and that 'England was never free. It was always a load of bullshit ... punks and Niggers are the same thing' (quoted in Gilroy 1987: 124).

In September of that year, Rock Against Racism was formed as a response by concerned activists to the racist comments of Clapton and other musicians, and the perception of an increasing turn towards racism and fascism within some sections of British society. Tony Parsons, writing in *Zigzag*, reported that the National Front 'intended to ban all music with black origins from the airwaves and replace the "jungle music", as they put it, with some Great British marching music' (*Zigzag* 1977, no. 76: 4). At the conjunction of music and politics, two trends of music history are often associated at the birth of RAR in the available record: the anti-everything anarchism of punk and the prominence of reggae with its anti-Babylon, anti-capitalist slacker messages. It is always difficult to assess political content and context for popular cultural forms, and never more so for those formations which attracted the moral panic that punk and Rastafari generated. Nonetheless, with many punk and reggae bands on the bills, Rock Against Racism managed to organise almost 800 events in Britain between 1976 and 1979. The largest of these 'carnivals' in collaboration with the Anti-Nazi League attracted 80,000 people in May 1978 (Gilroy 1987: 132) and 100,000 in September 1978 (Anti-Nazi League education pack).[7]

Paul Gilroy argues that the formation of a mass anti-racist movement in Britain 'has passed largely unacknowledged' (1987: 134).[8] It would be inappropriate to place too much emphasis on the lack of readily available histories of Rock Against Racism and the ANL, but the proliferation and significance of histories of the poll tax campaigns, anti-roads protests, and of the miners' and docker's strikes (from both anarchist and socialist presses) as documentations of counter-hegemonic struggle remind us it is important to recuperate multiple versions of what goes on in anti-racism in Britain. There are various interpretations of why the Rock Against Racism/Anti-Nazi League assemblage is important. One suggests that RAR and the ANL 'gave expression to the feelings of young people who had seen the inadequacy of racist explanation [and] revealed for all to see the implicit politics of youth cultures which were defined by and often copied from Black forms and traditions' (Gilroy and Lawrence 1988: 146). The SWP orthodoxy is that 'Rock Against Racism aimed at promoting racial harmony through music, and was one of the first organisations to mix black and white bands at gigs' (Anti-Nazi League educational pack), and with the ANL showed the way, indeed the 'lesson' of how, to fight fascism. More extravagant and optimistic assessments can be arrayed alongside these orthodoxies – most famous amongst them Tariq Ali's proclamation at an early RAR event that 'Lots of people will come for Rock Against Racism today and will see that it should be Rock Against the Stock Exchange tomorrow' (*NME*, 6 May 1978).

Although conjunctions of punk and reggae music inspired activists, it was the case that RAR remained mostly white boys' adventure rock for both organisers and performers – the Buzzcocks, the Clash, Tom Robinson. With the exception of lesser known and often obscure local reggae outfits, and perhaps Marion Elliot, aka Poly Styrene, from X-Ray-Specs (Marcus 1989: 77), RAR was into a more mainstream form of cross-over like UB40 and 'stars' like Elvis Costello and the Attractions, than a forum for local black cultural productions. It is worth noting that the British bhangra (Indy-pop) scene was running parallel to these developments, but there was no involvement of Asian bands in RAR. Bhangra bands were playing the circuits of weddings and community events in a context largely neglected by the organisers of RAR. Politically oriented Asian musicians, for example from the Indian Workers Association, might have been invited to events, but as the imagined Other were inaccessibly beyond translation.[9] In one example the RAR organisers abandoned plans to stage an event in Southall with Asian bands on the bill (Street 1986: 78–9). The potentially huge Asian audiences that might have been reached were all but ignored.[10] The diversity of the RAR crowds were often declared: 'punks with green and pink hair mingled with skins, hippies, students, and the occasional lonely representative of the middle-aged middle classes. A lot of black kids too, though fewer Asians' (*NME*, 30 September 1978).

Political Front or Popular Struggle?

A key issue of interpretation that impinges upon evaluations of the nature and usefulness of this mode of cultural work which is discussed in the available histories rests on the relation between the Anti-Nazi League as organised mainly by Socialist Workers Party cadre, and the Rock Against Racism collectives working throughout the country. While RAR was formed some time before the ANL, and organised many successful local gigs, it was when the two organisations joined forces to promote the large London marches and carnivals and a three-day 'festival' in Manchester that the movement gained widest public prominence.[11]

Gilroy's suggestion is that the difficult cross-over of punk and reggae,[12] manifest as a broad anti-capitalist anti-racism, dissolved in the face of the organisational bureaucracy of the Anti-Nazi League. He offers two explanations for this, both of which seem to have resonance in general black organisation complaints about the white left. First of all 'an emphasis on neo-fascism as the most dangerous embodiment of contemporary racism inevitably pulls discussion of "race" away from the centre of political culture and relocates it on the margins where these groups are doomed to remain' (Gilroy 1987: 148). Second, the neo-fascist use of the British flag and patriotism spawned an equally suspect nationalism on the part of the ANL (written elsewhere, but reclaimed?). 'The idea that the British Nazis were merely sham patriots who soiled the British flag by their use of it was a strong feature of ANL leaflets' (Gilroy 1987: 131). With the ANL's appeal to older voters with the slogan 'Never Again', an appeal to put Britain first and above the interests of 'foreigners' was not far behind.

The first of Gilroy's criticisms might be questioned on the grounds that the intention of the ANL/SWP was indeed to bring a version of RAR anti-racism to a wider constituency, although it is conceded that their methods and tactics were insufficient as they clumsily grasped the symbolism of Nazism, and therefore an anti-Nazi politics, and made it stand for anti-racism. The second criticism, of a nationalist undercurrent within the ANL itself, is difficult to refute since in the second manifestation of the ANL in the 1990s this tendency could again be found. The way in which the SWP's Chris Bambury claims the ANL organisation and the lessons of the 1970s are 'the model of how to organise against the Nazis' (Bambury 1992: 34) might be questioned when he even goes so far as to recommend an ANL structure to French anti-fascists, along with a large dose of anti-communist sectarianism.

This might raise suspicions that there is more hype in the SWP/ANL front than content – and especially so for those exposed to increasing racist attack on UK streets. Support for Gilroy's analysis could be found in the work of Bonnett who summed up: 'Unlike anti-Nazi anti-racism, the radical anti-racist perspective is firmly committed to some form of anti-capitalist critique' (Bonnett 1993: 120).

A common black criticism of organised left groups like the SWP and ANL was that they arrive with leaflets and resources to impose a different agenda upon local struggles which then develop in ways which are sometimes at odds with the broad aims of black groups. Writing of black mobilisations against racism in the aftermath of the Notting Hill 'riots', Farrukh Dhondy warned that 'there are well enough anti Nazi fronts in existence with well organised badges, posters and marching orders' (Dhondy 1978: 85). These fronts were otherwise characterised as 'a rag bag of local letterhead processors ... and project hatchers' (Bengali Housing Action Group 1978: 109). Although the sincerity of many of those SWP members who did get involved in local manifestations of anti-Nazi anti-racism could not be faulted, it is clear that often the limits of this perspective caused resentment and disruption to other anti-racist concerns. Describing such worries as 'hysterical', Graham Lock summarised: 'the argument goes that the ANL is *merely* a front for the Socialist Workers Party' (*NME*, 30 August 1978, italics in original). In *Sounds* the 'smiling, laughing, dancing, happy' carnival-ists gave 'the lie to all those cynics who try to paint the ANL as some sinister Socialist Workers Party plot' (*Sounds*, 30 September 1978). In a less credible association, the ANL/RAR was described as 'a wide ranging celebration of solidarity for freedom and against uniformity and bigotry, fired by the same spirit that fires dissidents in Russia and trade unionists in Chile' (*Sounds*, 30 September 1978).

The Spartacist League's pamphlet *Militant Labour's Touching Faith in the Capitalist State*, as already mentioned, slated 'the tradition of the ANL' popular-frontist practice of linking up with 'Anglican vicars and Labourite politicians' to confront fascism with dances. Spartacist assessment of the ANL in the late 1970s deserves consideration: 'When the fascist National Front marched through the East End in 1978, the ANL organised an 'anti-racist' carnival *ten miles across town* [SL italics], deliberately preventing thousands of anti-fascist militants from confronting and defeating the National Front' (*Touching Faith* 1994: 4). Lock, in the *NME*, reported that repeated calls at the carnival for 'volunteers to defend Brick Lane elicited little response. People preferred to lie in the sun and enjoy the music', and speculated that perhaps the absence of an Asian contingent at the carnival was thus explained: 'maybe they were in Brick Lane, or maybe it is their culture tends to get overlooked on occasions like this. Where are you now Ravi Shankar?' (*NME*, 30 September 1978). Other reports suggest that the SWP leadership intentionally ignored the Asian activists (and some SWP cadres) who had assembled to confront the fascists in Brick Lane. In this scenario the SWP central committee actively worked to close out those SWP local branches with tendencies towards 'squadism' (organised militant anti-fascist squads). Subsequently, many of these cadres broke with the SWP into other formations and micro-sects.[13] The Spartacist *Touching Faith* pamphlet pointed out that ANL equivocation was not confined to the 1970s, and had continued into the 1990s – going on to record that although the large October 1993 anti-fascist rally was a significant event (known as the Welling Riot by readers of the *Guardian*), the follow-up ANL carnival at Brockwell Park was nothing more than a rehearsal of this populist avoidance (more on this below).

Gilroy, writing with Errol Lawrence, characterised as ultra-leftist those criticisms of the RAR/ANL that argued it was mere 'fun music with no political connections beyond the private affiliations of the musicians'. A 'chorus of professional revolutionaries' (Gilroy and Lawrence 1988: 147) insisted that RAR had to be structured with delegates, conferences and cadres. That this 'ultra-leftism' did not organise RAR and that instead the SWP/ANL moved in with a popular front anti-Nazism does not seem an important distinction at this distance. Nevertheless, the calls of the Spartacist League for Workers' Defence squads as a response to the Nazis, and those of the Revolutionary Communist Tendency and other revolutionary communist groups, and the editorial collective of *Race Today*, for 'community defence' groups to combat racist attack, are considerably different from what the ANL offered.

Jump to 1991. The SWP moved to re-establish the ANL in the face of renewed awareness of increasing racism in Britain and escalating racial terror in Europe. Fascists were again standing for political positions and the British National Party was successful in gaining a council seat in one London Borough. In the face of this resurgent threat the SWP declared that Nazism was again an issue – the 'lessons of the 70s' (Bambury 1992) were to be rehearsed once again. Yet old problems remained, and the ANL was without, on this occasion, a national network of grassroots activists, previously provided by RAR, able to give organised left politics a hip edge. Where previously ANL/RAR rallies had been flamboyant affairs, the 1990s versions were still further dominated by mass-printed bright yellow lollipops. This was seriously uncool. Nevertheless, the popular support for anti-racist expression did draw considerable numbers to ANL rallies and the Welling demonstration in October 1993 was a success in terms of numbers mobilised, although police protection of fascists and confrontational tactics led to some disarray.

The 1990s 'new Asian dance music' or 'Indy-pop' demands to be understood in a historical context that recognises stops and starts in anti-racist campaigners' 'use' of cultural matter, exotica and ethnic identification as a recruitment vehicle. The re-formation of the Anti-Nazi League in the 1990s amounts to a rerun of the anti-racist mobilisations of the 1970s, including carnivals, except this time it is possible to note a change in the nature of the alliances formed. Astute Asian cultural workers made attempts to bridge the gap between locally organised self-defence/Asian political groupings and the popular front mobilisations of the white left. In the mid-1990s Asian musicians claimed a central place on the carnival platforms, addressed their concerns before both Asian and white audiences, took speaking places at rallies organised by the white left on other issues (especially anti-imperialist ones) and were generally more successful in countering the self-serving agendas of the Trotskyite formations.

Six months after Welling, the ANL organised another music carnival intentionally reminiscent of the populist Rock Against Racism events of the 1970s. It was huge. Yet there was little media attention. Only one music show, the youth culture programme *Naked City* which had also screened *Dog-Tribe*, saw fit to cover a public function which drew some 150,000 people, few other media even picked up the story. The *Guardian* only published a cynical dismissal, alleging people were only there for the free music, and then contradicting itself by pointing to politics:

> the Anti-Nazi League claim it was the biggest anti-fascist gathering ever staged ... but this crowd was never that specific. Judging from the banners along the march it was just anti. Anti-racism, anti-John Major, anti-unemployment, anti-student loans, anti-homelessness, anti-council tax ... Today's politics of protest have evolved into a kind of catch-all anti-establishmentism. (Bradley, *Guardian*, 30 May 1994)

It would, of course, be possible to read and publish against this conservative tone and valorise the anti-establishment, anti-capitalist spirit.

However, in the television debate on *Naked City*, Aki Nawaz and Sonya Aurora-Madan were critical of the event on several counts. There are grounds to believe that, to an extent, the carnival had been a feel-good publicity exercise for the ANL/SWP diverting attention away from more difficult complexities surrounding racial violence and the need to mobilise against its everyday occurrence. That the fascist BNP had not regained its London seat in the recent election was considered grounds for celebration, despite the fact that the most prominent BNP candidate's personal vote had gone up from 1,400 to 2,000. Further, the BNP vote nationwide had increased to some 16,000 votes, including 34 percent of the vote in Newham, with one other BNP candidate missing election by just 60 votes (*Revolutionary Fighter* 3). Mention might also be made of the way anti-BNP sentiment was used by reformist left groups such as Militant to campaign in favour of the Labour Party candidate. Nawaz complained that Fun^da^mental had been ignored by organisers of the carnival and 'should have been on the bill'. At Brockwell Park there was only one scheduled Asian band (Achanak) and they were on before the bulk of the march even reached the park. This is not the only reported instance of the 1990s ANL pissing Asian musicians off (the Kaliphz have similarly had cause for dispute with the organisers of another ANL carnival in Manchester). As it was, Fun^da^mental were subsequently reconciled to their omission from the carnival with an acclaimed (by Socialist Workers Party members) appearance at the SWP's annual conference, Marxism '94. By July, Nawaz had already been describing the Brockwell Park carnival within the context of the wider campaign:

> I think if 150,000 people go to a gig like that, then that's a petition. If 150,000 people are dissatisfied but can't change anything then something's wrong in our democracy. But are the Government listening? Are they F***! [*Melody Maker*'s asterisks] 150,000 people and there wasn't even one report in a daily newspaper. (*Melody Maker*, 16 July 1994)

This movement from critique to the desire to be involved actively in organised white politics is a strategic interventionism, but while the kind of politics offered by Asian-based bands resists any easy appropriation by the white left, simply dancing to Fun^da^mental does not constitute a serious engagement with the anti-racist/imperialist political stances central to these musical productions. The invitation to perform culture or politics at annual conferences and festivals ostensibly rocking against racism remains stalled in the move from visibility to redress.

What does all this have to do with the state of the planet? The ongoing plunder by the North of the South now includes destabilisations of geographical specificity such as the South in the North and neo-colonial comprador elites in the South. This should not, however, make it more difficult to see both the continuities and the changes in the history of resource extraction and 'coolie' labour regimes that stretch from the opium trade to the Contras, from Rio Tinto in Spain to the same in Bougainville, or from the Indian Civil Service to Microsoft in Hyderabad. So why is it that the distance between support and 'visibility' of South Asian activism in Britain does not extend to white left take-up of the internationalist causes these same activists espouse? Is it that Fun^da^mental and ADF, for example, are beyond the language competence of the SWP comrades? Obviously not, conniving *haramzada*'s aside. Is it that the solidarity work suitable for such a left requires specific relevances and clear recruitment constituency agendas? The SWP offers an 'anti-racism' that takes only the mild form of debt relief, calls upon the government to 'ban' the 'Nazis' and the tailing of Labour.

Jump to 1999. It would be false to suggest that discussion of these issues is not under way 'within' the left. In the wake of the murder of Stephen Lawrence at the hands of a group of white thugs, state-sponsored 'anti-racism' under Labour has also come in for critique. This occurs in interesting ways. In the *Weekly Worker* (1 July 1999, issue no. 295), Mark Fischer of the Communist Party of Great Britain (CPGB), discusses the 21 April 1999 issue of *Fighting Talk* put out by Anti-Fascist Action (AFA), and their warning that the agenda of post-Lawrence enquiry 'official' anti-racism is in danger of 'excluding the white working class' (p. 4) through the false assumption 'that there is a uniform access to power by all whites and uniform denial of access to power to all blacks' (p. 10). Such an assessment indicates that AFA's wider notion of anti-racism born of political experience and struggle, as opposed to legal or judicial inclinations of other groups (who would have all sorts of 'bannings' and increased police powers), offers more than the options approved of in policy circles. Fischer then condemns 'the dominant ideology of the institutional anti-racism' which drives the current British state agenda, at least from the rhetoric of the likes of Blair on down.

Fischer writes:

> Using concrete examples, *Fighting Talk* effectively illustrates how Labour councils in London have 'quite deliberately racialised' (p7) the competition for increasingly scarce resources and – 'in the name of anti-racism, presumably' – have 'pitted communities against each

other' (p8). This consequent 'racialisation of working class com-munity problems' provides a potentially rich vein of chauvinism and the plebeian racism which fringe organisations like the BNP can tap into. In the absence of a hegemonic class project, *Fighting Talk* correctly notes that 'a policy of redistributing the limited resources available to working class communities on ethnic grounds can only set the most impoverished against each other' (p10). (*Weekly Worker*, 1 July 1999)

This passage is worth quoting from the organ of the CPGB, rather than immediately from *Fighting Talk*[14] because it shows an avenue of class solidarity on the part of the small, but vigorous, CPGB group to address issues of race and class often glossed elsewhere on the left. The RCP-*Living Marxism* group seem to have completely forgotten their days in the organisation Workers Against Racism, the SWP mouth the usual anti-Nazi routines that tail the mainstream liberals, and Arthur Scargill's Socialist Labour Party seems beset with internal difficulties that preclude any positioning on these issues, unless the entry of the Indian Workers Association can offer the much-needed stability that Harpal Brah may bring them. The Revolutionary Communist Group paper *Fight Racism, Fight Imperialism* seems to maintain a standard, as does an associate organisation of AFA called Red Action, whose most recent magazine issue – *Red Action* – transmogrified from an inky tabloid to an A4 glossy at the end of 1998. *Red Action*'s April 1999 issue declares on its front cover that the question 'Race or Class?' is a 'fatal distraction'. Inside that issue the editorial notes that, despite liberal concern, the incidence of racial attack has been steadily on the increase. And alongside this they note that the stop and search incidents by the police increases in wealthy areas vis-à-vis poorer parts of London. The inference is clear: that the defence of the rich – class struggle – articulates itself today through police racism that is not simply to be solved by better police training and sensitivity in boroughs of high ethnic settlement, or by 150,000 people sitting in a park listening to drum and bass against racism.

Red Action writes:

in rejecting either the possibility and desirability of a redistribution of wealth from rich to poor, multi-culturalism instead places its entire emphasis on resources, such as they are, being shared on an equitable basis, thereby racialising social issues. A stratagem to deflect the consequences of increasing social inequality back into the section of society that bears the brunt of it. Fanning the flames of racial and cultural division, while systematically depriving the targeted communities of resources ... (*Red Action*, April 1999)

This text says more eloquently what Mark Fischer wanted to draw out from the *Fighting Talk* article. Though Fischer continues with a criticism where he claims that *Fighting Talk*'s analysis carries a weakness because it:

lacks an understanding that rightwing popularism-fascism need not come in a specifically racist form. An extreme reactionary movement in Britain will of course be chauvinist – it will be exclusivist, define itself against the 'outsider' – but not necessarily racist. Indeed, given the specifics of British history in the second half of this century, it will almost inevitably come draped in anti-Nazi and 'anti-racist' robes. (*Weekly Worker*, 1 July 1999)

It would not be impossible to imagine that Fischer is looking to exaggerate points of dispute in the interests of the almost sectarian separateness of his organisational location, rather than the professed rapprochement so often declared. The Red Action elaboration does not say that right-wing populism must be racist, indeed, it identifies establishment-approved anti-racism as the trick. This must lead us to annul the criticism, if not because of this, then at least because the reference to 'racial and cultural division' makes it clear that Red Action are aware of the kind of point Fischer wanted to make. We can agree with Fischer that 'much of the left tails establishment anti-racism, thus effectively contributing to the terrible fragmentation of some of the very poorest working class communities' (*Weekly Worker*, 1 July 1999), but there is no way this accusation can be levelled at the *Fighting Talk*/Red Action orientation. The roots of separation between these two camps lie elsewhere, and the annals of rapprochement would need to be mined to find them – there was a period early in the current reformation of the CPGB project where Red Action might have been further involved, and the Independent Working Class Association was an opportunity eschewed by the CPGB for its part. I am not however interested in apportioning blame or keeping sectarian scorecards.

Elsewhere in the *Weekly Worker* somewhat saner perspectives have been articulated. Eddie Ford writes, in the wake of the 1999 nail bombings in London, and the US high school teenage gun rampage massacres, of 'the consumer-driven conformity' of mainstream society and how this generates a 'fear of all "outsiders"' in the context of an educational apparatus that offers little but market training – where school is like 'a gigantic warehousing-cum-policing operation' (*Weekly Worker*, 6 May 1999). Ford is critical of those who call for 'bannings':

> After the first two nail bombs in Brixton and Brick Lane, Ken Livingstone wrote in *The Guardian*: 'The BNP should be banned from gaining the rights accorded to genuine political parties in the coming elections. We should ban the BNP, which is no more than a racist criminal conspiracy' (April 28) ... And after the Soho bombing, Michael Mansfield QC ... bellowed in *The Observer* (May 2) about 'proscribing' organisations like the BNP, in order 'to demonstrate to the Afro-Caribbeans, Jews, Asians and gays, and for that matter to the police themselves, that we mean business'. Mansfield conscientiously added: 'There is always the risk that such laws may be invoked against pure political dissent, but this risk post-Macpherson has been substantially reduced, now public recognition has been given to the need to define, identify and counter racism'. (*Weekly Worker*, 6 May 1999)

The sentiment here obviously leads to criticism of liberal anti-racism for its effectual 'dovetailing' with the interests of Blairite ideology, where it is left in 'impotency – shouting anti-racist slogans from the sidelines, slogans which the ruling class are only too happy to incorporate into their own vision of an impeccably anti-racist and inclusive bourgeois Britain' (*Weekly Worker*, 6 May 1999). As Marcus Larsen implies in his support for Ford a fortnight later, an 'ongoing critique of bourgeois anti-racism' seems to require more than a left that remains 'stuck in the past' and 'reduced to a mere leftwing echo of the emerging anti-racism of the bourgeoisie' (*Weekly Worker*, 20 May 1999). This sentiment then, perhaps needs to be learnt on both sides, by sectarian elements and well-intentioned anti-racists alike, in the context of actual involvement in the day-to-day practice of fighting the racists as part of an anti-capitalist project (and in opposition to asking racist cops to go easy for a while, at least until the dust of the latest enquiry blows over).

Credit as Bait

But does the notion of a 'proletarian' anti-racism as *part* of a general anti-capitalist project, advocated by some in the CPGB and as seen in the original sentiment of RAR, adequately respond to the necessities of the current conjuncture? Back to Spivak: Acknowledging the constraints of codification which force her to 'retreat' to work only in languages where she might even 'shift idiom' – because of her facility in Bengali as first language (Spivak 1999: 243n)[15] – it is the credit-baiting apparatus of finance capital reaching to the subaltern that attracts detailed analysis. This credit comes, without infrastructural involvement, to create a 'will for the financialization of the globe' which directs Spivak to look to her own separated backyard in Bangladesh (she is 'from' West Bengal, schismed by colonial mapping in 1947), and it comes in a way that is 'rather different from the visible violence of super-exploitation' (Spivak 1999: 343n), but is, interest-wise, the 'same'. Here 'if one wanted to intervene' it was necessary to 'know the language well enough to move with dialectical shifts', so that 'rather than stop at exchanging ideas with the activist leaders', it should be possible to 'learn' (Spivak 1999: 413) from local struggles against these financialisations, baitings, schemings. By the end of the book, which she has said was 'stalled' for many years (Spivak, talk at Goldsmiths College, London, May 1999), Spivak recognises that this learning comes through Bengali and she angrily denounces the deceits. That it is women who are now more than ever invited to participate in the get-rich-quick schemings of capital is only another fold in the comprador tale – 'credit-baiting' as the over-determined script of cultural intervention where capital sets itself up as cure for patriarchy. The alliance between capital and women does not make self-organisation of women as an entry into productive labour itself complicit, but, parallel to corporate music industry enthusiasm for 'ethnic' entertainers, the interest-seeking interest of the banks who will fund such credit schemes is in women who will pay up in the end. This is so not only because women are, through myriad long-standing cultural binds (Spivak 1999: 102) such as child care, household and family responsibilities, less risky as investments than desultory, possibly wayward, drunk, itinerant, etc., males. Of course this is the kind of stereotype and dreamtime on which global intervention thrives, and few women are likely to get rich in these schemes – but turnover will be generated, circulation, valorisation, with no regard to human costs. The further extension of capitalist relations into all domestic spheres and the reworking of old notions of the social is confirmed. The double play here is like the poisoned 'gift' that factory work offered to homebound women, since 'to enter a world without structural support is not an unquestioned good ... the encouragement of women's micro-enterprise – credit-baiting with no infrastructure – is a comparable phenomenon in the arena of finance capital' (Spivak 1999: 419).

The recognition of the importance of language specificity – we might add context too – opens into another, perhaps more specific, warning as regards teaching, research and criticism, where Spivak addresses the 'mania' for Third World literature anthologies which are taught, or discussed, in what she calls a 'sanctioned ignorance' where the student or reader cannot know the depth of the loss that is there in 'translation-as-violation' because the idiom of the original languages or the 'subject-constitution of the social and gendered agents in question' remains invisible. I would argue that 'official' anti-racism, and even some aspects of its 'left' critique, participate in a similar occlusion of more necessary internationalist work. That this 'sanctioned ignorance' is now sanctioned more than ever by reference to (cosmopolitan?) globality adds this to the list of parallels to the financialisation of the globe that might also be called embourgeoisment in Marx. The term 'sanctioned ignorance' might find other uses, doing work for the wilful acceptance of ideological rewritings of history, say of revolutionary movements, independence struggles, the lives of great thinkers, etc., or it might also name the specified levels of political analysis and informed participatory engagement that is the pride and joy of the democratic process, witnessed at best in television election broadcast coverage and SWP populist 'drop the debt' campaigning (i.e. not abolition of the debt system).

'Sanctioned ignorance' can take the most erudite forms. I think it is the appropriate term to use for those organisers of the white left who think that scheduling one 'Asian' band per carnival is a sufficiently inclusive 'alliance' anti-racism.[16] 'Sanctioned ignorance' is also to be seen in the selective forgetting that is the knowledge base of disciplines like anthropology, Indology, area studies and so on. Spivak notes that the 'specialists of the margin' often remain untouched in literary ideology critique. What is perhaps worse is that these disciplines are sometimes left alone to pursue their own self-criticisms and reflexive revaluations (*pace* Banerjea 1999: 18). In anthropology this has been both a boon and a trick – old anthropological voyeurism is dead, only to be reborn as the perpetuation of self (-obsessive) critique. In Indology, area studies, human geography, other such critical trajectories have taken up the work of Said as sanction for rehearsals, politically corrected, of the same backwards glance. Business as usual. Sanctioned ignorance enables well-meaning liberals to dance against capital and imagine that tinkering with levels of debt repayment is not an already calculated and accounted strategy of international capital. To think that inviting women into debt-production-capital-exchange is progressive in itself is just as ignorant. Sanctioned calls like this sell the planet into (wage) slavery.

So that there can be no doubt, it is worth emphasising the complicity of a critical anthropology, and often of Marxism etc., in what has to be called the imperialist project operated even at the moment that anthropologists and Marxists were most critically urging a defence of the people, the workers, culture, from imperialist rampage. This defence took various forms – relativism, dialectics and the shared source that can even be called Enlightenment thought – but complicity does not mean the work done under these, quite different, signifiers cannot be interrogated for still potent insights at a time when imperialism now acts in the very name of those 'others' that were to be defended from it. Today the international agencies of imperialism act with 'humanitarian' concern to bomb here, intervene there, impose sanctions and restrictions elsewhere. With the very best of anti-racist intentions,[17] the access-all-areas agenda of the free marketeers proceeds apace. Is it too late to ask if within complicity there is still a counter-hegemonic possibility?

The interrogation of disciplinary anthropology requires close examination of the way elementary pedagogy is related to disciplinary formation (Spivak 1999: 276). Even among those who would champion the cause of the oppressed, the requirement that the subject of oppression march into representation in progressive texts evokes a foreshortened version of the modes of production history that was the speculative morphology of Marx, reified in Marxisms. That anthropological pedagogy provides only quick-fire versions of this history, with details snatched from old classic texts such as *The Nuer*, *Argonauts*, perhaps even the Mashpee of Clifford's *Predicament*, does not teach a version of capitalist development that is transformatory. Graduates march willingly into the international agencies and NGOs, armed with good intentions and reflexivity, and perhaps even some degree of critical capacity vis-à-vis development. Reading *The Nuer* and *Argonauts* lets graduate students present themselves as cured of, or at least aware of, Eurocentric biases. But even critical 'diologic' exchanges with the subjects of development and otherly-constituted 'Others' can replicate older functionalisms. What chance is there for a dialectical reading of subsumption and transition in the history of the present here?

Sketch

Spivak provides her own sketch, and it is worth quoting in full since the parameters bring forward the critique of imperialism into the present-day arena of international aid, by way of the post-decolonisation period of subcontracting as it transmutes into neo-liberal financial free-fall, and it helps set the scene for the reading of international music commerce that follows. No doubt there are several other formulations possible, and the dynamics of transition and subsumption read out from *Capital* might usefully weave in with this passage, but nevertheless:

> The contemporary international division of labour is a displacement of the divided field of nineteenth-century territorial imperialism. Put in the abstractions of capital logic, in the wake of industrial capitalism and mercantile conquest, a group of countries, generally first-world, were in the position of investing capital; another group, generally third-world, provided the field for investment, both through the subordinate indigenous capitalists and through their ill-protected and shifting labour force. (Spivak 1999: 274)

Already the characteristics of comprador capital in the pay of circulation can be seen necessarily to sell its own labour into danger – the absence of extensive labour regulation in the 'Third World' becomes a prime channelling device for capitalist investment.

> In the interests of maintaining the circulation and growth of capital (and the concomitant task of administration within nineteenth-century territorial imperialism), transportation, law, and standardised education systems were developed – even as local industries were destroyed or restructured, land distribution was rearranged, and raw material was transferred to the colonizing country. With so-called decolonization, the growth of multinational capital, and the relief of the administrative charge, 'development' did not now involve wholesale state-level legislation and establishing education systems in a comparable way. This impedes the growth of consumerism in the former colonies. (Spivak 1999: 274–5)

The comprador class is formed, but does not have the same administrative tasks as in colonial times since it is not immediately in the interests of international capital to foster the same levels of consumption/consumerism in the Third World theatre as in the metropolitan sites, nor is the 'same' level of workplace legislation wanted. On the contrary, development does not follow the projected history (modes of production forward march narrative):

> With modern telecommunication and the emergence of advanced

capitalist economies at the two edges of Asia, maintaining the international division of labour serves to keep the supply of cheap labour in the periphery. The implosion of the Soviet Union in 1989 has smoothed the way for the financialization of the globe. Already in the mid-seventies, the newly electronified stock exchanges added to the growth of telecommunication, which allowed global capitalism to emerge through export-based subcontracting and post-fordism. 'Under this strategy, manufacturers based in developed countries subcontract the most labour intensive stages of pro-duction, for example, sewing or assembly, to the Third World nations where labour is cheap. Once assembled, the multinational re-imports the good – under generous tariff exemptions – to the developed country *instead of selling them to the local market*.' (Spivak 1999: 275, quoting, in the last part, from *Multinational Monitor*, August 1983)

Then, noting that human labour is not intrinsically 'cheap' or 'expensive', Spivak emphasises the absence of labour laws, or their en-forcement, and the totalitarian state often found in 'development' in the periphery, accompanied by 'minimal subsistence requirements on the part of the worker', that are the conditions which ensure 'cheapness' of that workforce (Spivak 1999: 275). Such a workforce cannot be 'systematically trained in the ideology of consumerism' (that classless ideal social dream) as – and this seems like a contradiction, but it fits – the 'Bretton Woods organisations, together with the United Nations, are beginning to legislate for a monstrous North/South global state' (Spivak 1999: 276). Bringing the modes-of-production dialectic up to date appears here as an urgent site for research and activity. The 'aid', humanitarian and administrative, that would facilitate this new fold in the fabric of imperialism, must be read dialectically as the continuity with the earlier mercantile extractions, and now mid-term sub-contracting developments.

It is in this context that the transition from colonial and mercantile capital which subsumes local forms – of tribute, bonded labour, super-exploitation – finds easier passage (does not require the same moralistic interventionism) when it comes to deregulation of markets under a global or universal neo-liberal rhetoric. Again, it is an important point that the formation of a middle level of intermediaries is what facilitates this process, the comprador class here being not so much the indigenous national elites, but now the, sometimes anthropology-trained, ex-marginal ex-migrants who work in the Bretton Woods sections or who market 'culture' or 'Indy-pop' in support of the abstract economic machine. Spivak's critique of this class fraction is ruthless. Is it innocent that it is only now, as IMF/World Bank tributary feudalism (Spivak 1999: 95) closes down the possibilities of normal capitalist 'development' in the South, that a culturalist diversity emerges as liberal ideological coefficient – a glorified divide and rule – which disarticulates metropolitans further from the periphery, inclusive of ex-migrants and ex-marginals, and about which anthropologists, among others, had better be articulate?

Spivak declares that 'an unquestioning privileging of the migrant may also turn out to be a figure of effacement of the native informant' (Spivak 1999: 18). This is not simply rectified by remembering that the 'minority' in the midst of the metropole is different from the people of the 'Third World', which is itself quite differentially fractured. The accusation is against one who claims authority to speak against the hegemonic order at the same time as electing themselves as the spokespersons for those who are subordinate in that order – and the danger is that this will reinforce that hegemony all the more by means of a diminutive inversion, a reversal not adequate to win, but merely verbose rehearsal of victimage. Who is it that reports on the 'Third World' if not those trained in a certain management of difference in a containment process that filtered difference into those languages the hegemonic power will comprehend and be able to codify, sort, administer, trade? And how many of these are not the international graduates of varied social science development and anthropology schools, most notably the graduate programmes of SOAS, LSE, Oxford and Cambridge – however critically informed by the soundtrack of new Asian dance, hip-hop, Live Aid, Womad, RAR or the like?

I like good music. But from Spivak we could learn a lesson for political struggle which is to 'not present the ethics of alterity as a politics of identity' (Spivak 1999: x). Yes, let us recognise that there are good intentions in the anthropological concern with, insofar as it is respect for, heterogeneity (and here leaving for other places the almost overwhelming complicity of that concern with a less benign imperialism), but if we were to think that this ethics for otherness provided sufficient grounds for a transformatory project we might be dangerously misled. Why? Because the limits already structured into a struggle that marks the exploited as victims means that it must fail. It rehearses a given structure, it administers a code. It codifies.

This returns us to the site of evaluation of the hyphenated ex-marginals now claiming space, and alterity, in the cultural industries and their associated telecommunications networks. Here, 'the upwardly mobile ex-marginal, justifiably searching for validation, can help commodify marginality' (Spivak 1999: 170). There are many examples relevant to this that could be read straight off the charts. As I write, Talvin Singh's album *OK* is named as winner of the Mercury Prize (*Guardian*, 28 July 1999). Executives smile. Cultural industry diversity has all too easily fed the trick in which we witness 'the multiculturalist masquerade of the privileged as the disenfranchised, or their liberator' (Spivak 1999: 176). Such deceits are the stuff of current production. Singh's comment on award night: 'It is a surprise, but then not a surprise, since my life has always been a struggle' (BBC News, 8 September 1999).[18] Perhaps the 'interventionist academic' can assist in opening the possibility of a critical fight against the depredations of global economic citizenship under transnationality by pointing to the seductions of 'unexamined culturalism' and a liberal multiculturalism which expands the corporate base (Spivak 1999: 402). All the 'narcissistic seductions of liberal multiculturalism notwithstanding, the so-called immediate experience of migrancy is not necessarily consonant with transnational literacy' (Spivak 1999: 402).

'Certain members of the Indian elite are of course native informants for first-world intellectuals interested in the voice of the Other. But one must nevertheless insist that the colonized subaltern subject is irretrievably heterogeneous' (Spivak 1999: 270). But it is further worth remembering that the ex-marginal located in the metropolitan West too often is only seen through the prism of a dubious and merely liberal 'interest' in the voice of the Other as well. This 'Other' silences by promoting people to speaking positions so long as they only say safe things, or so long as what they say will only be heard in ways that fit the 'interest' of those that control this marionette-like house-slave game. The house slave here is of course also heterogeneous, and listening more adequately perhaps would mean more than an appreciation of jazz, but would work through a pleasure in disruptions and dissonance, an identification-appropriation complex, and a reflexive revaluation of Other-love, and finally – and it takes far too long – to recognise self-determining and autonomous coexistence of the many of us implicated in these scenes. Perhaps a quicker way through these basic steps would be an education in communist universalism (to come).

A final 'example' that insists on the disaggregated role of 'Indy-pop' so that it cannot be so readily slotted together with George Harrison wailing 'My Sweet Lord', is one that insists on challenging the sanctioned ignorance of silenced oppression with loud public displays and protest on the streets. Indy-pop is not just a chart phenomenon, whether we think of self-defence vigilantism or Burnsalls strike anthems. Music politics cannot always be so readily co-opted into the carnival machine (except perhaps by way of academic commentary). What follows shows that what should be the run-of-the-mill causes for the wider British left are too often ignored. The parachute recruitment regimes of the SWP meant a passing interest, but never sustained internationalist anti-racism. But does my text yet achieve it? No, not yet, even as it reads cultural performance in Manchester – where Eid is celebrated by children of diaspora, the descendants of those brought to Britain to work the old industrial mills, now fed by undocumented ('illegal') curry-shifters as the current version of the same extraction – as the consequence of international labour flow. This story is possibly mere anthropological reportage, masquerading as activist anthropology writing tales of the heterogeneity of politicised postcolonial diasporic ex-migrancy, but it circulates a struggle that would otherwise recede into the memory of a few. It is recovered here because it honours comrades and unacknowledged work, and the excellence of a certain 'sound of drums'.

Amer

Amer Rafiq was a 21-year-old who worked as a part-time waiter in an Asian restaurant in Rusholme, Manchester. On the 21 February 1996 he finished work and was on his way home at 2.30 a.m. It was the Muslim festival of Eid. As a leaflet from the Amer Rafiq Defence Campaign puts it:

> Officers of the Tactical Aid Group arrested Amer and threw him into the back of their van. On arrival at the notorious Platt Lane police station Amer was covered with blood and pleading for help. He had been assaulted with such brute force that he suffered horrific injuries. His right eye was so badly smashed that surgeons had to remove it. They warned that he could still lose the sight of his remaining eye. (Amer Rafiq Defence Campaign leaflet 1996)

That this incident happened at all seems almost unsurprising given the long, long list of violence against black people at the hands of the police in the UK. That it occurred during Eid in Manchester is also unsurprising given the regular excessive over-policing of celebrations in Rusholme, an area with a long-established Asian commercial and residential presence. On relevant days, such as the 20 February 1996, the arrival of numerous large buses full of police, vans with police dogs and foot patrols occurs at about 6 p.m. (with back-up troops in readiness, waiting in vans parked in side-streets). Wilmslow Road is blocked off at both ends with barriers that had been delivered in the morning – the blocking of what is a main thoroughfare into central Manchester, along which are some 70 restaurants, take-aways, clothing and jewellery shops, must cause some considerable inconvenience – and in the car parks and spaces thus made available, a mini-festival occurs. In recent years this has been organised by groups such as Young Muslims UK which provide music and speeches. Towards midnight the police clear the street, including by baton charge, and the almost inevitable stand-off takes place in the area by the park designated for cars. It was for not moving his vehicle fast enough that Amer Rafiq was arrested and beaten.

Within a week a protest rally was organised leading to a larger demonstration drawing people and organisations from other parts of England to Manchester. Over 2,000 people attended this demonstration which was stewarded effectively by campaign organisers and volunteers from amongst the Rusholme community, Amer's family and friends, and regular anti-racist Manchester activists. The demonstration circled the police station, marched through Rusholme – where shops and restaurants closed in solidarity – and moved on to the Manchester town hall for a rally and speeches. At this rally the concerns of the community were outlined:

> Over the past few years, over policing and harassment of people celebrating Eid have become regular features. Riot squads, horses, dogs, baton charges and helicopters have been used to disperse peaceful gatherings. This confrontational policing is out of proportion compared to policing of New Years' celebrations. It is clearly designed to intimidate and create a violent situation. This is not community policing but policing against the community. The tragedy of Amer Rafiq was a disaster waiting to happen. (Amer Rafiq Defence Campaign leaflet 1996)

These are not inflammatory words, but rather describe the situation in a matter-of-fact way evident to anyone who has been in Rusholme during Eid festival. The area is an attraction to a wide cross-section of communities, and as such deserves greater attention than is often afforded it by the mass media, which only zeros in on the possibility of a riot story after such incidents. At different times the restaurants seem to have several main types of clientele – between approximately 6 and 8.30 in the evening Caucasian families dine, between 8 and 11 p.m. the clientele is predominantly Asian families, and from 11 till 12 those just out from pubs looking for a vindaloo arrive, washing it down with Kingfisher or Boddies. Later in the night the street is a mixed community of Asian youth and others. Throughout the daytime, and especially at the weekends, Rusholme is as 'multicultural' as any area can be in Britain. At the festival of Eid this character does not change significantly, although there are more people of the South Asian community in attendance than others, partly because the police presence turns others away. In this otherwise harmonious environment the numbers and ferocity of the cops exceed those evident at the most volatile of football confrontations between the Manchester derby rivals, City and United.

It was with incredulity that readers of the local press found that the police report – leaked to a journalist – contained the 'explanation' that when Amer was thrown into the back of the police van he hit his eye on a 'wham-ram' baton lying on the floor. Mostly, when someone is arrested, there are no weapons in the van, as presumably they could take out their frustrations by damaging police property or themselves. I leave it to the sceptics to work out why the police were throwing the lad into the van with such force that he may have damaged police equipment. The added irony of this report is that it came out on the same day as the coroner's report into the death in London of Brian Douglas – a black music promoter. The coroner found that Douglas had died 'accidentally' after his skull was cracked by a blow from the police's new long-handled LAPD-type batons, although – and I quote – 'the blow was not aimed at his head'. The coroner called for further baton training for police (so they can fix their aim I guess), but the Police Federation spokesperson claimed later that night that Britain already has the 'most efficient training programme possible within the available level of funding'.[19] It is no surprise that, in response, another militant and angry demonstration against police violence drew strong support in Manchester. Tempers were running high, yet discipline was maintained (in contrast to the well-trained police at Eid). As is normal with such events, there was some jockeying for position at the front of the march. As the march began at Platt Fields the SWP cadre attempted to set up at the front, which had been specifically designated as a place where Amer's family and women's groups would assemble. This matter however was soon resolved. Other organised groups in attendance included a large contingent from the Birmingham Indian Workers Association, the Pakistani Workers Association, the Association of Communist Workers, the CPGB, the RCP, Black Flag anarchists, some trade union groups, Militant and the Charterhouse Posse.

As a final coda, I want to describe the 'ethnographic' moment of significance at this demonstration, which has reference to the place of music in anti-racism and which seems to me to be worthy of mention not because of the music, but because of the expressive and creative energy displayed, because it is explicitly not exotica at point of sale, and because it is expressive solidarity that escalates. This moment does not summarise this chapter, it does not equate diasporic complicity with white anti-racism, and it does not evoke anti-establishment sentiment as activist panacea, but the moment does seem emblematic. The work of organising such a large demonstration is no picnic, requiring many nights of long meetings and sometimes finely argued polemic – especially where the organisation needs to negotiate amongst several shades of political persuasion. It is then, in part, an achievement of the organisers to gather people on the day, to keep people focused on making a strong statement without being drawn into further confrontation (at that stage considered an important tactical necessity) and to make a loud and large impact upon the otherwise quiet serenity of the Manchester shopping district (the place would be blown up by the IRA some weeks later in a still more impressively loud event). As the rally made its way from Rusholme to the town centre, a major focus for many marchers was the bhangra-honed drumming and chanting style of the Posse who organised the Amer Rafiq Defence Campaign. This was not simply rock against racism.

As the rally passed under the Arndale bus depot, the drumming and the voices reached a crescendo, echoing, resonance. Dancing, jumping, super-charged and angry black and white bodies which had been vibrant all afternoon gained a further charge of energy. The crowd packed in around an indefatigable drummer, surged and surged again. Police violence provokes justifiably angry reactions from the assaulted communities – and no one, but the racist coward – could fail to be moved in solidarity with those involved on this day. By contrast the SWP routine slogans about hating the Tories were meek and mild. One chant from the South Asian contingent taken up by all shows this with humour: 'Police *kute maro jute*'. In Panjabi this means something like: 'Police are dogs, slap them with your slipper'.[20] The exuberance and energy born of anger, frustration and organised militancy carried over from the anomie of isolation and despair and transformed fury into an affirmation of community and unity that could not be manufactured except through solidarity of purpose and struggle. It is just these things that are the legacy of political struggles (and musical skills) amd that I would want to mark and remember, if not also valorise and extend, throughout this book as a call to responsibility, justice and organisation, and which Sivanandan has more eloquently urged us to remember in his book *Communities of Resistance*:

> loyalty, solidarity, camaraderie, unity, all the great and simple things that make us human ... We have cultures of resistance to create, communities of resistance to build, a world to win. Now is the moment of socialism. And capital shall have no dominion. (Sivanandan 1990: 192–3).

Notes

1. Could there be an echo here of Adorno who described his work as a 'sort of rational appeal hearing against rationality' (in Wiggerhaus 1984/1994: 4)?
2. Possibly complicating this too much, can I speculate a little given that the scenario whereby modernity is allocated to Europe and America and the rest of the world condemned to act out an already written script is rightly criticised by Chatterjee in *The Nation and its Fragments* (1993: 5)? I would argue that it is also important to remember that the 'modular forms' of the nation, decreed from and by Europe and America, are of course not forms made solely there from the first. The West is co-constituted with the rest, and this is recognised more and more in the ways that every instance of national development is written in the blood of colonial-capital, already global, expropriation. The national modular form exemplified in the case of Britain, for example, could not be without the constitutive role of India, Africa, slavery, conquest and so on. The nation is also a product of the East. The capital of Empire was Calcutta, not London. Similar moves could also shift the history of France or Spain to another geography.
3. The Burnsalls strikers can be seen in a documentary video called *The Women from 10 Downing Street*. Made by Anne-Marie Sweeney, the film is available from The Labour Video Project, P.O. Box 425584, San Francisco CA 94142 USA, Email <lvpsf@igc.apc.org>.
4. I am taking the liberty of quoting this material from an article jointly written with Virinder and published as Kalra and Hutnyk (1998). The reworked lyrics, by Tariq Mehmood, were recorded by Virinder Kalra on the 3 July demonstration, Birmingham 1993.
5. For more on Asian Youth Movements, see Kalra et al. (1996) – a recovery history/writing project in Manchester from which this section on RAR also emerged.
6. *Fighting the Nazi Threat*, Anti-Nazi League educational pamphlet.
7. An SWP pamphlet claims each event attracted 100,000 (Bambury 1992: 33), *Sounds* reported an estimate by Lambeth Council of 150,000, ITV news said 60,000. Who knows?
8. Much of the material for discussion of musical anti-racism is found only in obscure pamphlets, the left press and in forgotten histories, but Paul Gilroy's 1987 book *There Ain't No Black in the Union Jack* usefully refuses to allow Rock Against Racism to be forgotten. David Widgery's study *Beating Time: Riot 'n*

Race 'n Rock 'n Roll (1986) has been out of print for several years; histories of punk only offer brief reminiscences, and histories of reggae and 'Two-Tone' remain either unwritten, or focus solely on the reggae of Anglo-British bands like The Police and associated personalities. Widgery was a co-founder of Rock Against Racism and member of the Socialist Workers Party, and although his book was described by Jon Savage in *England's Dreaming: Sex Pistols and Punk Rock* as 'full of insults for the groups who supported RAR' (Savage 1991: 484), it was the best of a small lot.

9. This point is emphasised in Kalra (2000a).

10. Doubtless this occlusion should not be overvalued since part of the explanation for the distance between bhangra and 'mainstream' English music culture was an intentional and organisational separation. It is worth mentioning that this continues today in bhangra, despite occasional major label signings.

11. Critical discussion of the relation between the ANL/SWP and RAR is important because it illustrates a difference of political practice that is common to the relations between the white and liberal left and black political activity. It is not without recognising this tension that Gilroy points out that RAR had an element of anti-capitalist critique which was effectively curtailed by the anti-Nazi focus of ANL – Gilroy writes that 'Rocking Against Racism had allowed space for youth to rant against the perceived iniquities of "Labour Party Capitalist Britain". The popular front tactics introduced by the ANL closed it down' (Gilroy 1987: 133). In contrast the SWP claim that the ANL support of Rock Against Racism was 'important in building support for anti-racism in schools, workplaces and the community, as well as exposing the Nazis of the National Front', and 'Of course this did not mean that institutionalised racism ... or racial harassment was stopped' (Anti-Nazi League educational kit). In reply to Gilroy's criticisms, Alex Callinicos says: 'It is in the nature of a united front that it brings together divergent political forces which are prepared to work together around a single issue, in this case combating the Nazis', and shows that he is aware of the need to shore up criticism of this single-issue focus when he adds that 'Focusing in this way on the fascists wasn't a retreat from the more general struggle against racism' (Callinicos 1993: 64).

12. Gilroy claims that the general anti-capitalist orientations of RAR came mostly from reggae and some aspects of punk rebellion, although this latter with ambiguities since some punks flirted with the iconography of the National Front. A June 1977 editorial in the punk fanzine *Sniffin' Glue* had characterised the National Front as 'crud', but also linked them with the 'commies, the Socialist fuckin' Workers, the head-in-the-sand brigade and the poxy Evening News' (*Sniffin' Glue*, 10 June 1977). Whatever the status of the Nazi symbols, it is acknowledged that punk brought an anti-authoritarian and anti-state orientation that complemented reggae's evocation of black urban militancy – Gilroy points out that the Notting Hill Carnival uprising coincided with the emergence of punk (Gilroy 1987: 125) – and so RAR came together in a way that broke from what was considered a 'dour and self-defeating' approach, 'devoid of fun' (Gilroy 1987: 127). An organiser of RAR commented in the *NME*, that 'for some reason or other the British left have always thought that anything electric couldn't possess any true political awareness and that acoustic folk was the only possible music

they could ally themselves with' (*NME*, 6 May 1978). There was no doubt that ANL and RAR were part of a moment in the political history of Britain that, alongside tumultuous musical developments, heralded a comprehensive change of tempo.

13. The more interesting of these are Anti-Fascist Action, Red Action and the Colin Roach Centre (see *ANL-Critical Examination* Pamphlet, Colin Roach Centre 1995).

14. It is possible to subscribe to *Fighting Talk* from London AFA BM1734 London WC1N 3XX.

15. Adorno again parallels this, having said of lyric music: 'Of Chinese, Japanese, Arabic lyrics I will not speak, as I cannot read them in the original and must suspect that translation deploys mechanisms of adaptation that preclude adequate understanding' (Adorno 1981: 52 quoted in Jameson 1990: 207). We should, however, also be wary of the possible ventriloquy in demanding that work in 'the vernacular' is best – language competence has been no guarantee against imperialism, orientalism, essentialism as the case of scholarly work would show, for example especially in Germany where the most detailed Indologies are to be seen, and the politics of speaking for others infrequently raised. Having said this, clearly the matter is important and although it is in footnotes that some of the keys to Spivak's thinking are revealed, perhaps this one should be elevated. Long footnotes are in vogue, are they? Look particularly at the one on Immanuel Kant's reference to 'Neuholländers' and the heterogeneity of Koories today (hint, not just Koorie, but also Murray, Nungah, etc). Here Spivak explains why it is not possible to pursue an analysis of Walpiri 'hybridity' in modernity because she cannot learn the languages with the care that she has learnt English and German ('to a lesser extent' [Spivak 1999: 27–8n]). This is after all an honest admitting of constraints not often found in cultural studies globalising commentary. In Spivak it is obviously also a constraint of time, and a small recognition of the multiplicity of the world mixed with respect-anguish for the loss of languages that is witnessed so often. But worth noting.

16. Aki Nawaz also points out that commercial festival organisers rerun this dumb routine, see the press release of August 1999 for the EP *Why America Will Go to Hell,* containing remixes of 'Jah Shataan' (Fun^da^mental).

17. To underline this, witness the Labour Party doing flips and twists to 'admit' its institutional racism after the McPherson Report into the murder of Stephen Lawrence. Now tell it to the parents of Ricky Reel – another black youth killed and only bumbling investigations by the cops.

18. Talvin Singh is an accomplished musician without doubt. My criticism is more for his apparent disavowal of political 'issues' and his conflation of such 'issues' with visibility and with his hedgingly embraced 'obligation' to be an 'Asian role model' – 'politics' with which he will engage with some degree of distance, but ... (*Guardian,* 10 September 1999).

19. For further information of the campaign for justice for Amer Rafiq see the article in *CARF* quoting Mukhtar Dar (April/May 1996 issue). To a mixed reception, but with some relief at the closure, Amer's family finally accepted a small compensation award after several years in the courts. The officers responsible were never charged or even reprimanded.

20. Thanks to Virinder Kalra for this translation. For a crash course in Panjabi see *Teach Yourself Panjabi* by Kalra and Purewal (1999).

7
'Naxalite'

A mass of sleeping villages
That's how they're pitching it
At least that's what they try to pretend
But check out our history
So rich and revolutionary
('Naxalite', from the album *Rafi's Revenge*, 1998. Asian Dub
Foundation. Lyrics, Das, Pandit, Zaman, Tailor, Savale, copyright
1997 by kind permission of Universal/MCA Music Ltd)

The marchers that day were party workers, students, and the
labourers themselves [paddy workers]. Touchables and
Untouchables. On their shoulders they carried a keg of ancient anger,
lit with a recent fuse. There was an edge to this anger that was
Naxalite, and new. (Arundhati Roy, *The God of Small Things* 1997: 69)

Openings

Cultural politics, in isolation from organisation capable of instituting
transformatory change, can be characterised as comprador, or at least
open too readily to co-option and appropriation within the logistics of
the culture industries. Sometimes, however, the convoluted histories of
'culture' confound all too easy assumptions about cultural products and
may surprise critics – especially where practitioners appear more
informed and astute, or wryly ironic, than commentators would credit.
The story related here shows again that pop music can have a deeper hue
than that apparent at first blush, however much we have become eager
to dismiss it as trifle.

This discussion is of the ways cultural and political 'matter' linked to
a small village in West Bengal can be conjured with in the circuits of

international publishing, the multinational music industry and within cultural studies academicism all at the same time. The discussion passes by way of literary, historical and musical sources, primarily a music track – 'Naxalite' – by London's own ADF. I make no apologies for singling out just one track from their prolific archive in this particular chapter,[1] nor for placing this track in a path that may not quite fit the easy-listening pretensions of the musicological fraternity. Nor is it the case that this work can be understood without clearing away a number of prejudicial conventions – which many will recognise – and making a space in which the track may be heard again. I do this first of all, as will by now be expected, in the context of the new audibility/visibility of things 'Asian' in the mainstream music scene. As I have noted in this book, the ways in which South Asian cultural forms in Europe have been celebrated through circuits of popular media have a long pedigree, from the translation of religious epics by Max Mueller and orientalists after him, through to the musical sitarism of the Beatle George, and today's soft-*hindutva* pop stars like Kula Shaker.[2] The popular narrative of Western fascination for the East can be countered by recognition that India never was the sleepy spiritual fantasy of imperial imaginings, nor the exotic cornucopia of adventure drama that brought Indiana Jones all the way to the Temple of Doom. Tranquil images and photogenic poverty aside, the idea of the sleepy Indian village, dancing temple girls, dusty sadhus and joss-stick waving *bhajan*-singing devotees is only the favoured perspective of a tourists' Eurocentric point of view, desperately blind to the consequences and realities of its own invasive glare. The villages were never so sleepy. In asking about the fit between a peasant struggle in rural India and either the circuits of the transnational cultural industries, or – at another level – with the specificities of community struggle in the East End of London, the attempt is to clarify some of the contradictions between cultural politics and its circulation. My argument is not that ADF do not 'know' the context or complexity in which the struggles sourced to the village of Naxalbari emerge, but that the deployment of this matter into the cultural industries may have rather different significances in circulation than it does in the circumstances of more localised anti-racist, anti-imperialist practice. Towards the end of this discussion I entertain a diversion into high profile literature and the awards circuit where these themes replay again. By providing a small coda on the works of Arundhati Roy and Mahasweta Devi, it is possible to emphasise how false the sleepy village ideology has been and to clinch the argument that attention to the specificities of struggle is worthwhile.

For some time it has been clear that the notion of India as esoteric paradise of spiritual and timeless tradition has been imported back into late imperial Britain, and not only by the tourist-descendants of Clive and Canning. The children of labour migrants, of citizen-refugees from the far-flung plantation empires (Kenya, Uganda), kith and kin of the elite Anglophiles and immiserated proletarian exports in search of whatever better options might be had in the northern mills, have now achieved what some proclaim as a successful degree of cultural visibility in multiculti Britain. This is of course challenged, and the evidence of continued racial attack and murder on the estates is sufficient to give pause to any hasty declaration that 'Asian Kool' translates into a significant transformation of the UK social mix. However, there are ways in which another version of fantasy South Asia is now deployed, to a greater or lesser extent as a strategic essentialism, and in a way that looks, at least from afar, as if the orientalist mindset has been made more intimate. And why not, we might ask? Although the requirements for a challenge to the exclusionary material politics of Britain, as opposed to its rhetorical inclusionary trickery, are somewhat greater than running a successful nightclub, style magazine or curry house, there is no necessity to argue with those who milk the honey of popular culture for payment, even if it means strapping on a union-jack print Nehru jacket and selling tabla tapes outside Camden tube. However, it is interesting to examine the way an inclusive rhetoric of a curry-loving culture in the UK serves as a smoke screen to occlude inequalities among the various constituencies of Britain, and the vast socioeconomic distance that separates those serving the curry-shifts from those who swallow the cardamom. The evidence for this last disjunction is all too visible, and it applies specifically to the urban context in which ADF operate, even as they themselves sign with a major company and rake in cash from chart success.

Designated an 'Official Tourist Zone' because of its abundance of South Asian eateries (reported in *Eastern Eye*, 19 September 1997, as mentioned at the end of Chapter 4), Brick Lane is one of the most high profile 'ethnic' markers of a larger London scene often characterised from afar in ways that owe more to scholarly and public policy demarcations than to actualities on the streets. This area of London has become an overdetermined symbol for a diverse and vibrant metropolis.[3] Adjacent to an emergent cyber and arts enclave,[4] Brick Lane's elevation as a tourist attraction raises all sorts of problematic questions about the marketing of difference at the very same time that 'Asian' cultural products begin to dominate the charts, are programmed on the telly and become strategic calculations in prime ministerial popularity campaigns. ADF have long resisted the simplifications that would make them icons of New Britain at the same time as they recognise the efficacy of promotions and marketing compromise within the industry which enables them to 'get through the gatekeeper's door' (interview, *Soundbox*, November 1997).[5] Recall that their lyric of 1995 runs: 'We ain't exotic, erotic or eclectic, the only E we use is electric' ('Jericho').

There is more to be said about the ways visibility on the cultural stage and the aestheticisation of previously excluded 'cultural matter' remain modes of papering over economic and political differentiation and the exploitative coordinates of the disunited kingdom. But I also want to locate the work of the band ADF alongside, or in contrast to, the history of political activism in European pop. Thirty years ago today, the European left was flirting with a kind of foreshortened, urbanised and cosmopolitainised Maoism. The story goes that students throughout the West were inspired to activism in the aftermath of France in May 1968, the Yippies levitating the Pentagon in America the same year, and Mick Jagger pouting the words to 'Street Fightin' Man' a year later: a song which complained that there was the sound of 'marchin' chargin' feet' everywhere and the summer was a time for street fighting.[6] The sound-track of the late 1960s was not only the saccharine rerun of Beatles melodies we are offered today in Britpop: wrong on any number of things, the cultural performance of acts like Joplin or Hendrix at least offered a much more confrontational and threatening stance to bourgeois complacency than the lads of Oasis, Pulp and Blur can ever achieve (not to mention the Spice Girls, saris and all, whose brand of feminism is funny only as a parody of parody). Even the forgotten difficult music of that time can be recuperated, but, of course, the sharper revolutionary examples of Third World class struggles in the 1960s were filtered into less dangerous forms by the time they reached from Vietnam or China to the metropolitan centres of London, Paris, Chicago and Woodstock, even as they wrought some effect. Country Joe McDonald sang out against the war, but he did so in multicoloured pantaloons. If the counterculture movement was the exoticisation of the West by means of incense-burning easternisation, the threat to global capitalist power came in those days from the anti-imperialist struggle also most effectively articulated by Maoists in the East (and Black Panthers wielding little red books in East Compton).[7] The East of the revolutionary movement was a rather different East than that admired by joss-stick poet Ginsberg and bed-protestor Lennon – one based on a long tradition of struggle and organisation, of dedicated fighters using whatever means necessary in the cause of throwing off the yoke of imperial power. That these movements did not succeed in precipitating revolutions in the West (even if it could be demonstrated that the impeachment of presidents, the decentring of hegemonies, and the undermining of segregations can be traced to their mediatised influence), it is still possible to imagine that the challenge to capitalist supremacy then continues to have its effects today, albeit in reactive forms. In this context an evaluation of the cultural politics of ADF is not simply an exercise in distanced cultural studies appreciation.

ADF

It is of course necessary to be cautious of the dangers involved in discussing culture industry product as some sort of indicator with special tactical and strategic importance for revolutionary and world-trans-forming activity. At the same time, it is important to take seriously what a group like Asian Dub Foundation are trying to do, and not to fall immediately into purity police sanctioned gut-response rejections. ADF 'like their politics' (Huq, *Footloose Magazine*, March 1998) and 'theirs is a no compromise in your face agitation. They offer the revolution on twelve inch plastic, on CD, and on cassettes' (anonymous reviewer, *Soundbox*, November 1997). When the *New Musical Express* managed to reassure us out of initial fears that 'Asian Dub Foundation were another "global techno" disaster waiting to happen', the exoticising curio focus of such a paper was plain to see, even as the success of the band challenged the 'received wisdom' that 'no-one would be interested in an Asian dub group preaching political change' (*NME*, 9 May 1998). The give-away word here which condemns the *NME* is 'preaching', a label often allocated to hard to categorise – that is to say, politically difficult – rap. *Q Magazine* writer Gillespie found the album *Rafi's Revenge* even more threatening, saying that ADF liked 'to gleefully bludgeon home messages (*Assassin, Hypocrite, Free Satpal Ram*) with full-pelt breakbeats, shouty vocals, guitar/sample viscerality and some warped injection of Indian folksounds that would send their dads into apoplexy' (*Q Magazine*, May 1998). Already the well rehearsed stereotypes of Asians in Britain stuck in the second-generation caught-between-two-cultures-routine explanation clashes loudly with the content of ADF's work.[8]

ADF in many ways fit the profile of any successful contemporary international music act. The band is fronted by Deedar (vocals) who raps in ways indebted to a politics learnt from an older generation. Much of the group's shared lyric writing draws on diverse experience and several years in other bands (ADF came out of the sound system milieu that included Jah-bhangra, in which Master D had an early role and from which State of Bengal and Fun^da^mental also emerged). Other members confirm that this history is an important aspect of coherence for the band's project: Chandrasonic (guitars), Dr Das (bass), Pandit G (decks) and Sun-J (technology and keyboards) complete the line-up. Perhaps a little more unusual, but not without precedent in Britain, has been ADF's enthusiastic support for various 'causes'. Their first gig was at a benefit for Quaddas Ali at the Hackney Empire in 1994 (*Fighting Talk*, April 1998).[9] After an EP, *Conscious*, on the Aki Nawaz-initiated Nation label, the first album in 1995, *Facts and Fictions,* achieved moderate success (see Sharma 1996). The next year they recorded the soundtrack for an anti-racist CD-Rom, *Homebeats*, produced by the Institute of Race Relations (who publish the journal *Race and Class*).[10] In 1997 they released the album *RAFI* in France. The extent of ADF's international appeal reaches into special publications in Germany (*Trax* no. 6 1998), several websites in France and even one in Japan,[11] invitations to work in New Zealand, Canada, great appeal in the USA, radio shows in Australia (2SER), and a fan base that grows exponentially and attracts good publicity not only for the band but also for the music project in which they honed their skills, East London's Community Music (the title of their most recent album).[12] The Community Music location is where things are considerably different. Unlike most music industry outfits, ADF are connected to a range of social projects and campaign groups in a way that goes beyond the odd vox pop appearance in support of the occasional good cause (other examples would be Fun^da^mental or The Levellers). The band's musical style was formed in the milieu of the music workshop located in Farringdon, and, as is often emphasised, in the East End of London: ADF's involvement with Community Music is more than as a contribution to an 'outreach' programme, but is explicitly linked to education, consolidation and politicisation work among youth of the East End. This work began with a programme in music making and media, MIDI techniques in a live situation, performance skills and mixing.

Community projects infuse many other aspects of ADF's work in a context that would understand anti-racism in Britain in continuity with the struggle against imperialism worldwide. It is for this reason that their music celebrates such figures as Udham Singh for his revenge against the assassin of Amritsar,[13] and the Naxalite revolutionaries (with whom the rest of this chapter will be concerned), as they remind us that their 'memories are long' ('Naxalite'). That tracks like 'Naxalite' are played across Europe to audiences not necessarily addressed by all the content of these commemorations is possibly irrelevant in the context where ADF's music industry success channels funding in turn back into the community music project ('Your pockets will be empty but you won't know why ... its a long term plan, teaching is the framework', 'Hypocrite' 1997).

Political organisation and revolutionary commitment is often worn as a badge (or t-shirt, or poster) and does not translate into anything more than style; radical chic is only one part of a spectrum of rehearsed responses that passively accept the co-option of all 'alternatives' within the overwhelming ubiquity of the one big system. How is it that reactions have become so predictable, and that protestations of 'politics' or activism must struggle from the first to get by already-knowing and closed-minded preconceptions? At the same time, how is it that the energy and enthusiasm of ADF can suddenly appear so sharp amongst/against the stagnant sounds of Britpop and the rehearsed but predictable rhythms of techno, house or even bhangra?[14] That ADF have been around for five years, but only after much work do they look like threatening the top of the charts, is not just a consequence of the new visibility of things Asian.[15] Rather than simply marvel at ADF's success, we might look to the way the vicissitudes of the market can be managed by alert cultural producers as a vehicle for promoting the most uncompromising of politics.[16]

What sort of politics? I would suggest that the distance between the 1960s in Bengal and the 1960s in Paris is about the same as the distance today between a Princess Diana memorial and the Satpal Ram campaign (explained below). By explicating the context and content of the 'Naxalite' single, we can see that the track 'Naxalite' was a difficult object for the media, despite its preppy beats. Music press reviews managed only to acknowledge the album liner explanation that the track is 'inspired by an uprising of landless peasants that took place in West Bengal at the end of the sixties and triggered other insurrections'. There are of course some wider contextual matters to be sorted out and some detail to be added. Discussion of the media travels of 'Naxalite' would need to do more than joke that 'A Peal of Spring Thunder has Broken over Brick Lane' – a simple transposition of the Chinese Communist Party's supportive greeting to the Naxalbari peasants in 1967. The 'Peal of Spring Thunder' line should not mystify the specificities of the Community Music Centre context of ADF's work and their involvement in anti-racist politics in the East End. This is a far cry from peasant insurgency in Bengal.[17] What needs to be done first then, is to examine the ways this band traverse several geographical contexts and the ways in which their product – the track 'Naxalite' – means different, and even contradictory things in different places.

These might be the dimensions of an understanding of ADF's politics of space: first, we would need to address the racial conflict endemic to the 'streets' of East London, and by extension other overlooked estates, and state racisms, in Britain and beyond. Here it is important to acknowledge the ways another track on the album, 'Free Satpal Ram', has raised the profile of the campaign to seek justice for a man imprisoned for defending himself from racist attack by white thugs at an South Asian restaurant.[18] The success of ADF in bringing the Satpal Ram Campaign to wider attention is evidenced in feature articles such as the one which graced the magazine *Dazed and Confused* (May 1998).[19] As I have already noted (in Chapter 3), ADF have also contributed to campaigns around the 1994 Criminal Justice Act, against Operation Eagle Eye, and numerous other UK campaigns. But it is also important not to confine ADF to an insular British context as the forms of political mobilisation they advocate are linked to the subcontinent at the same time that they bear upon community self-organisation and education in the UK.

The connections between here and there are not 'cultural' in the way that conventional anthropology 'brought home' might like to find replications of caste, tribe and village among the children of diasporic South Asia (as argued in Chapter 5), nor is it a matter of tracing only the favoured themes of historians who track the linkages of the Congress anti-colonial struggle to those famous names who studied law in England – Nehru, Gandhi, etc. Although important, it is not only the European heritage of the Comintern or even the ways more recent and contemporary movements, like the Tamil Tigers on the left, or BJP *hindutva* on the right, cross the waters with NRI remittances, cadres, publicity and sanctuary. Rather, ADF tends to a local politics organised in a more internationalist vein, and this has to be explained in several registers: in part the character of ADF's local politics is a response to the opportunism of the left in Europe – both the Comintern and the Trotskyite movement in Britain are examples. In part the politics of ADF is a heritage born of solidarity with oppressed peoples everywhere, but evidenced in the history of specific South Asian struggles. In this dual register, simultaneously local and global, I think we can understand both the anti-racist single-issue campaign of 'Free Satpal Ram', and the mass movement peasant solidarity politics of a track like 'Naxalite'.[20]

'Naxalite'. The track was released in an almost anonymous packaging as a single, and even on the album without contextual detail beyond the one-sentence liner note and the lyrics. This anonymity was not unimportant. Naxalite, as will of course be recognised by a majority of South Asians, but not everyone in the 'mixed audiences' of ADF in London or in other European clubs, is a name with great resonance for the communist revolutionary movement in India. Transnational perspectives on the movement of cultural objects and meanings suggest that this requires an attentive analysis, not simply a celebration of the to and fro of such objects. An extended attempt at elaboration is deserved. That I do this with a critique of the uses of such cultural/historical references, and within the horizon of revisiting problems much discussed in the anti-colonial and anti-imperialist movement up until today, I hope would not be considered contrary to the intentions of ADF in raising black and white consciousness through music and politics. The lyrics of the number one track on the album are:

This one is called 'Naxalite':
Brothers and sisters of the soil unite
We are one indivisible and strong
They may try to break us but they dare not underestimate us
They know our memories are long

A mass of sleeping villages
That's how they're pitching it
At least that's what they try to pretend
But check out our history
So rich and revolutionary
A prophecy that we will rise again

Chorus
Again and again until the land is ours
Again and again until we have taken the power
Again and again until the land is ours
Again and again until we have taken the power

Deep in the forest
High up in the mountains
To the future we will take an oath
Like springing tigers we encircle the cities
Our home is the undergrowth

Because I am just a Naxalite warrior
Fighting for survival and equality
Police man beating me up, my brother and my father
My mother crying can't believe this reality
And we will rise again...

[*Chorus*]

Jump into the future dub zone
Roots rockers
And we have taken the power
And the land is ours ...

[Repeat as per chorus and repeat stanza five]

Iron like a lion from Zion
This one going out to all the youth, man and woman
Original Master D upon the microphone stand
Cater for no sceptical man – me no give a damn
'cos me a Naxalite warrior.
('Naxalite', from the album *Rafi's Revenge*, Asian Dub Foundation
1998. Lyrics, Das, Pandit, Zaman, Tailor, Savale, copyright 1997 by
kind permission of Universal/MCA Music Ltd)

Towards Naxalbari

This story now travels by way of Indonesia, Germany, California, Mexico,
Uzbekistan, the Communist University in Moscow, rural Bengal, Andhara
Pradesh, Calcutta in 1971, Moscow again, and back to the UK, via Booker
prize-winners from Kerala and more Spring Thunder from Beijing.

Contradictions in the audience and reception of 'Naxalite' can
productively be understood in older registers. What I have in mind here
goes back through the internationally inflected history of communist
struggle in India. The debate between M.N. Roy and V.I. Lenin over the
role of the national bourgeoisie at the second Communist International
Congress would, on the evidence of the history of left politics in India,
not be resolved. The implications of this debate for strategy, tactics and
understanding of revolutionary politics still extends its influence.

The Communist Party of India (CPI) was formed in Tashkent,
Uzbekistan, by the Bengali communist M.N. Roy in 1921 (Roy 1988: 24).

Roy, politicised while a student at Aurobindo's Bengal National College, joined the Anushilan Samiti revolutionary group and in 1910 was tried for conspiracy (but discharged). Before 1921 he had travelled much, first to Dutch-occupied Indonesia, where he made contact with German arms suppliers on behalf of the Bengali Revolutionary Party, Jugantar (1914). Subsequently he was followed to the USA by the Calcuttan police in 1916 (where he met Evelyn Trent, whom he married in 1917 [Jayawardena 1995: 17]). Charged with conspiracy in San Francisco, the Roys moved on to Mexico to help found the Mexican Communist Party and, as the 'Hindu secretary' of the Mexican Party, Roy was invited by the emissary of the Comintern, Michael Borodin, to attend the second world congress of the Communist International (Roy 1988: ii). In Moscow in 1921, after a brief effort at setting up a training school for Asian revolutionaries in Tashkent, Roy founded 'The University of the Toiling Masses of the Eastern Autonomous Republics' with over 700 students studying economics, history and politics, and attended meetings of Asian revolutionaries in Moscow and in Berlin (Ho Chi Minh was a student of Roy and supported his position at the fifth congress of the Comintern on the importance of the exploited classes as a revolutionary force for decolonisation 'not only against imperialism, but also against its native allies, the capitalist and land-owning classes' [Roy 1988: 92]). Years in Moscow and inside the Comintern apparatus took their toll, and Roy was expelled in 1929 for writing critical articles. He returned to India in 1930 where he was promptly imprisoned by the British for five years from 1931. After release in 1936, Roy and his followers, some of whom joined the Congress Socialists and worked alongside Subhas Chandra Bose, with Roy urging him to provide an alternative leadership to Gandhi, remained within the Congress until 1940 (Roy 1988: 78). After defending Stalin's pact with Hitler, but at the same time warning of a future conflict between Russia and Germany (Roy 1988: 80), Roy argued for an anti-fascist position well before the CPI declared itself in relation to Britain and in defence of Russia (having previously sided with the Gandhian refusal to support the war effort against Germany). He was overlooked in the negotiations between the Congress and Britain regarding independence, and his political career was largely at an end (Roy 1988: 86).

The pre-history of communist struggle in India can be (and is, see Namboodiripad 1994) told in several ways, emphasising one prominent movement or figure here, or another there, for the obvious tactical, strategic or sectarian reasons. The Sanyassi Rebellion, the 'Mutiny' and the Rani of Jhansi, the early years of Congress, Subhas Chandra Bose, the Tebhaga and Telengana struggles, and so on. Differential emphasis is true of all histories, and my retelling here is partial and determined in the main by a focus on what led up to the Naxalite uprising and its significance in relation to what seems to me to be one of the important consequences of the so-called 'postcolonial condition'. The determining narrative constraints I choose here have to do with the development of elite or comprador classes vis-a-vis the interests of other sections of the population, and what this means for the character – or 'cultural politics' perhaps – of political struggle in general. Is it OK to consider these specific matters guided in such an abstract and distanced way? The materials of the revolutionary struggles are of course only the traces of lived experience, filtered through memories and documents, stories and histories, always contested. My guess is that the partisan character of my guiding questions means this particular investigation has more to do with cultural politics in the West than with the particularities of the Indian struggle. Yet in other ways I want to claim such struggles for an inter(trans?)nationalist movement, while noting the inevitable distortions of reified questioning.

There is much that set the stage for the fortunes of communist politics after independence in 1947. An adequate evaluation would consider how activists from various movements against imperialism found themselves in prison, and there learnt and forged a strong communist tradition through mutual influence, study and the educational experience of persecution. The history of organisations like the Revolutionary Socialist Party, the communists who worked with in the Congress (Chatterjee 1997a: 184), and the Congress Socialists, those forced to work 'underground' in the early years of the Second World War, and with 1942's Quit India movement, the publication of the weekly *People's War* by the CPI in Bombay, these form some of the significant references for this story. In 1942 the Bengal famine saw communists carry out relief work among the peasantry and in Andhara Pradesh during the war years communists had been active in opposition to forced labour, or the *vetti* system (Gupta 1997: 305). At this time the Central Committee of the Communist Party suspended class struggle and, in spite of the Gandhian agitation of the time, came out in support of the British, primarily to show solidarity with the Soviet fight against fascism. In the period when this 'suspension' was in force however, the Telengana communists engaged a successful battle in Andhara Pradesh which liberated extensive zones from Jotedar rule and continued until the late 1940s. The proper names of both Tebhaga and Telengana signify much of crucial importance in the fortunes of the movement, and rethinking of tactical decisions and errors related to these struggles remains a staple of debate today.

The Tebhaga (three parts) movement was initiated under the leadership of Communist Party dominated Kisan Sabhas and demanded a reduction in the share of crops that went to landowners from one-half to one-third. The peasants forcibly took away two-thirds of the harvested crops and were attacked by the police and mercenaries hired by the landlords. The movement spread throughout much of North Bengal but petered out because, according to CPI analysts, the party did not win over the middle peasants 'who often felt threatened by the demands of the share-croppers and crossed over to the enemy camp of the landlords' (Banerjee 1984: 18). Charu Mazumdar, who would later become the 'single most influential leader' of the Maoist party (Chatterjee 1997a: 89), suggested that the problem had been that the peasants had looked to the Centre (Party administration) for arms and 'we hesitated ... to carry forward the revolution by collecting arms locally and seize power area-wise' (Mazumdar quoted in Banerjee 1984: 18). These dual issues of localised organisational initiative and the vexed question of alliance with the middle peasantry were to figure again and again in Bengali politics.

Telengana, in the then Hyderabad State, was a more substantial event and its origins in 1946 in an agitation against forced labour and evictions 'developed into an agrarian liberation struggle to get rid of feudal landlordism and the Nizam's dynastic rule' (Banerjee 1984: 19). By 1947 the revolutionaries could mobilise a guerrilla army of 5,000 and the struggle continued until 1951 with a militia comprising 10,000 village squad members. Around 3,000 villages, comprising a population of roughly 3 million in an area of 16,000 square miles succeeded in setting up 'village soviets' or 'gram-raj' (Banerjee 1984: 19). After the Nizam violated some parts of a deal with the Nehru administration, the Congress government deployed the Indian army to the state. In five days the army occupied the area, although the communists held out in their strongholds while the central leadership of the CPI debated whether to fight or withdraw on the grounds, harking back to Roy's debate with Lenin, that the Nationalist government should be supported. In 1949– 50, a delegation of CPI leaders had travelled to Moscow for discussions and 'was sharply divided on general questions of revolutionary strategy and tactics of the Indian revolution and on the specific question of the future of the Telengana movement'. After the return from Moscow, Namboodiripad reports, 'it was agreed that the "Chinese path" was an impracticable proposition' for Telengana in the face of both the might of the Indian army and the people's view of the Nehru Congress as the leaders of the nation (Namboodiripad 1994: 105–6). The CPI Central Committee asked its Telengana cadres to surrender their weapons in 1951 (Banerjee 1984: 20). Some sections of the CPI worked on ways to defend the gains of the movement, but as Banerjee shows, it was the leadership of the party and the rich and middle peasants who 'in the absence of landlords in the villages' had led the receptions to welcome the Indian army (Banerjee 1984: 22 quoting Reddy), and it was their willingness to capitulate which prevailed.[21]

The 1964 split in the CPI led to a further split which had grave consequences in Bengal. In ways perhaps not unrelated to the ongoing fall-out over Telengana, the factional politics of the Communist movement in the 1960s were a see-saw affair. Mallick, citing the dissertation of Sudipta Kaviraj, reports how the centrist section of the then CPI – Jyoti Basu and Namboodiripad (EMS) – had followed the Maoist and radical left into the formation of the CPI(M):

> In the first stage [after the split towards the left from the CPI], EMS and Basu were clearly in the minority and in obvious disagreement with the party line. In the second phase, the rise of the more militant Naxalite ultra left made for reconciliation of the two sections of the leadership. In the third phase, after the Naxalite left had gone out of the party, and after the CPC [Communist Party of China] started open ideological attacks on the CPI(M), the exact reverse of the first process happened. Originally, the EMS-Basu section had conceded to the other section of the CPI(M). Historical circumstances made the main leadership gradually shift to the EMS position ten years later. (Kaviraj in Mallick 1993: 13)

It was critical for the future of the CPI(M) that, in the United Front period of government in the late 1960s, it did not support the Naxalite revolutionaries and came down on the side of reforms rather than revolution, eventually watching as the police, then under President's Rule, and the army, slaughtered the Maoists. That the CPI(M) was drawn into fratricidal and factional attrition is among the most tragic of consequences of participation in the parliamentary pathways.

Charu Mazumdar was born in 1918, studied at Edwards College at Pabna (now Bangladesh), and joined the CPI in 1938. He had been involved in the Tebhaga revolutionary movement and was arrested in its post-1947 phase (Banerjee 1984: 320). Later he worked as an organiser amongst tea plantation workers in Darjeeling's Siliguri area where he was born. For several years before 1967 he and other then CPI(M) comrades had been building connections amongst the Santal peasantry. It was with these people, in Naxalbari, in the Darjeeling foothills, that the uprising began which was to give its name to a range of militant struggles over the next ten years. That the Naxalbari uprising, which first consisted of seizure of lands from rich landlords, destruction of debt records for bonded labour and hounding of money-lenders from the area, was soon put down by the police, is a matter of record (Ram 1972; Sen Gupta 1972). Debate over the subsequent consequences and importance of the uprising raged. The development of a Maoist political movement, the formation of a new communist party – Communist Party of India (Marxist-Leninist), of which Mazumdar became the General Secretary – and the extension of agrarian struggles to other parts of India, especially Andhara Pradesh and the Panjab, were a greater legacy (see Chatterjee 1997a: 92).

The Naxalbari peasantry and tribal peoples had good cause to fight. Naxalite demands addressed frustration on the part of the peasantry with the years of 'high sounding words, grandiose plans, reforms galore' (Rai and Prasad 1973: 458) by the Nehru administration. While green revolution farming methods had opened opportunities for the middle and landowning classes, the tribal and peasant farmers had already been dispossessed of land and so also of the opportunity to invest in the fertilisers and seeds of the green revolution advance. Thus the disjunction between landowners and peasants led to a wider dissatisfaction. An early list of Naxalite demands was reported as:

> The first priority is ... forcible occupation of lands belonging to big landlords ... overthrow of the existing big bourgeoisie rule of the country ... and the immediate withdrawal of India from the Commonwealth ... so that India would range herself against American and British imperialism. (in Ghose 1971: 447–8)

The swift retaliation of the police against Naxalbari did not prevent leaders like Charu Mazumdar continuing and extending the struggle through the politicisation of other regions, of peasant, tribal and student sectors. This entailed calling on students not to let the 'electoral politics of the revisionist parties' divert them like an 'obscene film' and for them to attend to the 'century old cry of the landless poor peasantry' and stand by their side, moving forward 'with arms in our hands like the guerrillas of Vietnam' (from a leaflet entitled 'Students and Youth: Unite with Workers and Landless Peasants, Unite, Unite with Them', reproduced in Damas 1991: 206–8). The formation of the All-India Coordinating Committee of Communist Revolutionaries (AICCCR) and subsequently the Communist Party of India (Marxist-Leninist) in May 1969 were convoluted steps in this process. The new revolutionary party (CPI-ML) was announced by Kanu Sanyal from the rostrum of that year's May Day rally in the large expanse of Calcutta's Maidan park (Banerjee 1984: 131).

The extension of Maoist struggle to other areas did not proceed without internal tensions amongst the Naxalite cadres. The Andhara Naxalites, for example, did not join the new party formation because of a dispute over Mazumdar's interpretation of Mao Zedong's strategic principles (or MTTT: Mao Tse-Tung Thought [see Mohanty 1979]) – they were also possibly remembering the Central directive to capitulate at Telengana. It was reported that 'the domineering attitude of the leading figures ... from West Bengal alienated more and more Naxalite groups besides the Andhara Committee' (Rai and Prasad 1973: 473). Sushital Ray Chaudhury, from the Andhara group said that 'Mazumdar's interpretation of the word annihilation was without doubt against Mao Tse-Tung thought' (in Ghosh 1971: 136). The slogan of 'annihilation of the class enemy', celebrated in the war word *khatam* (see Banerjee 1984: 112; Seth 1995[22]), was thought to have led to 'indiscriminate killing [which] would only isolate the party from the masses by forfeiting their sympathy' (Rai and Prasad 1973: 477). The criticism was raised that Mazumdar was not relying on the masses as Mao had prescribed, as, according to Chatterjee (himself a Birbhum Naxalite) much of the peasant support of the movement had turned into passive sympathy by the end of 1969 (Ghosh 1971: 147). Against this Mazumdar countered that 'only after guerrilla squads had cleared an area of "class enemies" by annihilating some of them and forcing others to flee the countryside, should revolutionary peasant committees be formed' (Rai and Prasad 1973: 475).[23] The procedure of operating in small and secret cells was in part a necessity forced by the brutal response of the state as 'mass actions were likely to expose the guerrilla fighters to the forces of law and order' (Rai and Prasad 1973: 475). The move of the struggle into the urban metropolis of Calcutta after the decision of the Party in April 1970 to extend operations into industrial areas was designed to address the apparent failure of *hartals* (strikes) and other conventional methods of struggle which had been 'largely blunted against organised capitalist attacks in the form of lock-out, lay-off, and closures' (Ghosh 1971: 444).

This change of programme born of 'a certain suspicion of the communist preoccupation with trade unions', of their 'economism' (Seth 1995: 493), meant increased mobilisation of student revolutionaries which necessarily complicated internal party relations. Mass action was also difficult in the city, but in the years of 1970 and 1971 more and more frequent incidents escalated the conflict with the police who, having faced a number of 'annihilations' themselves, adopted a 'shoot to kill' policy (Damas 1991: 97). In response, those students who had followed the call of the CPI(ML) to leave the city and live and work in the peasant areas, drew the anger of the police upon themselves, conspicuous as they were as students living in villages and in the apparent absence of the secretive guerrillas, they bore the brunt of the repressive reaction.

The Chinese Communist Party had welcomed the Naxalites with banner headlines in 1969 – it was the *Peking Review* of 14 July 1967 that declared 'A peal of thunder has crashed over the land of India' (reproduced in Damas 1991: 276–9). But their support for the CPI(ML) lasted only two and a half years, after which they intervened in the conflict between Mazumdar and the other leaders: 'It was not until after Peking had indicated its serious reservations about Charu Mazumdar's leadership and tactical line that dissent in the party began snowballing into revolt, leading to his virtual isolation before his arrest' (Ram 1972). Mazumdar's life came to an end on 28 July 1972 as a result of a heart attack in police custody a few days after his arrest in – he was refused adequate medical treatment and was not taken to hospital until 27 July, a mere 24 hours before his demise (Banerjee 1984: 321). In assessing the tactical line of the CPI(ML), it is of course difficult to sort out the factional squabbles and attribute cause and blame. Certainly the fragmentation of the Naxalites into several separate groups has persisted up to the present, but this factor is not a sufficient explanation of the decline of the movement. Rather, the role of the police in 'conducting raids, tortures and indiscriminate arrests ... in order to force people to make a choice in favour of the police against the Naxalites' (Ghosh 1971: 155) was important alongside the conflict with the CPI(M). With its secret cell invisibility and displaced student cadres caught up in a factional war of attrition with other communists who should have been comrades, it is understandable that the 'romance' of the Naxalites faded under this pressure, as Duyker explains:

> the movement was doomed because the CPI(M-L) was no match for the ruthless organised power of the state. When the cost to the [Santal] tribal community (in casualties, arrested menfolk,

confiscated food supplies and disrupted cultivation) appeared too great to continue the struggle, Santal-Naxalite resistance crumbled. (Duyker 1981: 258–9)

When the movement 'developed cracks' the students and peasants on the fringe of the movement 'opted for Congress because no other party could protect them from the police' (Ghosh 1971: 129).

The role of the state in suppressing the Naxalite movement was one that extended across India, but in Bengal it was also fratricidal communist rivalries that had a hand in the slaughter. The received 'official' version has been distilled by Bandyopadhyay from Sumanta Banerjee's excellent book *In the Wake of Naxalbari*:[24]

With increasing help from the Centre and imported paramilitary and military forces, police retaliation against the CPI(M-L) urban guerrillas began to gain momentum from the last quarter of 1970. No mercy was shown to any CPI(M-L) cadre or supporter if caught ... The CPI(M) felt threatened because of another reason. The mid-term poll was scheduled to be held in March 1971. While the CPI(M) was preparing for the elections, the CPI(M-L) urban actions were disrupting the status quo and threatening the electoral polls ... To ensure smooth voting for its supporters, the CPI(M) sought to clear its strongholds of 'Naxalite elements' ... A bloody cycle of interminable assaults and counter-assaults, murders and vendetta was initiated. The ranks of both the CPI(M) and CPI(M-L) dissipated their militancy in mutual fighting leading to the elimination of a large number of their activists, and leaving the field open to the police. (Banerjee, excerpted in Bandyopadhyay 1986: x–xi)[25]

Does this story of factional strife, leadership squabble, and parliamentarist opportunism tell it how it was or is? Of course it is a partial account, and contestation by competing traditions makes any evaluation from afar difficult.[26]

The Struggle Continues in Britain with a Booker Prize-Winning Naxalite?

If recalling the 'rich and revolutionary' history of South Asia by telling (a version of) the story behind ADF's 'Naxalite' displaces aestheticised notions of sleeping villages, this is, after all, only a first step. Replacing those notions with a valorisation of peasant insurgency may still work to occlude the hard realities of exploitation and material inequality, both in India and, in only one of the several possible domains of this romance, in Britain also. Romanticised revolution may be received differently even within this theatre: for the children of diaspora it may occlude aspects of their own participation in systems which sell cultural product and technology (satellites, Music-Television programming, etc.) in the uneven global market (the image of ADF as comprador cosmonauts in the pay of Rupert Murdoch perhaps?); and for institutionalised academics (and of course, tenured Marxists, among others, me), the occlusion may be of the ways even radical advocacy works within the 'teaching machine' (Spivak 1993) to inculcate accommodations of cultural diversity. There are of course numerous examples which indicate that ADF are not alone.

The appearance of 'Naxalite' in the dance clubs of Europe is not an isolated curiosity as can be seen from other high profile eruptions of South Asian cultural product struggling between the interstices of exoticism and serious art. Two examples come immediately to mind as a coda for this discussion. Awarded the Booker Prize in 1997, Arundhati Roy's novel *The God of Small Things* (Roy 1997) has enjoyed incredible popularity among the chattering classes. In the domain of high theory, Mahasweta Devi's stories have been championed, in a sustained exercise of translation, by Gayatri Spivak (Spivak 1987, 1993, Devi 1990, 1993, 1997a, 1997b).

How and why do Naxalite revolutionaries appeal as cultural matter? I wonder at the interests that elevate such productions as cultural texts in the face of extreme contradictions – simultaneously celebrating 'difference' in a way that does not differentiate between poverty and romance, adversity and exotica. The 'cultural' and political are aestheticised once again. Against this, one dimension in which comparative themes around the signifier Naxalite might be considered is the way an extreme violence is visited upon the bodies of protagonists. The ADF lyric refers to police attacks upon Naxalites – me, my brother and father. This resonates with the fact of racist terror and police attack in Britain as well. But it is important to note that the track does not comment on the 'excesses' (Seth 1995: 486) on the part of the Naxalites themselves: it is the case that in the romantic narrative of struggle Naxalites were to visit violent death upon landlords and other class enemies, through the 'annihilation of the class enemy' strategy.[27] Yet again, as I have described above, far and away the greater violence was done in retribution against Naxalites, and indeed any leftists or even unwanted miscreants, by the police and army. Naxalites were killed in so-called 'encounters', only to be found dead with their hands tied behind their backs (Bandyopadhyay 1986: xi), tortured in the most hideous ways, raped and abused with a brutality that is still legendary. The terrible aggression visited upon peasant and student activists by that body of armed men in the employ of central and state governments, including coalitions containing 'Communists', was incomparable (the 'containment' of the communists in such coalitions has of course been a fount of debate over the viability of the 'parliamentary path' – subsequent Left Front coalitions in Bengal were less constrained). Whatever the twists and turns of tactical debate, it seems that the graphic violence of police attacks becomes almost a traumatic catharsis in the literary renderings of Naxalite storytelling.

The dénouement of Arundhati Roy's novel involves the summary execution of comrade Velutha, now a martyr in the goddery of leftist literacy. In an article in *Liberation* Kalpana Wilson has followed the debate around the reception of *The God of Small Things* and suggested that the negative responses on the part of some members of the left have to do with 'ill-advised' slights against the house of Namboodiripad (Roy fictionalises a future in which the Kerala comrade's ancestral home has become a tourist attraction with former communists as servants to the hordes). Although I think it is necessary to be cautious before claiming this novel as some sort of revolutionary text, Wilson shows that Roy's affinity with the left 'in the form of the Naxalite movement as she perceives it' (Wilson 1998: 30) can be seen in her treatment of the period of emergence of CPI(ML) and her critique of the practices of the CPI(M) in Kerala – characterised as a 'heady mix of Eastern Marxism and orthodox Hinduism, spiked with a shot of democracy' (Roy 1997: 67). Old Comrade Pillai's printing press is described as once the site for 'midnight study meetings' and 'rousing lyrics of Marxist Party songs', and it carried a flag which had once 'fluttered on the roof [but had now] grown limp and old. The red had bled away' (Roy 1997: 13). Central to such assessments of Roy's politics must be her sympathetic rendering of a Naxalite activist as one of the central characters. There is a much discussed (Wilson 1998: 30) evocative scene near the beginning of the book where the twins and family elders are delayed, while sitting in their 'skyblue Plymouth' car, by a Marxist Labour Union rally on its way to present a 'Charter of People's Demands to Comrade EMS [Namboodiripad] himself': 'There was an edge to [the marchers'] anger that was Naxalite, and new' (Roy 1987: 69). This sky-blue-red scene then enables a detailed introduction of the character Velutha, a Dalit carpenter (taught by a German missionary, Christianity sneeks in again, see Dube 1999), who had known the twins since they were young and he had come to deliver coconuts to the back door of their 'Touchable' house. At the end of the book the intrigues between members of the bourgeois household and their adopted, exploited, patronised, befriended, loved, resented, compromised Velutha ends with 'a posse of Touchable policemen' 'cracking an egg to make an omelette' with 'sober, steady and brutal' economy, destroying his life, fracturing his skull in three places, smashing both cheekbones and nose, splitting open his mouth and breaking six teeth:

> four of his ribs were splintered, one had pierced his left lung ... lower intestine ruptured and haemorrhaged ... spine damaged in two places, the concussion had paralysed his right arm and resulted in a loss of control over his bladder and rectum. Both his knee caps were shattered. Still they brought out the handcuffs. (Roy 1997: 310)

Roy's Booker Prize success was possibly presented not for this excess, but for the lyrical appeal of sentences like 'The river shrinks and black crows gorge on bright mangoes in still, dustgreen trees' or 'Jackfruits burst' and 'Dissolute bluebottles hum vacuously in the fruity air' (Roy 1997: 1). Yet, there is a more difficult politics working in her book, and though this may only be 'content', it evokes the violences of imperialism and racism far beyond the ken of Bookerish worlds. That the enactment of gross violence and death in Roy's book has complicated resonances with many such aggressions worldwide is obvious, but the extent to which they parallel the sorts of racist death and violence at the hands of the police that the activism of ADF documents in its music and campaigns should not be missed. 'Free Satpal Ram' must be the call that can be read alongside the anti-colonial and class politics of these so-called postcolonial (Naxalite) literatures.

The scene in Mahesweta Devi's story 'Draupadi', discussed by Spivak, where the heroine of the story confronts the army officer Senanyak, is another example of the excess of violence irrupting into texts. Here the officer faces the tribal comrade raped and bloodied, but still able to spit a gob of defiant blood on his clean shirtfront; he feels fear for the first time, at the same moment he does his duty in crushing her. It may indeed be useful to recall this as a parable about the relation of the First World scholar in search of the Third World (Spivak does this well enough in her introduction, showing that the representative of the exploitative power is also a pluralist aesthete, and that this doublethink is shared by all do-gooder souls in the First World enclosure [Spivak 1997b: 2]). In addition I would also want to see this 'teaching text' as one of several emissaries of the politics of Naxalbari circulating through a range of global sites, reaching feminist study groups, anti-racists and anti-imperialists, First- and Fourth-Worlders as well as continuist communist activists ranged across the planet, and still reading the history of people's struggles as an illustrative guide for political activity today. Would it be too much to suggest that this brutality remains an all-too-grim inspiration for the necessity of a renewed class and race politics that 'will rise again'?

Of course this is something that I want to relate to the contemporary British context, where the violence is played out on the bodies of Bengali youth with excessive force by both police and other racists (and note the possible role here of the First World anthropologist 'at home' who documents, or not, such matters). It is not an aestheticisation of culture or a romanticisation of the revolutionary narrative of 'Naxalite' that suggests we should do more than nod sagely as cultural studies makes an object of analysis and publication of world music, world culture and exotica. The matters under discussion here require more than discussion.[28]

Devi herself takes a critical, even hectoring, tone when discussing the radical chic of Calcutta-based intellectuals and their attitudes to the tribal peoples of whom she writes:

> We do not know the tribals nor do we care to know them ... a large majority of the educated have a stereotyped image of the tribals, promoted largely by films and plays. Tribals on the screen or the stage inevitably wear feathered head-dresses if they are males and flowers if they are women, wear scanty clothing – near-nakedness is compulsory – just to emphasize their innocence. And lastly the typical dance and music. Not that these are not part of tribal life, but certainly not in the way shown ... the following is typical of exchanges I have often gone through:
> 'Are there Mundas in West Bengal?'
> 'Yes. Many.'
> 'In which language do you speak to them?'
> 'Bengali, of course.'
> 'Bengali? How surprising!' (Devi 1997b: 105)

Even in solidarities of the South romanticisation prevails (and indeed probably got a number of students killed in the 1967–71 period). 'Such notions are prevalent among West Bengal intellectuals', Devi continues:

as far as they are concerned, tribals can have their sympathy as long as they remain half-clad, starving and illiterate. Such intellectuals are admirers of Adivasi culture and they expect starving Adivasis to forget their misery in *mahua*, music and group dances. Their knowledge of tribals is derived from books and magazines. After a few decades exposure to the general education stream, many tribals ... are officials, educationalists, doctors and engineers. Their lifestyle has expectedly undergone changes. But they, according to the people I am referring to, are no longer true tribals. (Devi 1997b: 88)

No doubt in the end a degree of romanticisation must be levelled at the door of ADF. Having not visited Naxalbari (as I have not) the valorisation of peasant struggle must remain ignorant of the harsh specificities of rural revolutionary lives. What then to make of the several slippages in the lyric: 'and the land is ours', 'we will take the power'? At the same time, that contradictory tendency which prevails where ADF are seen to be no longer true Asians, somehow hybrid, corrupted by the very syncretism that some forms of 'anthropology at home' would celebrate as curious, is also a violence. When asked the question why would East End Londoners be interested in Bengali peasant insurgents, the answer is not *just* a revolutionary romanticism. No doubt, in the celebration of Naxalbari from afar there is too much of such romance and little appreciation of the bloody reality of *that* kind of struggle. However, the experience of violence in Britain in not alien to the politics of ADF. Their call for a revolutionary political unity – for example in the tracks 'Black White' (1998) or in 'Rebel Warrior' (1995) – is made in the face of ongoing racialised violence and inequality evident in everyday experience in their neighbourhood and across the UK, and the whole of Fortress Europe. This does not mean I am labelling ADF as crazed Maoist ultras; clearly a coherent Naxalite programme would be difficult to read in their mix of community-based politics, anti-racism and music performance. It's also somewhat absurd to think of the connection between ADF and their audience as in any way commensurate with the relation of Naxalite guerrilla cells to the masses, however glamorous the idea of media guerrillas and 'Digital Underclass' (the name of an ADF B-side track, reverse of the 1998 single 'Buzzin') may sometimes be. Brick Lane is not the new Yenan, despite the lyric 'we encircle the cities' ('Naxalite').

Castigating the non-resistive role of cultural workers, Spivak extends Devi's critique of those who, through support of projects like the

'Festival of India', promote 'an elaborate museumized international self-representation of Indian culture as arrested pre-capitalist tradition of folk-artisanal ethnic simplicity' (Spivak, introduction to Devi 1997b: ix). Yet the uses of academic criticism are equally contingent, as questioning as a skill, and the critique of exoticism, are not the be all and end all of a politics, even within the institutional spaces where theory counts for more than praxis. The parallels deserve noting so long as the limits are not reified into paralysis for other areas of activity. Consider also what uses urban-theory reading Euro-American-Australian students will make of the extension of Mahesweta Devi's fiction into the postcolonial reading salons.[29] Obviously many will agree that reading Rushdie or Marquez as magic realism does not necessarily lead to a politics of transformation (but it may), yet when stories of peasant insurrection appear in the magic realist space, is this an interruption without deep significance? Are these peasants 'countered' by incorporation?

Authenticity

It should at least be clear that the concern with 'authenticity' that leads to a critique of trinketising exotic versions of South Asian musics is not one which insists upon the purity of traditional forms or the relativistic egalitarianism of an anthropology blind to material inequality. The danger is always that the worries about appropriation and com-mercialisation are contradictory insofar as authenticity critique may sometimes slide into less savoury valorisations of cultural boundedness, nationalisms and conservatism. Instead, the critique of inauthentic and aestheticised versions of South Asian cultural production should be geared towards clearing a space for hearing the 'secret omnipresence' of resistance to which Theodor Adorno refers. The resistances in this case might be against the co-option by commodifying forces at the same time as those media are utilised to get the word out and get in touch with others; against the homogenising, simplifying, universalising pressures of the world music system and its requirement that 'cultural' product fit into neat nationally demarcated packets; or against the denial of actual oppositional struggles as part of lived history and the present – such that: ADF *are* Naxalite warriors, even at the same time as they are so very distant from the revolutionary struggle of the Bengali peasantry, and with the contradictory effects of having their music beamed by satellite into the Calcuttan sitting rooms of the very bourgeoisie that continues to oppress that peasantry (not that London and the IMF and so on are not also complicit in this).[30] What is noteworthy here is that ADF persevere with their use of music as an organising tool, despite the protocols of the music industry, culturalist commentators and the state force arrayed against them and like-minded activists. *For* a cultural politics that does not drown us all in a bland world music masala culture, but which respects and acts with unity in difference in pursuit of justice, social transformation and an end to tyranny.

A return to the Maoism of the 1960s is as susceptible to a critique based on the romanticisation of resistance as the 'Vindaloo' and *bindi* versions of Asian kool visibility in Britain are susceptible to authenticity critique. Questions of leadership strategy, the role of the bourgeoisie, of comprador co-option and factional fragmentation all complicate the mix. Nevertheless, the struggle to work through these contradictions is not one we should refuse. To do so is to retire from politics and accept the rewriting of history that would wipe away Naxalbari and replace it with only the Maharishi Mahesh Yogi, *hindutva* and the glories of the Raj. We can begin by asking why it is that the politics of a truly internationalist 1960s is not made into the content of the new nostalgia? What sort of revision is it that rests content with a corporate-sponsored commemoration of Woodstock or Live Aid but forgets completely the disruptions of 1968, or for that matter 1971 in Calcutta, or 1975 in Saigon? Is it because we have elevated culture to the field of some rhetorical equivalence and cannot even see today the material inequalities that persist, and which are perhaps even more urgent, than they were thirty years ago? *For* a renewed counter-culture, this time transnationally.

Notes

1. ADF at this writing have produced three albums and a slew of single and EP releases. *Facts and Fictions* was their first album, discussed in Sharma et al. (1996), and *RAFI* (*Real Areas For Investigation*) (French version 1997) or *Rafi's Revenge* (UK release 1998) was the second. A third album, *Communisty Music*, was released as this book goes to press, containing some familiar material and much that is new. The band's EPs are too numerous to mention, but see especially the *Militant Science* presented by 'Botchit and Scarper' (1997) and the *Rhythmic Intelligence* offering from 'Sub Rosa' (1997). The ADF website contains soundfiles from the albums, including a version of the track under discussion here <www.asiandubfoundation.com/>. Two versions appear on the EP entitled *Naxalite* (1997).
2. My critique of Kula Shaker was made in terms of a contemporary and ongoing orientalism, complicated by the co-existence of avowed good intentions and hazy far-right sympathies (see Chapter 4). With ADF the contradictions are still more complicated: far-left sympathies and good intentions deployed via the very same media technologies and music

industry structures used by Kula Shaker. I address these contradictions more fully in the conclusion.

3. Indicative of a wider resurgence under the current process of capitalist restructuring, Britain is made over anew as a site of cultural creativity, information-technology and media–driven regeneration of the stagnating economy. It is more likely that this process is only the end-game of a defunct capital project unable to reinvest at levels adequate to turn over new profit, thus it reaches for a quick speculative recoup via infotainment and cultural industry services. That this is presented as a move forward, and includes new gestures of inclusion and representation for Britain's 'ethnic' communities, is only evidence that 'a complex but flexible political structure is highly suitable for maintaining the internal balance in the ruing class coalition' (Chatterjee 1997b: 56 – taken slightly out of context).

4. The arrival of entrepreneurial property speculators on the heels of the East End artistic quarter development pushed warehouse rents up from £3 a square metre to £10 in two years (personal communication from Josie Berry). See also Banerjea (2000).

5. In a similar way it might be noted how Fun^da^mental accede to the world music project of Peter Gabriel in order to take opportunities to contact and work with other progressive musicians from around the world, such as Prophets of the City (South Africa), Consolidated (on the 1996 album *This is Fascism*, Blue Source, AFA) and of course Nusrut Fateh Ali Khan – who recorded often for Real World and whose *Ta Deem* was remixed by ADF for the album *Star Rise* (Real World 1997).

6. The lyric of course continues with discussion of what a poor boy can do with only the option of singing rock 'n roll in a 'sleepy London' which offers 'no place' for the heroic 'Street Fightin' Man'. It is a matter of record that sleepy London did not awake to the inspirational revolutionary call of the Stones. At the end of the track the (then) most stoned stone, Brian Jones, can be heard plucking at a sitar. Mick Jagger of course was no poor boy by this stage, nor merely the singer in a band, rather the head of a publishing and recording empire that is today sponsored by the likes of VW and the Coca-Cola Corporation.

7. Curious note of transnational exchange: Gail Omvedt reports on a group called the Dalit Panthers, who built upon the anti-caste politics of Ambedkar and who styled their struggle after the Black Panther Party of the USA. This group, formed in Bombay, began using Naxalite imagery in their 1968 Manifesto to expose the ways 'the entire state machinery is dominated by feudal interests' and the 'same hands who for thousands of years under religious sanctions controlled all the wealth and power, today own most of the agricultural land, industry, economic resources and all other instruments of power' (Omvedt 1994: 337). They anticipated a revolutionary mass which would 'rouse the people' and advance the 'tide of revolution' (Omvedt 1994: 337). In her book, Omvedt points out the importance of non-wage labour and slavery 'in the periphery' as integral for capitalist accumulation on a world scale (Omvedt 1994: 82). A further peripheralisation applies in that analysis of the Dalit movement has suffered from being seen as: 'diversionary either from the economic class struggle because of its argument for the necessity of struggling against social oppression, or in terms of the needs of

national struggle because of its insistence on putting the needs of the most oppressed/exploited group first and because of its willingness to treat the Indian elite, not foreign powers, as the "main enemy"' (Omvedt 1994: 14).

8. The reduction of the cultural politics of racialized ethnic groups ... to first-generation/second-generation struggles displaces social differences into a privatized familial opposition. Such reductions contribute to the aestheticizing commodification of ... cultural differences, while denying ... immigrant histories of material exclusion and differentiation. (Lowe 1996: 63)

9. *Fighting Talk* is available from Anti-Fascist Action, UK. National Office, tel: 0976 406 870. Quaddas Ali: yet another black man in Britain brutally attacked by a gang of racist thugs – mentioned in the Hustlers HC lyric 'Vigilante' see *Dis-Orienting Rhythms* (Sharma et al. 1996).

10. *Homebeats* and *Race and Class* are available from the Institute of Race Relations, Owen Eyles, 92 High St, Berkhamsted, Herts, HP4 2BL, UK.

11. <www.vinet.or.jp/~y-ish/*9801htm/adf.html>.

12. Get in touch with Community Music via the web: <www.communitymusic.org/>.

13. Udham Singh is celebrated for taking out the, then repatriated, Brigadier General Dyer, who had officiated over the mass slaughter of Jallianwala Bagh (see Banerjea and Barn 1996; Kaur 1999; Kalra 2000a). ADF's lyric: 'A bullet to his head won't bring back the dead, but it will lift the spirit of my people' ('Assassin' 1998).

14. Of course this denunciation of predictable rhythms is also a personal preference on my part – designations of taste in music are a consequence of varied educations of the ear and heart, and in no way can my preferences be considered recommendations *in universum*. Buy the album and see. My tendency to dislike house, techno and 'even' bhangra, comes after having attended far too many club nights, raves and *melas* and, while those times were fun 'back in the days', my nostalgia does not extend to feeling I should hesitate to call bad bhangra bad when I hear it (I have in mind things like *Beam Up the Bhangra* by Captain Kirk).

15. Although this visibility is by now well-documented (Sharma et al. 1996; Kalra and Hutnyk 1998), the extent to which this inaugurates a 'politics' is to be debated, especially in the context where the 'cross-over' character of ADF comes in for questioning because they are somehow not authentic enough. Or because their audiences are mixed, as Keele University anthropologist Pnina Werbner implied at a British Association of South Asian Studies seminar (BASAS) with her question about the number of Asians in ADF's audience. The prevalence of cultural essentialisms that are not strategic in any way that could be called positive, but instead rehearse racist essentialisms and narratives of exclusion, are especially dubious in the hands of establishment academics. It is a small step from thinking all Asian bands should have all-Asian audiences to initiating calls to have them sent to all-Asian places to do all-Asian gigs – the subtle slippage version of Pakis Go Home. That Werbner would prefer her anthropological informants to remain 'ethnic', exotic and non-electric (nostalgia for the non-threatening otherness of acoustic and 'traditional' forms) is of course an operation more to do with preserving outmoded anthropological verities – that all South Asians are to

be understood in terms of religion, caste and 'culture', modified for the British context with categories of generational clash, cultural dislocation and, at best, syncretic creativity (again a small step from here to advocating repatriation). It is disturbing that this kind of homogenisation bordering on racism still prevails in academic work. See also Chapter 1, note 3.

16. The threat that ADF represent is that their political motivation as anti-racists and anti-imperialists working in solidarity across a range of disenfranchised, racialised, exploited groupings is in fact contiguous with that of earlier generations of Asians, including in Britain, in a mode that the capitalist British state would want to be forgotten. Still smarting at the winding back of empire and trying desperately to reconfigure relations of production to restore Britain's place in the imperial marketplace, the ruling elite would prefer nicely assimilated polite ethnics over a raucous militant junglist agit-prop band any day. It should be no surprise that cultural commentators would, however inadvertently, provide the ideological armoury for this active forgetting of both the political continuities and the exclusionary reality. Whatever the case, the politics ADF articulate strikes a chord.

17. Making an object of fascination out of Naxalbari is more complicated and fraught with contradictions than the ADF tribute track itself. On the one hand it does serve to disrupt archetypes of passive Asia, be it sleepy villages or aestheticised hybridity; on the other hand, if this work remains only a scholarly appreciation of revolution, for writer and readers, it replicates aestheticisation and trinketisation. Here I would only point to the importance of the addresses in the footnotes to this text, which direct the reader not only to further resources for study of the history of struggles, but also to extant organisations worthy of active support.

18. From leaflets from the Free Satpal Campaign, and articles in the magazines *Lalkar, Fight Racism, Fight Imperialism, Fighting Talk,* and the *Transl-Asia* website; <les.man.ac.uk/~transl-asia/index.htm>, it is possible to draw up a composite picture of the issue: presently Satpal Ram is in his eleventh year of imprisonment in the racist UK prison system. At a Birmingham restaurant in November 1986 Satpal was attacked by six whites, one of whom glassed him in the face. This attacker was injured as Satpal defended himself and this man later died after refusing medical treatment. In British law, self-defence is no offence, but Satpal was imprisoned for murder. An appeal was heard, but rejected, in November 1995, and the Free Satpal Campaign organised several lively demos at the High Court. Satpal was refused the right to speak in the court and was dragged out shouting, 'No Justice No Peace!'

Subsequent requests for appeal and review have been declined despite evidence that defence witnesses in the original trial were not understood – the Judge saying he would translate despite being unable to speak Bengali. Persecution of Satpal within the prison system is unrelenting – he cannot be considered for parole because he has not 'shown remorse' (for something that cannot be considered a crime). The campaign continues for Justice for Satpal Ram. The campaign address is: Free Satpal Campaign, c/o Handsworth Law Centre, 101 Villa Rd, Birmingham, B19 1NH England.

A section of the lyrics of 'Free Satpal Ram':
Self defence is no offence
The Scales of Justice are weighed down on one side

> Freemasons on the case you know you're gonna get a rough ride
> Hold tight, even if you know your rights
> It's just a piece of paper unless you're prepared to fight
> For ten years, one hell of long time
> To rot in a cell when you've committed no crime
> Another innocent man forced to carry the can
> Free Satpal Ram.

('Free Satpal Ram', from the album *Rafi's Revenge*, Asian Dub Foundation 1998. Lyrics, Das, Pandit, Zaman, Tailor, Savale, copyright 1997 by kind permission of Universal/MCA Music Ltd)

19. Including a full page photograph of Satpal after having been 'allegedly' beaten by prison officers – all too ironically appropriate as a comment on the magazine's name, *Dazed and Confused* ('allegedly'? – it's doubtful that he could do that damage to himself).

20. The local is where struggle is engaged, the resources used are those of a local history – that these resources are located on different sides of the planet does not make them any less local, just as it does not simply make them global – a too easy resolution.

21. Criticisms of the communist movement have often been that they have had, in Kathleen Gough's phrase, a policy to 'curb' militancy and to 'persuade [labourers, the poor] to rely on constitutional channels for redressing grievances' (Gough 1981: 252). The issue of the role of the national elite continually emerges as a site of debate in relation to political tactics. Omvedt notes that in the years after independence from Britain, in the context of the Telengana agitation, 'only a visit to Moscow and the intervention of Stalin himself ... could create a consensus in the party that the path of the Indian revolution would be "neither the Russian path nor the Chinese path"' (Omvedt 1994: 308). That, at the behest of the Cominform, the CPI withdrew the Telengana movement turns out to have been one of the key moves of the story. The practitioners of 'not the Chinese path' served to create the conditions in which the police were able to eliminate the Naxalite threat. The grounds for M.N. Roy's debate with V.I. Lenin stir once more.

22. Charu Mazumdar proposed a liquidation of 'the political, economic and social authority of the class enemy' (Mazumdar 1969: 13, quoted in Seth 1995: 498), and this started:

> only by liquidating the feudal classes in the countryside ... this campaign for the annihilation of the class enemy can be carried out only by inspiring the poor and landless peasants with the politics of establishing the political powser of the peasants in the countryside by destroying the dominant feudal classes. (Mazumdar December 1969 quoted in Banerjee 1984: 112)

23. It is worth noting that these are interpretations of interpretations. Even to the extent that Charu Mazumdar can be considered representative of one kind of Naxalite, this has no chance but to be (mis)read through the thickets of sect and faction, and outsider commentary, that have accrued in the 30 years since the founding of the CPI(M-L). This of course is the problem with all contested history – my interest here is only to note that my readings would also read in a particular and partial way, my interest being not merely to encourage informed attention to communist struggle.

24. This was first published in 1980 in Calcutta, but reissued in 1984 under the title *India's Simmering Revolution: The Naxalite Uprising* by Zed Books, London.
25. Sumanta Banerjee goes further than the excerpted passage quoted here. Referring to then Home Minister Jyoti Basu seeking assistance from the Eastern Frontier Rifles, a central force, to suppress the movement, he writes:

    The party [CPI(M)] believed in controlled violence in rural areas aimed at minor goals, like wage increase for agricultural labourers or restitution of land ... A certain amount of agitation, often bordering on violence, suited the CPI(M) or the other parliamentary leftist parties, as long as it was contained within limits and controlled by the leaders, and did not attack the roots of the prevailing system by trying to seize political power. Since they were members of a united front of heterogeneous classes, the CPI(M) wanted to make the peasants believe that they were carrying the flag of the revolution and were out to destroy the status quo, and the middle class believe that they were arresting the danger which threatened them, and the Centre that they were faithful to the Constitution. (Banerjee 1984: 140)

26. For example, it is tempting to make a judgement as to the contemporary fortunes of the Basu-led CPI(M) Communists in Bengal. Mallick suggests their effort has failed, they themselves of course suggest a degree of success. Here, although the examples of communist struggle that might be cited do not always, or indeed primarily, refer to parliamentarism, it is true that a degree of electoral success, at least in terms of years in power, has long been the preserve of this section of the Communist movement in Bengal. Though it was not always so. Since 1967 CPI(M) Communists have dominated the state government for all but a few years of President's rule (and Jyoti Basu has now been in charge for over 20 years). This context introduces specific conditions for any evaluation of struggles. Mallick writes:

    The Indian Communist movement is unique in operating within the institutions of a parliamentary democracy not unlike that of the industrialised West, while trying to develop a base in conditions of extreme poverty and exploitation. India combines many of the institutions of an advanced capitalist state with cultural and economic conditions often not far removed from feudalism. (Mallick 1993: 21)

    That these 'feudal' conditions were the main contradiction faced by activists in India is the most obvious context in which to evaluate parliamentarism. The poor, those in bonded labour, the landless peasantry, the disenfranchised labourers on tea estates, plantations, in rural agriculture and urban industry – formal and informal sectors – provides a massive constituency of a communist politics.
27. It is sometimes thought this included, at times, ritualised elements, most famously that of requiring all new cadres to participate in the execution of a landlord and immerse their arms up to the elbow in the blood of the enemy. Unfortunately my reference for this incendiary factum has evaporated into mythology.
28. The text of *Dis-Orienting Rhythms* (Sharma et al. 1996) is one such attempt to suggest more than discussion, as are the special issues of *Post-Colonial Studies* (1998) and *Theory, Culture & Society* (2000) devoted to similar themes. It should be unnecessary to say that not all activity relevant to this point can be, nor should be, documented in such forums. *For* a secret cell structure!

29. Devi's own assessment of the context of her writing deserves attention:
     All parties, those to the left and those to the right alike, have failed to
     keep their promises to the common people. There is little prospect of any
     significant change in these things, at least in my lifetime. Hence I have to
     go on writing to the best of my ability in defence of the dispossessed and
     the disinherited, so that I may never have reason to feel ashamed to face
     myself. For all writers are accountable to their own generation and have to
     answer for themselves. (Devi 1990: xx–xxi)

30. With an almost audible sigh of relief [the privileged classes in India] ...
     have decided to embrace and celebrate [the discovery] ... that it is in the
     very nature of Indian modernity that the latest consumer goods coexist
     with extreme poverty, and that the information superhighway celebrated
     in their magazines runs parallel to dirt tracks. (Seth 1995: 503)

   It is not necessary to report that this dual structure befits British modernity
   also.

8
Conclusion: The Culture Industry and the Globalisation of Struggles

> Not everywhere by any means, but in some of the most advanced parts of the globalization process what one finds are new regimes of accumulation, much more flexible regimes founded not simply on the logics of mass production and of mass consumption but on new flexible accumulation strategies, on segmented markets, on post-Fordist styles of organisation, of lifestyle and *identity-specific forms of marketing*, driven by the market, driven by just-in-time production, driven by the ability to address not the mass audience, or the mass consumer, but penetrating to the very specific smaller groups, to individuals in its appeal. (Hall 1991: 30, my italics)

Stuart Hall reminds us that globalisation has done a very good job in the manufacture of hybridity and the niche market as the loci for the latest round of transformation of the mode of production. Difference and fragmentation, multiplicity and multiculture are in. At the very same time everybody everywhere participates, in no doubt singular and specific ways (to be specified, anthropologists shall be deployed)[1] in the same process of doing those flips and twists to get into the blue jeans, etc. There must be more to it than this push and pull.

By now it should be readily recognised that factors of economic and forced migration (and blocked travel), demand for ideas, 'crazy for foreign', abundance of goods, militant rights, excessive freedoms, creative solidarity, communality, community, connection, all amount to a driving momentum that could be called the other side of globalisation. At the same time as we hear talk of new enclosures we also hear of new 'visibilities'. There is much to be said about the micro-differences and multiplying apparitions of a heterogeneity of expression that circulates the world (albeit via technologies of communication dominated by capital). Is it possible to read this in a way that does not first start with allocating the momentum to the exploiters? I think so. There is another story in the globalisation narrative to be told, and it is not simply one of alternatives or romanticised resistances for their own sake. This other telling would entail a host of interconnectivities and circulations that make up an counter-history of the present. A process of political globalisation for the last hundred years might reach from October 1917 and the sentiment of the Baku Congress, anti-imperialist struggles, independence movements, Bandung conference, internationalism of all stripes, through to social, cultural and political solidarities of our own time, to an other history which might be sampled, conjured, commemorated as the primary driving force of (all of) our lives, and which capital battles to crush or co-opt.

I would mark this story with names: M.N. Roy, as discussed in the previous chapter, but maybe also Ho Chi Minh, who already embodied this internationalising globalising tendency which transformed the local – at 21 he went visiting Lenin's Moscow, Clara Zetlin's Paris, Marcus Garvey's Harlem (Prashad 1999). The obvious contemporary correlate of these internationals would follow music and culture in its circuits. It's not just your Mahatmas and Pandits studying law in *Vileyti*[2] that can claim global identity, it's not just the material girl who has worldwide fame.[3]

Clearly, cultural workers who attempt to tell difficult histories from elsewhere are not pure and simple conduits of exotica into the culture industry. It would not do to be wholly critical of efforts to bring a little cultural depth into the mass manufacture entertainments machine. Neither, however, would simple celebration of cultural activity and public sphere visibility guarantee either 'healthy' and sustained political involvement, continuity of activism, education or long-term solidarity. Something more is needed to counter the attrition that bedevils all issue-based and campaign struggles in the face of the dangers of appropriation, tokenism, authenticity reification and marketing rip-off. It matters, though, that the beginnings of an internationalist politics can grow here where conventional tales of globalising force close down. Secret omnipresence plus transnational literacy instead.

Cultural work also might be used to show what I mean by the possibility of another history of globalisation and would work at exactly the point where institutionalised histories exclude. Some of the work of the new Asian dance scene serves as exemplary instances of creative initiative that links up a globalising resistance. In the sonic histories of struggle Fun^da^mental and ADF et al. cross divisions and borders,

Hindu, Muslim and Sikh; East/West; London, Bengal, Zion; black/white; Electric, eclectic ... Some provisos first however. That this music, and other less danceable/likeable forms are discussed in this book as a way to open up questions of identity and politics is something that requires several hedged bets and circumscribed limits. My project is not in any way a comprehensive music survey, but rather attends to the dialectic of co-option in commerce and commercialisation in politics. This text takes seriously the idea that any essentialism that assigns a musical culture to a specific group is, if ever justified, merely a strategic claim, so that the working out of difference and unity becomes fluid and negotiated. Exotica deployed through music, in various ways, is not confined to lyric texts (even as these have been overtly privileged in this analysis) and the overlaps of representation and visibility, cultural space and anti-racism, survival and organisation are not at all exhausted. What I am trying to do is ask myself questions, and write towards answers, using certain musics (appropriating them) as the convenient vehicle of an analysis heading somewhere else (from where we are now). This is why, even within the field of music, exotica exceeds neat categorisation, and this entire book is, if anything, a partial catalogue of this excess. As an example of the difficulty that categorisation will get us into, take yet another so-called 'Asian Kool' star and see how culture is reduced and packaged regardless of any specificity. Nitin Sawhney now tours the country playing such events as the Oxford Festival of Contemporary Jazz where his music is described as a mix of 'Contemporary and traditional sounds, acid-rap-jazz, tranquil ambient groove ... drum'n'bass', so that he can be characterised as an 'Asian modernist', although it seems the exotic does not boil down into the (post?)modern so neatly as 'tabla is juxtaposed with techno bass and a rich array of original voices, all bound together by a strong element of improvisation' (leaflet, May 1998). 'Juxtaposition' here is the key to sell tabla and techno to jazz fans – a curious hybrid indeed – and it is clear that Nitin is misrepresented if reduced in this way. He presents himself as 'beyond politics' and 'beyond nationality, beyond religion and beyond skin' (liner notes for *Beyond Skin*, 1999). Of course the hyperbole of this 'beyond' might be questioned as it appears on a successful media product even as the album contains consistent anti-nuclear declarations and a denunciation of Combat 18 and the BNP in relation to the nail bombing on Brick Lane. Juxtaposition also works here in the presentation of the music and the musician, but explicitly the 'beyond' of this politics is a more complex versioning which does not settle for the primacy of the secular.

Similar comparative questions might be raised in other registers. Just as exotica finds a market, or serves to facilitate market categories that sell diverse products, it is strange that content doesn't lend itself to other marketings in more obvious ways. Why, for example, was the attempt by Manchester's Band on the Wall club to present a Qawwali night not able to draw a sell-out crowd from the region's huge Qawwali-loving South Asian audience? Not because the Rizwan Group were unknown, but perhaps because conventional 'ethnic arts' social projects have not thought through the best ways to promote such events. Ignoring the design aesthetics of Qawwali promotion in the North of England, unable to distribute information to the locations frequented by Qawwali's fan base, and overcharging at the door, meant that a potentially good night was a select event for a very few alert fans. Neither did this more 'traditional' mode of South Asian music deliver the 'cool' crowd of white funsters that the recent trendiness of Asian sounds (Cornershop, ADF, Nitin) might have promised such a venue. Is it that the late June Monday night was a dud (when in other cities early weeknight events have been very successful, and not only because this might be the night waiters have time off from their curry shifts), or is it that the stock trinketising styles of promotion favoured by well-meaning world music liberalism are unpredictable and confused?

Exotica remains blind to its own hypocrisy all the more in the face of explicit politics that runs ahead of 'the music'. The continual recourse of music commentators to explain away Fun^da^mental as an 'Asian Public Enemy' (Frith being the most prominent; Gilroy has hinted at the same) casts Asian politics and culture in Britain in a demoted place of mimicry, imitation and derivative decay.[4] This is ironic given that European cultures – extending the list again: tea, coffee, sugar, chocolate, rock and roll, potatoes, *Neighbours*, jazz clubs, balti restaurants, critical writing, demographic process, skill at cricket, etc. – are all derivative of other places. What is obscured is the possibility that a repertoire of styles is made available by hip-hop in ways that do not displace the specificity of Asian political experience in Britain, nor the vast musical, stylistic and political differences that are evident to the attentive observer. Of course mimicry can also have a strategic element, no doubt it serves as some degree of useful notoriety for Fun^da^mental to be able to complain they are not understood by the likes of Frith. That much is clear. But there is no reason to reduce rather than recognise the solidarities that are possible across the quite different formations of US rap and the Fun^da^mental sound.

So with a multitudinous (dubious) critique of exoticism in mind, I want something of Paul Gilroy's project to be the terrain towards which my own work also points. He suggests that 'a comprehensive history of that special period in which phonographic technology first made black music into a planetary force remains to be written' (Gilroy 1999: 261). I would argue that one of the contexts in which this history can begin includes refashioning the parameters of planetary consciousness within a certain kind of political commitment, though I would be neither so pessimistic or nostalgic perhaps. Of course what I have in mind will not just be a history of the technology, but rather of its agents.[5] Music offers the ground for this, alongside technology, because it is central to the communicability necessary to the cultural industries.[6] For me this is a possibility, not something to regret as Gilroy mournfully argues:

> more recently, digital audio, stagnation, and what we could politely call recycling have intervened to make live music less pleasurable, and, in my view, less live, than it once was ... a lost ethical flavour in our face-to-face, pre-video transculture. (Gilroy 1999: 262)

For me, this pre-video transculture was always mediated by technology in some way as well,[7] so if I ask who this 'we' is that politely mourns, I can't help but think it's not 'my' crowd.[8] Whatever, the video format of the current conjuncture is crucial.

The shift from live performance to recorded, sampled and rearranged 'mixing' in popular music from the late 1970s advent of disco up to the dominance of dance music and the DJ today is not necessarily a loss. If Gilroy wants to commemorate the passing of a more social form of musical enjoyment, that is fine, but consider – how spontaneous were the lip syncs of live performance, the rehearsed and scripted routines of the great stagers? Further back along the musical timeline live performance was note-perfectly pre-arranged, with conductors in control and the audience rattling their jewellery in the balcony. The audience experience and sociality in dance music is not less, perhaps is even more, today than it was under the sway of the rock formation. Drum 'n bass or rave crowds are the group. Undifferentiated. Though of course, at the same time, this too is a resistance site easily co-opted by commercial considerations. In any case, the irrelevance of mourning for some lost authenticity of live music is concealed only by the elegant formulations of its expressive form. Nothing is lost here that wasn't already subsumed. Liberation lies elsewhere than the club in this scene. 'Even music that is different can survive economically and hence socially only under the wing of the Culture Industry it detests' (Adorno 1999: 13).

Thus, the new tele-technological means circulates a new resistance contradictorily through diasporic 'community'. This book tacks back and forth between searching for the ways cultural performance of a certain character can provide a critique of complacent academic work and official anti-racism in the metropolitan centre, and making critiques of the ways sometimes (more or less) similar cultural work from the same domain, progressive in one context, can have dubious and devastating effects via the telematically transmitted internationally distributed cultural industry in another. The term 'diasporic community' as *one* context deserves to be bracketed however, as it is made the location, for all the wrong reasons, of the 'exotica' identified as an enabling (and constraining) fiction in this work. Community may be reified and is subject to many of the same incorporations that play this to-and-fro game.[9] Community means the coming together of people, but, of course, the collation of world population also cannot simply be dissolved into something we can call diaspora and the rest, even as this perhaps, but not likely, provides a 'contemporary vision of cosmopolitanism based on a quasi-planetary dispersion of bounded identities' (Anderson 1998: 45). As Kalra and Kaur argue, diaspora is a problematic term for collecting together all South Asians in Britain, and indeed, in its implied reference to a notion of origin and or *return*, it carries an affinity with the text of Enoch Powell. In another context Gilroy has suggested the term is useful only in a quite restricted sense, referring specifically to forced dispersal (spoken communication at PACSF conference at Goldsmiths June 1999). The problem with this is obviously the sliding scale of decisions about compulsion, as it is not always clear why people want or have to move. Further, this notion could be taken away from Gilroy's restricted definition, as diaspora as forced dispersal retains a hint of bounded, although dispersed, identity unless it is accompanied by recognition of the specificities of, for example, the founding African dispersal – which was a violent abduction and often deadly or near death trauma of kidnap and transport visited upon the multiplicity and diversity of a continent. In my argument, as an emissary from a local version of globalising or planetary initiative, where the cross-hatched threads of international solidarity and struggle still weave expressive magic and power, 'Naxalite' is just one example that could be used to illustrate this, the video of 'Dog-Tribe' another. There are multiple choices, not all equal. From East London to Bengal, with no first privileged site of 'diasporic homeland', the work of ADF and other such cultural activists cannot be so easily located in some simple push and pull model of a globalising culture industry, though of course there are contradictions. In the space called 'transl-asia' (Kaur and Kalra 1996), no doubt there are dozens of other possible examples where the reifications and slippages of identity and essence, ownership and authenticity claims, cultural style and codification fall prey to a conservative co-option. And of course. The point merely has been to document some of these instances, but also to do so alongside a recognition that the conventional registers for understanding cultural production and resistance, under conditions of the global market, might not be the best suited for either understanding and interpretation or for actually doing something about it. Another way of telling the story can be useful here.

TV

Shiv Visvanathan notes that 'it was in Gandhi's public meetings that the loudspeaker first entered India' (Visvanathan 1997: 224). Despite the intentional mischief of this echoing reference to Hitler and radio, I think such historical points deserve attention. Film technology made a very early appearance in India, with Dadasaheb Phalke making his first feature, *Raja Harishchandra*, in 1913, and with others ensuring that the latest developments of Western cinema were almost simultaneously available in urban India. With an equally rapid take-up initially, television was found to be especially useful for news and 'development' work, while colour TV came to the subcontinent for the 1982 ASIAD Games. Television was seen as 'an arm of the nation-state ... an obvious means for projecting a glorified vision of national identity' (Rajagopal 1993: 93). In the 1980s the arrival of 'VCR' was celebrated almost to parody as the consumer item of the growing middle class (2 million units sold by the end of the decade), and with satellite television's extension to India in the early 1990s, the speed of new media take-up remained swift.[10] The big stories of television in India up to this period had been development and nationalist soap operas (educational narratives or 'cultural-historical' ones), sport (cricket of course) and religious serials (such as *Mahabharata* and *Ramayana*).[11] The 'introduction of satellite and cable television services in the early 1990s was very sudden, and small unregulated private cable systems to distribute satellite broadcast signals were rapidly constructed throughout many urban areas' (McDowell 1997: 2). Music television drew upon the previously unrivalled (even by VCRs) Bollywood film industry to provide content for a host of new channels. Along with music television came other info-entertainment services, and the beginnings of a new investment sector. Driven by import liberalisation in a context of trade restructuring, direct foreign investment and privatisation through an IMF-encouraged 'opening up' to international markets, the telecommunications, entertainment and information sectors continue to expand. Computer and software industries, as well as other telecommunications technologies (software and hardware), have subsequently become a significant sectoral industry. Import liberalisation may have been a factor in the success of satellite delivery, while the strength of the telecommunications labour sector is considered to have served to limit policy liberalisation, at least up until recent years. In response to satellite broadcasting from Murdoch's Star TV and the like, transformation of the state-run television system, Doordarshan, has also been rapid in the last decade, with the development of regional Doordarshan offerings and multiple urban choices, as well as Doordarshan availability on satellite, and including plans to challenge Zee TV in Europe and Africa.

It would not do to picture India as a totally wired community however. Access rates to telecommunications per capita are low by world standards. Wagle reports that by 1993 there were some 7 million telephones for a population of 860 million (1993: 29).[12] It would not be difficult to imagine the even smaller percentages of the population that would thus have any access to dedicated lines for Internet usage or other specialised telecommunications functions. The numbers make a mockery of 'globalisation' hype and the limited horizons of web-fanatics who think the Internet will transform the 'entire' world.[13] Nonetheless, the gross numbers are important, whatever the percentages. A substantial Indian middle-class segment has availed itself of new technologies at every turn and today, as much as anywhere, the media is enthusiastically engaged in production of satellite and Internet good news stories and propaganda.[14] Yet, since the introduction of satellite provision was largely unregulated, the 'widespread investment by small private firms in cable distribution systems' suggests that the preponderance of 'low quality, informal mini-networks' will not have sufficient capital to support higher quality development (McDowell 1997: 221). Already the process of takeover and collapse operates in the microcosms of diverse levels of provision.

Does the involvement of South Asian musicians, and others – technicians, producers, sound engineers, distributors A&R, etc. – in the culture industry amount to the accommodation of South Asian cultural production to a hybridising capitalism that sells culture and technology to India in the same way capital once sold cotton and mass production looms? This question obviously evokes the argument of Gayatri Spivak discussed in Chapter 6 and of course requires an evaluation of the ways in which diasporised persons are recruited to do media business for capital. In relation to such persons, and also clearly indebted to Spivak, Chen Kuan-Hsing promises a future work on the trade off between 'diasporic opportunism and native collaborationism' (Chen 1998: 5):

The former term refers to those who reside in the imperial centre space: not only selling their PC (multicultural identity), they mono-polise speaking positions to block voices coming from 'home'; and the latter points to those 'returnees' from the neo-colonial empire who have clearly projected a desire to 'return' to the centre: they become native informant (drawing on theories produced in the empire, partly enunciated by the diasporic opportunists), and become academic brokers in collaboration with the centre powers, diasporic or otherwise, left or right (Chen 1998: 48).

There are possibly more positions available than the two, however convoluted, that Chen offers here. Diasporised types, both returnees and centre-dwelling, may also be engaged in political work that cannot be so readily recuperated into the empire's multicultural project. Chen's notion of the broker owes perhaps too much to anthropological notions of the in-between subject, and his critique of opportunists elevates the notion of 'home' to determining status, even within quotation marks. The critique of opportunism and brokerage, surely, makes sense only when made from the standpoint of organising against these modes of diasporic collaboration. Without a political programme such criticisms are also easily contained within the reflexive scholarly apparatus. However, as I will discuss below, the extension of South Asian musics into South Asia itself does not necessarily conform to the expected pattern of globalising cultural imperialism theses. While television in the UK has been 'Asianised' slowly,[15] this occurred somewhat organically in the subcontinent itself.

Yet even if it is possible to valorise *some* of the new media and media activists ranged across diasporic space, often the story is a grim one. Let's insist on not romanticising. The hegemonic capacity of capital does globalise across the scenes of international exchange, cultural work, solidarity and heterogeneous visibility as well – parasitically. I see the cultural deployment of Madonna or Kula Shaker, or the various impresarios of world music, as similar to those who do the work of comprador NGOs, with well-meaning but naïve notions of solidarity. They also circulate (the globe, the conference circuit) with resources and liberal compromises on offer – similar also to that package deal supposed to deliver humanitarian rights through UN military intervention. Or semi-feudal cyber-imperialism and Internet access for the civil society. Sign up, sign up. The choice between Mahatma and Uncle Ho was never clearer; one comes with the apparatus of the law structured as a trick glossed as 'freedom', the other comes with struggle and possibility. The Naxalite story can be inserted here as a possible destabilisation, but a fragile one as well. Many have died in the telling.

Of course it has to be emphasised that bands like ADF and Fun^da^mental also enter into this contradictory complex with a 'community' and 'internationalist' politics which is forced to circulate through the same satellite-enhanced cultural industry. Thus ADF's tribute track to peasant insurgency in the Darjeeling foothills is beamed via satellite simultaneously to middle-class MTV-enhanced living rooms in both Calcutta and Croydon, Carlton and Cape Town. There are points at which their track leaves all possible plausible artistic control and could do service for the most antithetical of ends – in the same way that use of the soundtrack of 'Dog-Tribe' by MTV (mentioned in Chapter 3) excavates intention and reverses meaning: 'What is the thing that makes a Black man insane?' was the lyric, advertisements for fashion House style magazines the result.

Similar contradictory structures can be found in an Internet activism which sells Bill Gates's computer units with exemplary radical cachet. Lefty laptop activists are the other side of profiteering electronic expansionism.[16] The trick of well-meaning brokerage facilitates transitions towards capital through the no-nonsense anarchism of non-denominational charity volunteers in Calcutta (Hutnyk 1996a), or in the calls of the anti-debt campaigns – insofar as they are incapable of calling for abolition of the entire debt system and rest only with the wiping clean of a slate so as to renew the payment cycle again. This impacts also upon the content of this book: it is too easy to sit in London, or in front of a screen linked to London, and consider multicultural futures as emancipation. It is not much more than a romantic self-deluding tale of congratulation. What a disaster if eating curry masquerades as personal political declaration and if this replaces any other exploration of solidarity work, of even the small contributions of intellectual 'speaking out' about the atrocities of imperial plunder that might hint at the extent of the struggle against an integrated multiple-sited system – from smart bombs defending human rights to that extraction which brings the curry ingredients to table in the first place. That this is a kind of disciplinary racism shared by both anthropologists, developmentalists and activists is forgotten in the rush to think immediately that the person who could become an 'informant' is only or necessarily forever to be thought of that way. It might be worth remembering that really existing people should not automatically become primary resources for book production. This cannot be overstated.

Thus 'content' issues are important in several immediate ways and should be examined on a larger scale than that offered by audience reception or market research studies. The broadest framework for such research would be to examine the reach of certain marketed products, and the differential product lives of certain offerings in the context of market restructuring and a dynamic imposed by a logic that has little to do with music as such. The music industry, like any industry, operates according to a structure that can be analysed and described, even though with difficulty. Adorno as ever is useful here:

> sociological research that would prefer to avoid the problems of analysing production and to confine itself to questions of distribution or consumption remains imprisoned in the mechanisms of the market and hence gives its sanction to the primacy of the commodity character of music. (Adorno 1999: 6)

The point has been that more than music is at stake, whether the analysis be of cultural politics transmuted through music, or market logistics feeding thereon. It is not always necessarily clear that 'taken globally, the function of music in society is mainly to act as a diversion' (Adorno 1999: 4), but

> to attempt to combat [the cultural veil and chit chat that is its] neutralisation by simply invoking the living power of music to affect people, without realising the extent to which music depends on society as a whole, is to capitulate to ideology even more abjectly. (Adorno 1999: 5)

This ideological capitulation appears in audience studies as much as in critical transnational cultural work – it comes replete with incorporations and articulations with all manner of institutional trends:

> Empirical studies that take audience responses as their starting point, on the assumption that they constitute the ultimate, secure foundation for scientific data, lose validity because they fail to see these responses for what they have become, that is to say, as functions of production. (Adorno 1999: 6)

So, given a desire to think beyond the disciplinary stricture, but caught within it, why not ask just how the necessary economics of profit and loss does impact upon global flows of music industry product?

One narrative might explain this as follows:[17] the industrialisation of creativity – even seen in the organised and premeditated recorded spontaneity of Peter Gabriel's *Real World Box* sessions – is a production process uninterested in how music is used, heard, consumed, so long as it is consumed. It must circulate so as to recoup profit for the investors. This reflects the situation more generally, where the technological hyper-development required in the advanced centres of the market, which is pursued in research and development labs of large corporations so as to ensure competitive advantage, disrupts the possibility of any neat geo-spatial containment of capitalist production. Technological development makes certain products obsolete in the advanced markets well before it is possible to recoup development expenditure and profits through the regular process of circulation and exchange (competition, fashion and technological redundancies drive down prices, cheap CDs, bootlegging, jukeboxes are all peripheral effects of this process). Expansion to new markets that is the consequent outcome necessitates the maintenance of these new markets as a depressed Third World theatre for older and outmoded commercial product – be these television sets, computers or telecommunications systems, weaponry or nuclear reactors (perhaps even rock' n' roll bands, country and western music and Sharon Stone). The point is that these zones of delayed development provide opportunities for profit recoupment even after the conditions of technological development in the centre have moved beyond these products (the contracting of nuclear technology to South East Asian earthquake areas, the dubbing of *Jurassic Park* into Hindi, the anxiety of record and fashion companies to protect copyright in China or Thailand, are all examples of this opportunistic recoupment process). The specific positions allocated to differing persons and classes in this picture may be more complex in any particular example, since the boundaries of the actual cannot be so neat as the abstract model, but the divisions between service provider and served, advanced consumer and producer, developed and exploited, are fairly evident to the eye. Consequent upon the unevenness ranged across the world market are conditions of depressed labour and environment regulation, exploitative and opportunist hit-and-run marketing (with no product support), dumping, pollution, extortion and corruption. The entire world is not a neat department store.

'Even Beethoven's most authentic compositions ... have been debased into cultural commodities by the music industry' (Adorno 1999: 2).

Music has a use-value of course, but it enters the music industry as an exchange value, as a commodified form. Music is ideological not so much in what it may say – its lyrics – and not in its non-conceptual elements, musicality, technique – though the bass beat may be identified by left and right as 'repetitive beats' or 'devilish' jazz (see Kaur and Banerjea 2000) – but music is, as Adorno points out, ideological in the 'use made of music by politicians and other authorities who regard it as a cohesive social force, as something capable of creating the illusion of immediate community within a reified and alienated society' (Adorno 1999: 3). Grumpy old Adorno links 'youth music' and its 'cult of social bonding', and the 'integration of the individual into busy communal activities', with the totalitarian tendency that must be watched vigilantly today as musics 'of the most varied kinds are made increasingly subservient to unexplained trends and needs – mainly those of domination' (Adorno 1999: 3). The examples of Clinton or Blair photographed with the accoutrements of – somewhat outdated – youth culture, the saxophone, the Fender guitar, would be as much illustration of this subservience, as the blocking off of Oxford Street in London outside the Virgin Megastore for a 'record signing' by Ricky Martin would be an example of commercialisation untamed.[18] For Ricky Martin, the police were out in force to quell the irritation of motorists and to herd pedestrians in orderly fashion into just one lane of the thoroughfare. The same police beat Amer Rafiq, killed Brian Douglas, persecute Satpal Ram. Is this comparative lurch too real?

Politics is never far away. The collapse of the USSR and rapprochement with China were the necessary conditions for transnational investment in the cheap labour enclaves of Asia – for while a strong communist sentiment existed, or threatened the possibility of revolution or electoral success leading to changes which would impose taxation, labour regulation, nationalisation, etc., there could be no guarantee for 'offshore' capitalist investment. The subsequent collapse of the economies of Asia and the paralysed anxiousness of the USA over the possibility that Indonesia might 'fall' to the left (with Australia deployed this time as out-of-its-depth regional police force) only underlines how important the threat of communism had been up until 1991.

Identity

The failure of cultural studies, audience studies and media an'
to examine these disjunctions at a global level, or at the level

street violence become epidemic, extends the complicity of these approaches with the myopic blindness to exploitation typical of culturalist agendas. This is especially so where valorisations of tribalism and 'ethnic styles' operate in the world music literature to dress up ignorance of socioeconomic divisions and expropriation as progressive relativism. The 'civilised' Euro-capitalist culture that could inflict such massive violent destruction upon itself and others across the planet over the past hundred years – through a series of wars ever more precise in their brutality – must surely be treated with suspicion when it proposes a happy world of consumption for all, with a world music soundtrack and ethnic print bedspreads. In a narrower time-frame we might notice that it is no accident that diversity and culturalist politics emerged after the decline of the European workers' movement and the realignment of capitalist polarity between Asia and the USA. Culture in the big picture gave way to cultures in the post-1968 period. In a century whose history should rather be read as the success and betrayal of so many anti-imperialist and proletarian struggles against capital, fascination too often remained at the level of stereotypes and simplifications. Identity politics and postmodernism arrive together not because the grand narratives lost their coherence and hegemonic force, but because they were pushed. The end of empire (or rather its forced realignments), the Cold War lunacy, Hiroshima, Nagasaki and the anti-nuclear movement, fear and loss of confidence in science and competence – all this destabilised the establishment story, but this does not do away with narrative altogether. It is plausible to consider how anti-colonial, anti-essentialist, polymorphously perverse and autonomous struggles were the greater driving forces in this century, which should be understood as the dialectic of struggle and reaction on the part of the people and those who wield power.

Within this general characterisation it would become important not to be deceived into agreeing to acceptable limits, into realpolitik accommodation to the parameters of approved discourse, the replication of copy-cat forms of small-scale understanding and part-time response. A return to new moralisms and Victorian values is not a viable response to the critique of homogeneity. Rather, we are enjoined to construct greater narrations, inclusive and liberatory, capable of embracing the hetero-geneity of humanity without jettisoning the advances of technology, the capacities of production and the creativity of the many. Heterogeneity in itself would be a dangerous idea if it came to hegemony outside a programme of redistributive justice and advanced development. It is important to politicise difference in such a context.

By design, the creation of a world market opens the way for the capitalist class to consolidate its dominance and, according to differences amongst this class, and in various sectors, to assert a continued hegemony in much the same way that various national capitalist elites were able to benefit from the development of national markets produced in the early phases of imperialism. As Partha Chatterjee notes: 'It was colonial capital and the British colonial state which created an "all-India" market for the operation of big capital, whether commercial, financial or industrial. It was this "all-India" market which the big bourgeoisie subsequently took over and consolidated' (Chatterjee 1997b: 15). Of course the all-India market did not, just as the global market does not, include everyone – being available only to the upper layer of relatively well-off 'consumers'. But just as the upper bourgeoisie managed to articulate its interests as those of the nation-state, so too do the interests of the global capitalists come to stand in for those of the entire world – so long as we put up with this. The degree to which middle-class cultural production and co-opted working-class entertainments are increasingly subsumed to the workings of corporate hegemony is often acknowledged, yet is it still possible to hold out for attention to alternative possibilities, to that secret omnipresence of resistance, or to the counter-hegemonic eruptions of those with quite different 'objective' interests, even on a world scale, and work for transformational change?

Why does identity and culture seem to exclude politics, or at least reduce politics to cultural identity and the competition of various manifestations of difference for the limited resources of the nation's allocated public welfare (arts council grants and the like, space in the sun, a trick)? Where did the politics of material equality and the project of transformatory justice go in the work of the 'identity' theorists? Has the international division of labour, social inequality, material wealth for some and shit jobs for the rest, etc., all disappeared with the advent of the information economy, difference and hybrid culture? Theorists of cultural identity locate politics at the level of self-fashioning, rhetorical fabulation, discursive construction of self and consumption of images. In a way we are all seen to be subject to the theory of shopping. But even those who would identify the rise of difference and identity as a manifestation of the move to a post-industrial information and service-economy (Castells 1998) cannot be blind to the fact that the service jobs that have replaced industrial production primarily in the metropolitan West are less secure and less well-remunerated Mc-jobs, and that, for the rest of the world, increasing industrialisation still implies immiseration and exploitation based upon astonishingly high levels of surplus extraction (formal subsumption and accumulation at mercantile levels in the Third World exceeds the trick of surplus value appropriation and real subsumption in the First).

As James Heartfield writes in his booklet *Need and Desire in the Post-Material Economy* (1998), there can be 'No catwalk without a rag trade, no Britpop without a plastics industry, no Internet without an assembly line in Korea or Silicon Valley' (Heartfield 1998: 22). His withering critique is aimed at those who would keep their analysis of culture only on the level of consumption, and thus forget that the relations of wages to capital, and labourer to capitalist, are relations that also determine – in that lonely last instance which Althusser said may never come – the struggle of identities that passes for politics today. Without the appropriation, on a massive scale, of surplus, there could be no experimentation – 'the cultural experimentation that identity theory thrives upon' would be unlikely. 'No surplus, no endless play of difference' (Heartfield 1998: 28). The situation is, however, perhaps not all as Heartfield argues, although I agree that identity theory, the post-industrial information economy and the endless play of difference reflects the interests of the metropolitan class who see theory-production as the driving force of society. Where he lampoons the neo-Hegelian hype of those who offer a 'description of the world of work in which the future belongs to writers, administrators and the intelligentsia – the very people writing the advertising copy ... [people from] think-tanks which see the country peopled entirely by people who work in think-tanks' (Heartfield 1988: 10), I would argue a stronger case. I think the extension of the information and service economy, especially insofar as it operates out of the metropolitan West, but also in tourism, cinema and the so-called placeless virtual of the Internet, amounts to a set of historically specific responses to the stagnation of world capitalist production and that, rather than invest in a new round of productive activity in the West, the smart money is on the quick recuperation of profits via encouragement of consumption, circulation and expenditure. Of course, in this scenario the chattering classes of London, and the layer of intellectuals, artists and advertising executives live a luxurious life of parties, cocaine and bubble.dot.com exuberance, but the real accumulation still occurs in the accounts column of old Moneybags, with East-as-a-career profiteering in the 'Third World', recouping what profit can be had through mergers at 'home'. That Cool Britannia, with Tony on guitar, or even Urbane USA, with Bill on sax, merely provides the covering soundtrack (Nero fiddles while the city burns), does not indicate more than the participation in this rip-off riff on the part of the executive committee of the bourgeoisie, and the complicit deception of the chattering classes who provide the theoretical smoke screen.

Mesmerised by the new horizons of the informational economy, it is perhaps the capacity to exploit English-language technology and world-wide markets for English-language cultural products that provides investors in the cultural, information and service industries with new opportunities for profit (without reinvestment in production in the metropolitan zones). No longer having a competitive edge in industry, nation-states such as Britain, or industrial conglomerates like RCA, rely on the sale of 'culture' as a locus for recuperative turnover. To the extent that 'industry' exists in contemporary capital and its slump condition, massive profitable productive investment occurs elsewhere (and slides further into stagnation with each turn at 'crisis'). The factor which governs the larger shifts of life for most of us on the planet is that an obscure elite few able to extract wealth from the world system are now engaged in a bitter endgame to re-cash their capital reserves through speculative investment in the cultural arts, in the warehouses of the East End of London, in Internet and multimedia technology investment and in information and service industry ventures ... and continued 'old school' plunder elsewhere. There is no reason not to enjoy the efflorescence of culture, but it is also incumbent upon analysts to point out that extension of the service economy, whether it be the proliferation of South Asian restaurants fuelling the culinary transformation of Britain, or of hip-hop from the USA, is dependent on this stagnation of overall world production. And, as I keep saying, listening to Chumbawumba, Public Enemy, Fun^da^mental or ADF is not yet in itself a revolutionary politics.

If the efflorescence of cultural industries, identity, style and 'information' looks at second glance to be a move of capital to quickly cash in accumulated stock in conditions of global stagnation, it should not be thought that this imposes any homogenised character upon the contemporary scene.[19] It is evident that several different modes of capitalist production can coexist (both to complement and compete) within the uneven world system. Several levels of technology and logics of exchange simultaneously develop at their own pace. While some capitals expand and invest in new plant and in new locations, others concern themselves with surviving the buy-off sell-off routine of merger and acquisition favoured in the period of restructuring. The oil crisis, debt crisis, peso crisis, '87 crash, Japanese slow down and the South-East Asian 'crisis', including its threatened extension to Europe, are all comprehensible examples of the fall-out of competition in periods of restructuring. Though the uneven temporal pattern may complicate the calculations, it is clear that these movements obey a brutal market 'truth' that not all extant capitals can survive into the next round of reinvestment and accumulation. The ledger of who moves through and when is not necessarily neat.

If in this scenario, predominantly English-language multimedia, information technology and 'service' products have served as a rapid 'laundering' service for stagnant capital, it is also too early to tell if these forms – especially telematics – will also provide the necessary new opportunities (technology, competitive advantages) for the next expansion phase or not. Many have gambled that there will be such a phase (science parks and other 'incubation' ventures receive massive state subsidies in the hope of 'take-off', the Gallaghers visit 10 Downing Street), but the extent to which the masses of the people (potential stake-holders, consumers, customers) accept or reject the new trick remains uncertain – and it is exactly at this secret point where things come undone – it is of course a trick, initiating a new round of exploitation, and of course not everyone is equally deceived, as increased political mobilisations (Indonesia, Korea, USA, etc.) substantiate.

Coda

The entry of European-based Asian practitioners into media develop-ment work corresponds with a commercial ambition that reveals considerable contradictions. It is possible to take up issues of techno-logical development and remote area access within the framework of outreach and NGO activity. Here culture is recruited to technological development and articulated as progress by means of crossing borders – examples of such border crossings would include large state and commercial operations such as the Australian government ATV beaming 'education programmes' across Asia; the dubbing of Hollywood film into Hindi/Urdu for release in Indian and Pakistani cinema halls; or Rupert Murdoch's Star TV beaming into China and India from Hong Kong. Smaller-scale versions of the same border violations involve NGO documentary work, self-starter Internet evangelists setting up cybercafes and website design, entrepreneurial service provision via Internet and typing pool (the vast dictation transcription services that deliver typed text of spoken recordings overnight between New York and Bangalore). Obviously transnational media offer opportunities for the evaluation of developing globalisation processes which cannot be ignored, although it would be a miscalculation indeed to overlook the strong state and policy influence shaping these flows. The specificities of these developments must also be taken into account. Recent debates in the UK and Australia regarding Murdoch's media empire and his 'influence' on both culture (as a sports broadcaster transforming the shape of rugby) and politics (as best mate of Brother Number One Blair) have suggested possible restrictions upon his activities. The issues of content and influence have not been as fiercely contested in Asia, or rather, as Murdoch's relationship with China shows, have been contested differently – the issue of content and influence relatively quickly resolved, the problem of licensing, technology transfer and contractual obligations less simple. One of the reasons for this difference, it is suggested, is that music television plays a greater role in Asian programming and therefore music formats have provided a somewhat easier translated access into foreign markets for Western providers.

It still remains the case, however, that locally produced music television had capitalised on the music and dance orientation of Asian audiences to a much greater extent until – and this is the key point – Europe-based Asian practitioners found openings and opportunities in the overseas music market. Here the complex position of self-described radical and alternative music practitioners who make forays into Asian markets in ways that some might label imperialist bears ideological implications not easily negotiated by European performers. At the same time as a certain suspicion of the media empires prevails in many quarters, the extension of media literacy and innovative media technology use throughout the region has important consequences for 'access' debates and allows Europe-based artists to justify some of their activities that might otherwise look lame, as Gopinath's discussion of Apache Indian's 'cultural identity' possibly shows:

> Apache opens his set [Delhi June 1993] by gazing out at an audience of several thousand Indian youths, and shouting, 'I do not come to you as a pop star or a reggae star. I come to you as an Indian ... who loves his country and loves his people, all over the world!' ... 'Indianness' here is being defined from outside the geographic boundaries of the nation while being consumed within it. The fact that this hybrid notion of 'Indianness' is produced within and deployed from the former colonial power, and is being consumed within the former colony, complicates a standard cultural imperialism argument, in which Britain could be seen as merely exporting another commodity – this time Indian identity – to India.

Rather, the movement [bhangra in Britain, etc.] gestures towards a refashioning of what it means to be British through a refashioning of what it means to be Indian, and vice versa. (Gopinath 1995: 314)

The point to make about international broadcast and distribution for the cultural products of British South Asian bands is that any political slant that may be evident or intended within the British context often travels less well to other sites. Obviously unpredictable consequences and commercial distortions are the more likely outcome, at the expense of comprehension or educational persuasion. The clincher for this point would be to consider just how the specific campaign politics and organisational form of self-defence anti-racism or, for example, the Satpal Ram campaign, could translate across viewing constituencies. Militant self-defence in one situation could be interpreted quite otherwise in another. Site-specific struggle could become token of radical credentialism in another context. The high-powered financial interests that control international distribution and media are not the only forces to contend with here. As Gupta notes in the context of a discussion of the ways public services are restricted to obey the directives of political states, while commercial agencies are not, the 'framework of trans-national telecasting is encouraging commercial transactions, rather than cultural ones' (Gupta 1998: 84). Or, more precisely, cultural transactions are subject to the directives and distortions of commercial priority. Given the present and expected future (economic) importance of this cultural domain, the failure of social scientists to address these issues must be challenged in the interests of a progressive politics. In this regard, Jacques Derrida has already pointed to the necessity of such work: 'one of the most serious problems today' is 'responsibility before the current forms of the mass media and especially before their mono-polisation, their framing, their axiomatics'. This is a demand for political vigilance before the media, but he adds a rider in that for him this 'does not at all mean ... a protest against the media in general'. He is, he argues, always for the multiplication of forms of media ('there are never enough of them') and he is 'especially for their diversification', but his main argument is that he will be:

resolutely against their normalisation, against the various take-overs ... which have in fact reduced to silence everything that does not conform to very determinate and very powerful frames or codes, or still yet to phantasms of what is 'receivable'. But the first problem of the 'media' is posed by what does not get translated, or even published in the dominant political languages, the ones that dictate the laws of receivability. (Derrida 1995: 87)

This may be only the first move of 'visibility' but Asian media competence and expertise is not translated (see Kalra 2000a). An under-acknowledged and little understood aspect of 'ethnic' cultural and political activity in Europe is now revealed to have far-reaching global consequences evidenced in, albeit limited, export of South Asian musics 'back' to Asia itself. The expertise of Asian youth from groupings involved in international communications and marketing today demands a reconceptualisation of the resources available to and used by so-called minority organisations, and a reconceptualisation of the directional flows characteristic of so-called globalisation. The full impact of tele-technological competence upon the cultural practices of 'ethnic' communities in Europe and amongst these communities in the trans-national diaspora (or 'transl-asia') remains on the agenda of disciplinary attentiveness even as the modes in which these disciplines approach the material are stuck. Undoubtedly, these matters bear economic and ideological implications in the sphere of international communications and commerce which require a rethinking of 'responsibility before the current forms of media', as Derrida says, which will not be race blind, or myopically focused only upon a single nation-state or bounded 'ethnographic' group. By bringing more dynamic (politicised? partisan?) participant observation methods to the technological coordinates of cultural production and to debates about ethnicity and diaspora in the context of music-video production across international borders, the desire has been to reconfigure these debates on the basis of engaged understandings.

There is a double bind of crossing the border of the global and local.[20]

In a 1924 article, Ho Chi Minh noted that 'colonialism is a leech with two suckers, one of which sucks the metropolitan proletariat and the other that of the colonies. If we want to kill this monster, we must cut off both suckers at the same time. If only one is cut off, the other will continue to suck the blood of the proletariat, the animal will continue to live, and the cut-off sucker will grow again. (cited in Prashad 1999)

Complicity, and the double-tentacled character of the enemy, will also hardly be news, except maybe to those entirely caught up in the irrelevance of their analysis. ADF's community project in East London links up with rural Bengal for good 'internationalist' reasons. Kula Shaker's travelogue in India misses the point for all the wrong reasons. Let us never imagine globalisation as either wholly one-way or simply uncoordinated multiplicity. It is not a model that can be easily worked, but it is one that offers us the possibility, or indeed requires we take the opportunity, of rethinking just what it is that is going on. To rest uncritically in appreciation of the extent to which some images are able to compete with the likes of Madonna or Murdoch is to cede the chance at the very point where something might be built. The time for more than haphazard culturalism and difference-mongering is nigh. Thus, Gilroy's circulation, plus Spivak's vigilance, plus militant transnational cultural studies, plus Fun^da^mental's vigilantism, plus ADF's educational community organising, plus wariness of difference-mongering, plus critique of opportunism and commercial alibi-ism – all this still requires an obtusely angled ruthless critique (plus the party of the new type – open and organised). Of course we need to be not too serious, to find time for jokes too. Ha ha. But perhaps teaching literate First-Worlders that the struggle against global terror is fragmentary and local, might merely be another alibi to get them off the hook. Is universalism out of bounds? Certainly mere interpretive competence does not address the problem that 'found' political alliances are neither a guarantee of progressive politics, nor grounds for sustaining political struggle. What keeps those with the best chance of opportunistic regression or co-options of comfort 'in' struggle? Isn't the political party form, recognising its past violences (see Chapters 6 and 7), in need of renovation, but also still necessary? What other strategies are adequate for a struggle that has lasted over a hundred years already? Is the record of this struggle, the road travelled thus far, one of instruction and inspiration? A different telling of the globalisation narrative might say so. On the other hand, prescriptive political optimism is akin to the self congratulation of the celebrants of cultural visibility – another narcissistic egoism. There is not much room for sloppy politics there. Should we be so surprised that the mass media environment in which we live leads us to egoistic narcissism? The exoticised and trinketised images it sells us encourage only this soft self-focus. Just as, when talking of the paranoia engendered among the citizens of atomic era capitalism, Adorno noted 'a strong reality basis for everybody's sense of being persecuted' (Adorno 1994: 122). But nothing says we cannot still fight. Let us clearly recognise that assessments of capital, its origins and directionality, and questions of 'what to do' about it, and our capacity to sublate paranoia into action, require identification of sites of struggle and circulation and their valorisation. The task is to name the shape and specificity of the current conjuncture and explore and extend ways to intervene. Not to cower in the face of some rampant 'complexity' or 'uncertainty'.

Globalisation that proceeds lyrically through the crucible of acknowledged internationalisms seems to offer a chance of rethinking. Complicity and transnational context is a move towards ... Where? Let's go there.

Notes

1. Despite a considerable and impressive early involvement in media by anthropologists, this has not translated into contemporary competence in cultural studies. The older anthropologies of 'remote' peoples were media literate in their fashion – Spencer and Gillen's photography in Australia at the beginning of the century (Mulvaney et al. 1997), Bateson and Mead with cameras in Bali in mid-century (1942). But when anthropology turned to urban issues it did not capitalise on these beginnings. Eiselin and Topper made much the same point a long time ago in relation to television: 'urban anthropologists seem to have an anti-television bias, which, coupled with an overconcern for studying the "primitive" or "exotic" aspects or urban life, has left them blind to the fact that television is a major social and cultural force' (Eiselin and Topper 1976: 131). As will be clear from the argument in this chapter, urban populations characterised as 'ethnic' have always been competent in long-distance communications technologies. In the new hype about transnational communities and telecommunications, about 'digital diasporas' and multimedia minorities (I prefer comprador cosmonauts), the 'newness' of the media participation of 'minority' cultures carries with it a pathologising tendency. It is as if white supremacist use of advanced technology is legitimate and normal, use of video cameras by indigenous groups, or of advanced computing systems by South Asian junglist musicians, is at best a curiosity and, at worst, contrary to some 'natural' ethnic disposition.

2. *Vileyti* might be conceived as a Panjabi and bhangra transliteration of the word 'Blighty', as discussed by Virinder Kalra who tells us that in 'Bhangra texts, England is referred to as "*vilayet*"' and continues by noting that 'Saifullah Khan [1976], somewhat contentiously traces the genealogy of this word to the description of England as "Old Blighty", *vilayeti* is therefore the Panjabified version of the word "Blighty"' (Kalra 2000a).

3. This globalisation malarky could take a myriad of forms. A text that tells a similar tale most eloquently and which provides an excellent read is Kumari Jayawardene's *The White Woman's Other Burden*. This is the story of the lovers of South Asian communists, though it never disrespects the work of those men, its focus is on acknowledging the solidarity of women who made serious internationalist liaisons. To go for such connections, to insist on international solidarity at all levels – this is not something that exists as mere footnote or gossip, but deserving of respect (Jayawardene 1995).

4. This is not an isolated tactic, Tony Mitchell presents the Italian rap band

Assalti Frontali as 'the hard-core style of Public Enemy' (Mitchell 1996: 152 in Wright 2000). Wright offers a more nuanced treatment.

5. I leave aside the question of who works who here. In Marx's chapter 'The Rate and Mass of Surplus Value' the discussion turns towards complex production processes and valorisation: 'It is now no longer the labourer that employs the means of production, but the means of production that employ the labourer.' The labourer is consumed as 'the ferment necessary' to the life process of capital as self-valorising value (Marx 1867/1967: 310). The key to unpack this would be to focus on the valorisation entailed, and recognise (perhaps hope?) that this does not exhaust the possible uses of technology. Capitalism, after all, cannot last forever. Let's end it.

6. Marx and Engels are also interesting here, in a well-known passage:
   'The bourgeoisie, by the rapid improvement of all the instruments of production, *by the immensely facilitated means of communications*, draws all, even the most barbarian nations into civilisation. The cheap prices of its commodities are the heavy artillery with which it batters down all Chinese walls, with which it forces the barbarians' intensely obstinate hatred of foreigners to capitulate. It compels all nations, on pain of extinction, to adopt the bourgeois mode of production; it compels them to introduce what it calls civilisation into their midst, i.e., to become bourgeois themselves. In a word, it creates a world after its own *image*. (Marx and Engels 1848/1952: 47, my emphasis)
   Interestingly, the 'immensely facilitated' means of communications of the English translation might also be rendered with a stronger affirmation when translated as 'infinite release' – the *unendlich erleichterten'* (Marx and Engels 1848/1970: 47) suggests also the release of a never-ending opening of communications that already anticipates the continually developing communications environment characteristic of the information order today.

7. Auto-reference, please excuse: my whole life has been elaborated in the communications system. From learning the alphabet at school, reading those propaganda war and adventure comics, a part-time job as newspaper boy, which got me up at 5 a.m., more school, more entertainment, a first full-time job as a picture framer, then work assembling display shelves in supermarkets, return to university, teaching, politics, the Internet – there is no outside anymore. My visits to India are scripted too, as so many films, documentaries and videos, predispose the visitor with programmed expectations (see Hutnyk 1996a, and Chapter 4 note 4 of this volume).

8. Gilroy has mentioned the (self-declared ageing) rock and roll professor Larry Grossberg – the 'we' here is not necessarily one that includes fans of contemporary music, and the autobiographical compulsion seems peculiarly something that afflicts professorial level authors in late tenure.

9. The to-and-fro has not been explicitly examined in terms of this double play, but it is obviously there in so many of the examples I've used: Kula Shaker, Madonna, Nusrat, Fun^da^mental. Consider how this might be extended through the ways Atom Agoyan's film *Exotica* uses playback film music and Qawwali extensively as aural backdrop for the sex club lap dancing scenes. With hypnotic lighting effects, but a lousy DJ, the film both flaunts, and underplays its charge.

10. Satellite television, beyond CNN, became available in South Asia with the

launch of Star TV in 1991 (Satellite Television Asia Region) including BBC, MTV, sports and entertainment, and from 1992 Zee TV in Hindi. Rupert Murdoch bought 63 per cent of Star in 1993.

11. The serialisation of the Ramayana and Mahabharata on television in India was occasion for copious speculation about the future of television. Viewing figures of 90 per cent, possibly apocryphal stories of televisions made into shrines, and burnt down under weight of candles, rioting after an ill-timed power cut, and forced reschedulings of Communist Party meetings and church services which clashed with the programming give a flavour of the incredulous-spectacular tone adopted (see Gupta 1998: 47; some of the above examples are from my own memory of the time, details not retained). Reflecting on this however, I take heed of Chetan Bhatt's warning that 'we should not assume an uncritical consumption of electronic idolatry' amongst the 80 millions who watched *Mahabharata* and *Ramayana* in 1987–9 (Bhatt 1997: 247–8).

12. This figure does seem low. I would even suspect that there are that many not-working telephones in India. In Calcutta there is a monument erected by the city's telecommunications workers commemorating the 'dead telephone' – in honour of the particularly appalling connection record of Calcutta's system.

13. See my discussion of Derrida's version of exactly this hype where he says email will 'transform the entire public and private space of humanity' (Derrida 1995/6; Hutnyk 1997b).

14. Without providing detailed explanations of divisions of labour, class hierarchy, urban–rural and informal economy considerations, middle class, privilege, cultural enclaves, employment options and poverty, exploitation and survival, it is obvious that huge sections of the population of any locality in India are not the most relevant subjects for a study concerned with music video product consumption. This is not to say that those for whom day-to-day survival in rural or urban India is a primary struggle are not also consumers of such media, but rather that the purchase of CD recordings, or watching hours of music video via satellite pertains to a rather restricted section of the community relative to the population as a whole. While acknowledging the size and growth of the Indian middle-class and their consumption of the kinds of cultural products discussed here, it is also worth remembering some of the basic co-ordinates within which this rarefied consumption takes place. In urban areas especially, sections of the lowest classes do have some access to satellite television and its associated products, and more so to the Hindi film song examples that cut across this sector – with the cheapest tickets to cinema still only a few rupees, Bollywood film music remains the widest distributor of sounds to the general population. Recent developments, where films are released with an accompanying promotional campaign via the music television stations – special programmes, videos of the film's songs re-shot for TV cassettes, tours and merchandising have not yet displaced the importance of local cinemas. However, while televisions with satellite connections in some form are increasingly available outside middle-class urban homes, it is important to remember that possibly half the population of India has yet to be 'connected' to the communications revolution technologies that are so hyped today. Many live their lives

without access to a telephone, may have never made a call, at most have seen television at the home of the village *sarpanch*. The Internet and the world wide web superhighway has affected them only to the degree that related globalisation and liberalisation of the Indian economy has knock-on effects such as inflation and increased cost of rice, greater exploitation, new jobs in multinational mining ventures, further reductions in quality of life, immiserisation, increased pauperisation and so on.

15. Not so many years ago it was possible for South Asian cultural commentators to be astonished when the occasional Asian face popped up on British TV, as Sanjay Sharma commented at the 1996 launch of *Dis-Orienting Rhythms: The Politics of the New Asian Dance Music*: 'You'd see Sheila Chandra and go "Oh look, Asians on the telly".' Just the year before Nabeel Zuberi wrote:

    Growing up in Britain in the 1970s, the last thing one expected to see on the telly was an Asian performer on *Top of the Pops* ... Asians were confined to the BBC's Sunday morning ghetto slot on *Nai Zindagi Naya Jeevan* (translated as *New Ways, New Life* by the Beeb's English announcer). (Zuberi 1995: 36)

16. Not that I would ever want to deny anyone electrification, something that seems useful and necessary indeed. We have to agree that the relentless extension of electronic media across the webs of our lives is there to be used, enjoyed, captured, redeployed. But sometimes the speed-hype that is in fact a sales pitch blurs possibilities. Sometimes new media work may require different speeds – slower reading, longer planning, temporal depth ... An overdetermined image of net-activism, faxivism, and the like, has all too often been singled out for attention by the mass media in ways that furthered a conspicuously liberal cause. What was the underlying agenda? In continuity with the Californian Ideology, it seems no accident that faxivism so neatly fits the ongoing communications transition – the extension of a new mode of production to the entire social fabric. Everyone – even those who make it their business to resist – now needs to buy a computer, sign up for a provider account, set up a website, and dedicate themselves to net time (time on the net, not just <nettime> the list). In this context, celebrations of the Internet as a 'public discussion' forum are somewhat hollow in the face of economic constraints. The question of 'access' is not simple, and never without convolutions. In many cases even the most media-active NGOs are unable to participate in this discussion without considerable investment which simultaneously acts to limit activity. The investment is not only in terms of hardware, but also the software of person-hours required to read, and reply to, digest and regurgitate net correspondence (or editing time making documentary news for global media). It must be considered that it is also a 'cost' that time spent engaged with new media is also time disconnected from other activities of organising that may be of greater priority for the organisation (a fact far too often overlooked by the organs of well-meaning solidarity who request 'news from the front' reports from under-financed groupings). There needs always to be a dedicated person in an organisation who will feed information to the rest. Is this practical? What mechanisms might facilitate this work? Resource requirements for participation in net activism are sometimes beyond the capacity of a small 'Third World' organisation. In addition, there is the fluctuation cost of net

access at levels accepted at an 'industry standard' which always seems on the move. Add to this the exponentially growing cost to the organisation in time and person-hours to respond to requests for information in the ever increasing 'online world' and webification of the struggle seems a decreasingly appealing option. A second order of problem has to do with discursive reach. Whatever the level of 'crisis' which may be recognised from near and from afar, and whatever the solutions proclaimed or ordained by the lap-toppers and webucated elites, if the general population have no access, no time, no resources or no habit of making sense of the discourses of 'crisis', responses or mobilisation, then net activism feeds only itself. The danger of the big hype of the new media and Internet is that it is wide open to a tendency to distract attention from the immediacy of political and organisational practicality. There may or may not be all sorts of alternative news and counter-hegemonic communications and reporting advocated by net activists and those who proclaim the need for a 'free media', but without a political base for developing a context for these claims, this can be nothing but fantasy. Clearly more education and more organisation is more important than more information. Though of course the new media and the need to organise come together. It would be absurd to suggest that the information resources of new media are not to be embraced, but, as with all technologies, the point is to utilise these to best effect. (I'd like to acknowledge Anna Har with whom I wrote an article along the lines argued for in this note, but in that case specific to South-East Asian struggles. It was written for the 'Workbook' of the <Nettime> N5M3 conference, Amsterdam 1999, see <www.saksi.com/jul99/huynyk.htm> where some of the marks of that context remain.

17. This narrative is a speculation after the fashion of Gayatri Spivak's 'Scattered Speculations on the Question of Value' (Spivak 1993).

18. On 'Youth' and the culture industry: when Angela McRobbie asks 'how much music and how many musicians can the new culture-society accommodate?' (McRobbie 1999: 41), surely it is not so much an issue of calculating how much the hyped 'escape from the ghetto' does become available to working-class youth, black or northern, male or female, but rather that this hype is very much the preserve of a class fraction of the very 'youth market' that consumes the culture-society product worldwide. McRobbie is quite (intentionally) over the top when she notes that proclamation of 'any' number of new opportunities to work in the night-time economy is a utopian scenario 'similar to the one Marx himself looked forward to: cooking, looking after the children, and doing the ironing in the morning, writing lyrics and composing tracks on the home computer in the afternoon, and playing them for money in the evening' (McRobbie 1999: 42). There is no need to say here that Marx would likely be into a rather more radical groove than this.

19. Lisa Lowe notes:

> The need to understand the differentiated forms through which capital profits through mixing and combining different modes of production suggests, too, that the complex structures of a new social formation may indeed require interventions and modes of opposition specific to those structures. (Lowe 1996: 161)

Readers will recall that Mao Zedong was the one who made a career out of just this thought, followed up by action.

20. The difficulty of crossing borders even for the most benighted of economic refugees is still a privilege compared with those who have no possibility of getting under the wire (for discussion of this in relation to Whaggis on the Indo-Pak border see Kalra and Purewal 1999).

Bibliography

Abu-Lighod, Lila (1993) 'Finding a Place for Islam: Egyptian Television Serials and the National Interest', *Public Culture* 11: 493–513.

Adorno, Theodor (1941/1990) 'On Popular Music', in Frith, Simon and Goodwin, Andrew (eds) *On Record: Rock, Pop, and the Written Word*, London: Routledge, pp. 301–14.

Adorno, Theodor (1951/1974) *Minima Moralia*, London: Verso.

Adorno, Theodor (1973) *Negative Dialectics*, London: Routledge.

Adorno, Theodor (1981) *Noten zur Literatur*, Frankfurt: Suhrkamp.

Adorno, Theodor (1983) *Prisms*, Cambridge, MA: MIT Press.

Adorno, Theodor (1991) *The Culture Industry: Selected Essays on Mass Culture*, ed. J.M. Bernstein, Routledge: London.

Adorno, Theodor (1994) *The Stars Down to Earth and Other Essays on the Irrational in Culture*, London: Routledge.

Adorno, Theodor (1999) *Sound Figures*, Stanford, CA: Stanford University Press (originally *Musikalische Schriften* 1–3, *Gesammelte Schriften*, vol. 16, 1978, Frankfurt: Suhrkamp Verlag).

Adorno, Theodor and Horkheimer, Max (1944/1979) *The Dialectic of Enlightenment*, London: Verso.

Adorno, Theodor, Benjamin, Walter, Bloch, Ernst, Brecht, Bertolt and Lukács, Georg (1977) *Aesthetics and Politics*, London: Verso.

Ahmad, Aijaz (1992) *In Theory: Classes, Nations, Literatures*, London: Verso.

Ahmad, Aijaz (1995) 'The Politics of Literary Postcoloniality', *Race and Class* 36(3): 1–20.

Ahmad, Aijaz (1996) *Lineages of the Present: Political Essays*, New Delhi: Tulika.

Anderson, Benedict (1998) *Spectres of Comparison: Nationalism, Southeast Asia and the World*, London: Verso.

Ang, Ien (1996) *Living Room Wars: Rethinking Media Audiences for a Postmodern World*, London: Routledge.

Appadurai, Arjun (1990) 'Disjuncture and Difference in the Global Cultural Economy', in Featherstone, M. (ed.) *Global Culture: Nationalism, Globalization and Modernity*, London: Sage.

Back, Les (1996) *New Ethnicities and Urban Culture: Racisms and Multiculture in Young Lives*, London: UCL Press.

Back, Les and Nayak, Anoop (eds) (1993) *Invisible Europeans? Black People in the 'New Europe'*, Birmingham: AFFOR.

Baily, John (1990/1993) 'Qawwali in Bradford: Traditional Music in a Muslim Community', in Oliver, Paul (ed.) *Black Music in Britain: Essays on the Afro-Asian Contribution to Popular Music*, Milton Keynes: Open University Press, pp. 153–65.

Bambury (1992) *Killing the Nazi Menace: How to Stop the Fascists*, Socialist Workers Party pamphlet.

Bandyopadhyay, Samik (1986) 'Introduction' to Devi, Mahesweta, *Five Plays*, Calcutta: Seagull Books, pp. v–xvii.

Banerjea, Koushik (1998) 'Sonic Diaspora and its Dissident Footfalls', *Postcolonial Studies* 1(3): 389–400.

Banerjea, Koushik (1999) 'Ni-Ten-Ichi-Ryu: Enter the World of the Smart-Stepper', in Kaur, Raminder and Hutnyk, John (eds) *Travel Worlds: Journeys in Contemporary Cultural Politics*, London: Zed Books, pp. 14–28.

Banerjea, Koushik (2000) 'Diaspora in the Age of Mechanical Reproduction', *Theory, Culture & Society* 17(3): 67–82.

Banerjea, Koushik and Banerjea, Partha (1996) 'Psyche and Soul: A View from the "South"', in Sharma, Sanjay, Hutnyk, John and Sharma, Ashwani (eds) *Dis-Orienting Rhythms: The Politics of the New Asian Dance Music*, London: Zed Books, pp. 105–24.

Banerjea, Koushik and Barn, Jatinder (1996) 'Versioning Terror: Jallianwala Bagh and the Jungle', in Sharma, Sanjay, Hutnyk, John and Sharma, Ashwani (eds) *Dis-Orienting Rhythms: The Politics of the New Asian Dance Music*, London: Zed Books, pp. 193–216.

Banerjee, Sumanta (1984) *India's Simmering Revolution: The Naxalite Uprising*, London: Zed Books.

Banerji, Sabita (1988) 'Ghazals to Bhangra in Great Britain', *Popular Music* 7(2): 207–13.

Banerji, Sabita and Baumann, Gerd (1993) 'Bhangra 1984–8: Fusion and Professionalisation in a Genre of South Asian Dance Music', in Oliver, Paul (ed.) *Black Music in Britain: Essays on the Afro-Asian Contribution to Popular Music*, Milton Keynes: Open University Press, pp. 137–52.

Barthes, Roland (1982) *The Empire of Signs*, New York: Hill and Wang.

Basu, Dipa (1998) 'What is Real about "Keepin' it Real"?', *Postcolonial Studies* 1(3): 371–88.

Bateson, Gregory and Mead, Margaret (1942) *Balinese Character*, New York: New York Academy of Sciences.

Baudrillard, Jean (1983) *Simulations*, New York: Semiotext(e).

Baumann, Gerd (1990) 'The Re-invention of Bhangra: Social Change and Aesthetic Shifts in a Punjabi Music in Britain', *Journal of the International Institute for Comparative Music Studies and Documentation* 32(2): 81–97.

Baumann, Gerd (1996) *Contesting Culture: Discourses of 'Culture' and 'Community' in Multi-Ethnic London*, Cambridge: Cambridge University Press.

Benn, Melissa (1993) 'Women and Democracy: Thoughts on the Last Ten Years', *Women: A Cultural Review* 4(3): 237.

Bhabha, Homi (1988) 'The Commitment to Theory', *New Formations* 5: 5–23.

Bhabha, Homi (1994) *The Location of Culture*, London: Routledge.

Bhatt, Chetan (1997) *Liberation and Purity: Race, New Religious Movements and the Ethics of Postmodernity*, London: UCL Press.

Bonnett, Alastair (1993) *Radicalism, Anti-Racism and Representation*, London: Routledge.

Brah, Avtar (1996) *Cartographies of Diaspora: Contesting Identities*, London: Routledge.

Brodsky-Porges, E. (1981) 'The Grand Tour: Travel as an Educational Device, 1600–1800', *Annals of Tourism Research* 8(3): 318–29.

Butler, Mark (1994) 'Whitewashing Racism', *Living Marxism* 70 <http://www/informinc.co.uk/LM/LM70/LM70 Race.html>

Calcutt, Andrew (1998) *Arrested Development*, London: Cassel.

Callinicos, Alex (1993) *Race and Class*, London: Bookmarks.

CARF (1981) *Southall: The Birth of Black Community*. London: Campaign Against Racism and Fascism, Institute of Race Relations.

Castells, Manuel (1998) *The Power of Identity: The Information Age*, vol. 2, Oxford, Blackwell.

CCCS (1982) *The Empire Strikes Back*, London: Hutchinson.

Chakravarty, Rangan (1999) 'The Global and the Local in the Post-Colonial: Popular Music in Calcutta 1992–1997', PhD dissertation, University of Sussex.

Chambers, Iain (1994) *Migrancy, Culture, Identity*, London: Routledge.

Chatterjee, Partha (1993) *The Nation and its Fragments*, London: Zed Books.

Chatterjee, Partha (1997a) *The Present History of West Bengal: Essays in Political Criticism*, Delhi: Oxford University Press.

Chatterjee, Partha (1997b) *A Possible India*, Delhi: Oxford University Press.

Cheah, Pheng (1998) 'Given Culture: Rethinking Cosmopolitical Freedom in Transnationalism', in Cheah, Pheng and Robbins, Bruce (eds) *Cosmopolitics: Thinking and Feeling Beyond the Nation*, Minneapolis: University of Minnesota Press, pp. 290–328.

Chen, Kuan-Hsing (1998) 'Introduction: The Decolonization Question', in *Trajectories: Inter-Asian Cultural Studies*, London: Routledge.

Chow, Rey (1993) *Writing Diaspora: Tactics of Intervention in Contemporary Cultural Studies*, Bloomington: Indiana University Press.

Chow, Rey (1998) *Ethics after Idealism: Theory-Culture-Ethnicity-Reading*, Bloomington: Indiana University Press.

Cleaver, Harry (1979) *Reading Capital Politically*. Brighton: Harvester Press.

Clifford, James (1986) 'On Ethnographic Self-Fashioning: Conrad and Malinowski', in Heller, T.C, Sonsa, M. and Welbery, D.E. (eds) *Reconstructing Individualism: Autonomy, Individuality and the Self in Western Thought*, Stanford, CA: Stanford University Press.

Clifford, James (1988) *The Predicament of Culture: Twentieth-Century Ethnography, Literature and Art*, Cambridge, MA: Harvard University Press.

Clifford, James (1989) 'Notes on Travel and Theory', *Inscriptions* 5: 177–88.

Clifford, James (1994) 'Diasporas', *Cultural Anthropology* 9(3): 302–38.

Clifford, James (1997) *Routes: Travel and Translation in the Late Twentieth Century*, Cambridge, MA: Harvard University Press.

Cohen, Eric (1972) 'Towards a Sociology of International Tourism', *Social Research* 39.

Cohen, Eric (1979a) 'A Phenomenology of Tourist Experience', *Sociology* 13: 179–201.

Cohen, Eric (1979b) 'Rethinking the Sociology of Tourism', *Annals of Tourism Research* 4(4): 184–94.

Cohen, Philip (1992) '"It's Racism What Dunnit": Hidden Narratives in Theories of Racism', in Donald, James and Rattansi, Ali (eds) *'Race', Culture and Difference*, London: Sage.

Cohen, Sara (1994) 'Identity, Place and the "Liverpool Sound"', in Stokes, Martin (ed.) *Ethnicity, Identity and Music: The Musical Construction of Place*. Oxford: Berg.

Crick, Malcolm (1985) '"Tracing" the Anthropological Self: Quizzical Reflections on Fieldwork, Tourism and the Ludic', *Social Analysis* 17: 71–92.

Crick, Malcolm (1988) 'Sun, Sex, Sights, Savings and Servility: Representations of International Tourism in the Social Sciences', *Criticism, Heresy and Interpretation* 1: 37–76.

Crick, Malcolm (1994) *Resplendent Sites, Discordant Voices: Sri Lankans in International Tourism*. Chur: Harwood Academic.

Damas, Marius (1991) *Approaching Naxalbari*, Calcutta: Radical Impression.

Davis, Angela (1997) 'Interview' in Lisa Lowe and David Lloyd (eds) *The Politics of Culture in the Shadow of Capital*, Durham, NC: Duke University Press.

DeCurtis, Anthony (1999) 'Lost in the Supermarket: Myth and Commerce in the Music Business', *Stars Don't Stand Still in the Sky: Music and Myth* London: Routledge.

Derrida, Jacques (1995/1996) *Archive Fever*. Chicago: University of Chicago Press.

Derrida, Jacques (1995) *Points: Interviews 1974–1994*, Stanford, CA: Stanford University Press.

Devi, Mahasweta (1990) *Bashai Tudu*, trans. Samik Bandyopadhyay and Gayatri Chakravorty Spivak, Calcutta: Thema.

Devi, Mahasweta (1993) *Imaginary Maps*, trans. Gayatri Chakravorty Spivak, Calcutta: Thema.

Devi, Mahesweta (1997a) *Breast Stories*, trans. Gayatri Chakravorty Spivak, Calcutta: Seagull Books.

Devi, Mahasweta (1997b) *Dust in the Road: The Activist Writings of Mahasweta Devi*, ed. Maitreya Ghatak, Calcutta: Seagull Books.

Dhondy, Farrukh (1978) 'Teaching Young Blacks', *Race Today* 10(4): 80–6.

Disraeli, Benamin (1871) *Collected Edition of the Novels and Tales by the Right Honourable B. Disraeli, vol. IV: Tancred or the New Crusade*, London: Longmans, Green.

Donald, James and Rattansi, Ali (eds) (1992) *'Race', Culture and Difference*, London: Sage.

du Gay, Paul, Hall, Stuart, Janes, Linda, Mackay, Hugh and Negus, Keith (1997) *Doing Cultural Studies: The Story of Sony Walkman*, London: Sage.

Dube, Saurabh (1999) 'Travelling Light: Missionary Musings, Colonial Cultures and Anthropological Anxieties', in Kaur, Raminder and Hutnyk, John (eds) *Travel Worlds: Journeys in Contemporary Cultural Politics*, London: Zed Books, pp. 29–50.

DuBois, W.E.B. (1965) *The World and Africa: An Enquiry into the Part which Africa Has Played in World History*, New York: International Publishers.

Dunayevskaya, Raya (1973) *Philosophy and Revolution*, New York: Columbia University Press.

Dunayevskaya, Raya (1981/1991) *Rosa Luxemburg: Women's Liberation, and Marx's Philosophy of Revolution*, Urbana: University of Illinois Press.

Duyker, Edward (1981) 'Tribal Guerrillas: West Bengal's Santals and the Naxalite Movement', PhD thesis, University of Melbourne.

Eiselein, E.B and Topper, Martin (1976) 'A Brief History of Media Anthropology', *Human Organization* 35(2): 123–34.

Featherstone, Mike (1995) *Undoing Culture: Globalisation, Postmodernism and Identity*, London: Sage.

Fekete, Liz (1998) 'Let Them Eat Cake', *Race and Class* 39(3): 77–82.

Finnegan, Ruth (1989) *The Hidden Musicians*, Cambridge: Cambridge University Press.

Foucault, Michel (1978) *The History of Sexuality*, vol. 1, Harmondsworth: Penguin.

Frith, Simon and Goodwin, Andrew (eds) (1990) *On Record: Rock, Pop, and the Written Word*, London: Routledge.

Frith, Simon, Goodwin, A. and Grossberg, L. (eds) (1993) *Sound and Vision: The Music Video Reader*, New York: Routledge.

Gandhi, Leela, Seth, Sanjay and Dutton, Michael (1998) 'Introduction', *Postcolonial Studies* 1: 1–9.

Garafalo, (1994) 'Culture versus Commerce: The Marketing of Black Popular Music', *Public Culture* 7(1): 275–87.

Ghose, S. (1971) *Socialism and Communism in India*, Delhi: Allied Publishers.

Ghosh, S. (1971) *The Naxalite Movement*, Delhi: Firma KLM.

Gillespie, Marie (1995) *Television, Ethnicity and Cultural Change*, London: Routledge.

Gilroy, Paul (1987) *There Ain't No Black in the Union Jack*, London: Routledge.

Gilroy, Paul (1988) 'Cruciality and the Frog's Perspective: An Agenda of Difficulties for the Black Arts Movement in Britain', *Third Text* 5: 33–44.

Gilroy, Paul (1993a) *The Black Atlantic: Modernity and Double Consciousness*, London: Routledge.

Gilroy, Paul (1993b) *Small Acts: Thoughts on the Politics of Black Cultures*, London: Serpent's Tail.

Gilroy, Paul (1994) 'Black Cultural Politics: An Interview with Paul Gilroy by Timmy Lott', *Found Object* 4: 46–81.

Gilroy, Paul (1999) 'Analogues of Mourning, Mourning the Analog', in *Stars Don't Stand Still in the Sky: Music and Myth*, London: Routledge.

Gilroy, Paul and Lawrence, Erol (1988) 'Two-Tone Britain: White and Black Youth and the Politics of Racism', in Cohen, P. and Bains, H.S. (eds) *Multi-Racist Britain*, Basingstoke: Macmillan, pp. 121–55.

Gledhill, John (1994) *Power and its Disguises: Anthropological Perspectives on Politics*, London: Pluto Press.

Goodwin, Andrew (1988/1990) 'Sample and Hold: Pop Music in the Digital Age of Reproduction', in Frith, Simon and Goodwin, Andrew (eds) *On Record: Rock, Pop, and the Written Word*, London: Routledge. pp. 259–73.

Gopinath, Gayatri (1995) '"Bombay, U.K. Yuba City!": Bhangra Music and the Engineering of Diaspora', *Diaspora* 4(3): 303–21.

Gough, Kathleen (1981) *Rural Society in Southeast India*, Cambridge: Cambridge University Press.

Graburn, Nelson (1977) 'Tourism: The Sacred Journey', in Smith, Valene (ed.) *Hosts and Guests*, Oxford: Blackwell.

Grandin, Ingemar (1994) 'Nepalese Urbanism: Musical Elaborations', in Allen, Michael (ed.) *The Anthropology of Nepal: Peoples, Problems and Processes*, Kathmandu: Mandala Book Point.

Guattari, Félix (1996) *The Guattari Reader*, ed. Gary Genosko, Oxford: Blackwell.

Guattari, Félix and Negri, Antonio (1990) *Communists Like Us*, New York: Semiotext(e).

Gupta, Amit Kumar (1997) *The Agrarian Drama: The Leftists and the Rural Poor in India 1934–1951*, New Delhi: Manohar.

Gupta, Nilanjana (1998) *Ideologies of Television in India Delhi*, Oxford: Oxford University Press.

Habermas, Jurgen (1987) *The Philosophical Discourse of Modernity*, Cambridge: Polity Press.

Hall, Stuart (1980) 'Race, Articulation and Societies Structured in Dominance', in UNESCO, *Sociological Theories: Race and Colonialism*, Paris: UNESCO.

Hall, Stuart (1989) 'New Ethnicities', *Black Film, British Cinema*, ICA Documents 7, London: ICA.

Hall, Stuart (1990/1993) 'Cultural Identity and Diaspora', in Williams, Patrick and Chrisman, Laura (eds) *Colonial Discourse and Post-colonial Theory*, Hertfordshire: Harvester Wheatsheaf, pp. 392–403.

Hall, Stuart (1991) 'The Local and the Global: Globalization and Ethnicity', in King, Anthony (ed.) *Culture, Globalization and the World System*, London: Macmillan.

Hall, Stuart (1992) 'The Question of Cultural Identity', in Hall, S., Held, D. and McGrew, A. (eds) *Modernity and its Futures*, London: Polity Press.

Hall, Stuart (1995) 'Black and White Television', in Givanni, June (ed.) *Remote Control: Dilemmas of Black Intervention in British Film and TV*, London: British Film Institute, pp. 13–28.

Hall, Stuart (1996) *Stuart Hall: Critical Dialogues in Cultural Studies*, London: Routledge.

Hamilton, Annette (1993) 'Video Crackdown, or the Sacrificial Pirate: Censorship and Cultural Consequences in Thailand', *Public Culture* 11: 515–31.

Hardt, Michael and Negri, Antonio (1994) *The Labour of Dionysus*, Minneapolis, University of Minnesota Press.

Hayward, Philip (1997) *Music at the Borders: Not Drowning Waving and their Engagement with Papua New Guinean Culture*, Sydney: John Libbey and Co.

Heartfield, James (1998) *Need and Desire in the Post-Material Economy*, Sheffield: SHU Press.

Hebdige, Dick (1996) 'Digging for Britain: An Excavation in Seven Parts', in Baker, Houston, Diawara, Manthia and Lindenborg, Ruth (eds) *Black British Cultural Studies: A Reader*, Chicago: University of Chicago Press.

Hesmondhalgh, David (1995) paper given at the International Association for the Study of Popular Music, Glasgow conference, September.

hooks, bell (1994) *Outlaw Culture: Resisting Representations*, London: Routledge.

hooks, bell (1995) *Killing Rage, Ending Racism*, Harmondsworth: Penguin.

hooks, bell (1998) 'The Feminazi Mystique', *Transition* 73: 156–63.

Horne, Donald (1984) *The Great Museum: the Re-Presentation of History*, London: Pluto Press.

Housee, Shirin and Dar, Mukhtar (1996) 'Re-Mixing Identities: Off the Turntable', in Sharma, Sanjay, Hutnyk, John and Sharma, Ashwani (eds) *Dis-Orienting*

Rhythms: The Politics of the New Asian Dance Music, London: Zed Books.

Hutnyk, John (1987) 'The Authority of Style', *Social Analysis* 21: 59–79.

Hutnyk, John (1995) 'The Revolutionary Structure of Sound', *Versus* 2 (Leeds).

Hutnyk, John (1996a) *The Rumour of Calcutta: Tourism, Charity and the Poverty of Representation*, London: Zed Books.

Hutnyk, John (1996b) 'Repetitive Beatings or Criminal Justice', in Sharma, Sanjay, Hutnyk, John and Sharma, Ashwani (eds) *Dis-Orienting Rhythms: the Politics of the New Asian Dance Music*, London: Zed Books, pp. 156–89.

Hutnyk, John (1996c) 'Media, Research, Politics, Culture', *Critique of Anthropology* 16(4): 417–28.

Hutnyk, John (1997a) 'Adorno at Womad: South Asian Crossovers and the Limits of Hybridity', in Werbner, P. and Modood, T. (eds) *Debating Cultural Hybridity: Multi-Cultural Identities and the Politics of Anti-Racism*, London: Zed Books.

Hutnyk, John (1997b) 'derrida@marx.archive', *Space and Culture* 2: 95–122.

Hutnyk, John (1998) 'Jim Clifford's Ethnographica', *Critique of Anthropology* 18(4): 339–78.

Hutnyk, John (1999a) 'Magical Mystical Tourism', in Kaur, Raminder and Hutnyk, John (eds) *Travel Worlds: Journeys in Contemporary Cultural Politics*, London: Zed Books, pp. 94–119.

Hutnyk, John (1999b) 'Semi-Feudal Cyber-Colonialism: The Multimedia Super Corridor for Malaysia', in J. Bosma et al. (eds) *Read Me!: Ascii Culture and the Revenge of Knowledge*, New York: Semiotext(e).

Hutnyk, John (2000a) 'Hybridity Saves: Authenticity and/or the Critique of Appropriation', *Amer-Asia* 25(3): 39–56.

Hutnyk, John (2000b) 'Capital Calcutta: Coins, Maps and Monuments', in Bell, David and Haddour, Azzadine (eds) *City Visions*, London: Longman, pp. 27–43.

Jameson, Fredric (1990) *Late Marxism, Adorno, or, The Persistence of the Dialectic*, London: Verso.

Jayawardene, Kumari (1995) *The White Woman's Other Burden: Western Women and South Asia During British Rule*, New York: Routledge.

Kalra, Surjit Singh and Purewal, Navtej (1999) *Teach Yourself Panjabi*, London: Hodder and Stoughton.

Kalra, Virinder (1997) 'From Textiles Mills to Taxi Ranks: Experiences of Labour among Mirpuris/(Azad) Kashmiris in Oldham', PhD thesis, Department of Religions and Theology, University of Manchester.

Kalra, Virinder (2000a) 'Vilayeti Rhythms: Beyond Bhangra's Emblematic Status to a Translation of Lyrical Texts', *Theory Culture & Society* 17(3): 83–105.

Kalra, Virinder (2000b) *From Textile Mills to Taxi Ranks: The Local Impact of Global Economic Change*, Aldershot: Ashgate.

Kalra, Virinder and Hutnyk, John (1998) 'Brimful of Agitation, Authenticity and Appropriation: Madonna's "Asian Kool"', *Postcolonial Studies* 1(3): 339–56.

Kalra, Virinder and Purewal, Navtej (1999) 'The Strut of the Peacock', in Kaur, Raminder and Hutnyk, John (eds) *Travel Worlds: Journeys in Contemporary Cultural Politics*, London: Zed Books, pp. 54–67.

Kalra, Virinder, Hutnyk, John and Sharma, Sanjay (1996) 'Re-Sounding (Anti)Racism or Concordant Politics: Revolutionary Antecedents', in Sharma, Sanjay, Hutnyk, John and Sharma, Ashwani (eds) *Dis-Orienting Rhythms: The Politics of the New Asian Dance Music*, London: Zed Books, pp. 127–55.

Kaplan, Caren (1996) *Questions of Travel: Postmodern Discourses of Displacement*

Durham, NC: Duke University Press.

Kaplan, E. Ann (1987) *Rocking Around the Clock: Music Television, Postmodernism and Consumer Culture*, New York: Routledge.

Kaur, Raminder (1999) 'Skinned Alive', in Kaur, Raminder and Hutnyk, John (eds) *Travel Worlds: Journeys in Contemporary Cultural Politics*, London: Zed Books, pp. 155–72.

Kaur, Raminder and Banerjea, Partha (2000) 'Jazzgeist', *Theory, Culture & Society* 17(1): 159–80.

Kaur, Raminder and Hutnyk, John (1999) *Travel-Worlds: Journeys in Contemporary Cultural Politics*, London: Zed Books.

Kaur, Raminder and Kalra, Virinder (1996) 'New Paths for South Asian Music and Creativity', in Sharma, Sanjay, Hutnyk, John and Sharma, Ashwani (eds) *Dis-Orienting Rhythms: The Politics of the New Asian Dance Music*, London: Zed Books, pp. 217–31.

Knowles, Caroline (1992) *Race, Discourse and Labourism*, London: Routledge.

Koepping, Klaus Peter (1989) 'Mind, Body, Text: Not Quite Satirical Reflections on the Trickster', *Criticism, Heresy and Interpretation* 2: 37–76.

Kovel, Joel (1994) *Red-Hunting in a Promised Land*, New York: Basic Books.

Lenin, Vladimir (1917/1951) 'State and Revolution', in *Selected Works*, Moscow: Foreign Languages Publishing House.

Lipsitz, George (1994) *Dangerous Crossroads: Popular Music, Postmodernism and the Poetics of Place*, London: Verso.

Lowe, Lisa (1996) *Immigration Acts: On Asian American Cultural Politics*, Durham, NC: Duke University Press.

Lydon, John (1983) *Rotten: No Irish, No Blacks, No Dogs*, London: Hodder and Stoughton.

MacCannell, Dean (1976) *The Tourist: A New Theory of the Leisure Class*, New York: Schocken Books.

McDowell, Stephen D. (1997) *Globalization, Liberalization and Policy Change: A Political Economy of India's Communications Sector*, Basingstoke: Macmillan.

McLoughlin, Sean and Kalra, Virinder (1999) '"Wish You Were(n't) Here": Discrepant Representations of Mirpur in Narratives of Migration, Diaspora and Travel', in Kaur, Raminder and Hutnyk, John (eds) *Travel Worlds: Journeys in Contemporary Cultural Politics*, London: Zed Books, pp. 120–36.

McQuire, Scott (1995) 'The Go-for-broke Game of History: The Camera, the Community and the Scene of Politics', *Arena Journal* 4: 201–27.

McQuire, Scott (1997) *Visions of Modernity: Representation, Memory, Time and Space in the Age of the Camera*, London: Sage.

McRobbie, Angela (1999) 'Thinking With Music', in *Stars Don't Stand Still in the Sky: Music and Myth*, London: Routledge.

Maharajan, Keshav Lal, (1994) 'Effects of Modernisation on Periurban Families in Kathmandu Valley', in Allen, Michael (ed.) *The Anthropology of Nepal: Peoples, Problems and Processes*, Kathmandu: Mandala Book Point.

Maira, Sunaina (1998) 'Desis Reprazent: Bhangra Remix and Hip Hop in New York City', *Postcolonial Studies* 1(3): 357–70.

Malinowski, Bronislaw (1922) *Argonauts of the Western Pacific: An Account of Native Enterprise and Adventure in the Archipelagos of Melanesian New Guinea*, London: Routledge.

Mallick, Ross (1993) *Development Policy of a Communist Government: West Bengal since 1977*, Cambridge: Cambridge University Press.

Marcus, George (1995) 'Ethnography in/of the World System: The Emergence of Multi-Sited Ethnography', *Annual Review of Anthropology* 24: 95–140.

Marcus, Greil (1989) *Lipstick Traces: A Secret History of the 20th Century*, Cambridge, MA: Harvard University Press.

Marcuse, Herbert (1970) 'The End of Utopia', *Ramparts* April: 28–34.

Marx, Karl (1844/1979) *The Economic and Philosophical Manuscripts of 1844*, Moscow: Progress Press.

Marx, Karl (1857/1974) *Grundrisse der Kritik der Politischen Ökonomie*, Berlin: Dietz Verlag.

Marx, Karl (1857/1986) 'Economic Manuscripts of 1857–8', in Marx, K. and Engels, F., *Collected Works* vol. 28, London: Lawrence and Wishart.

Marx, Karl (1867/1967) *Capital: A Critique of Political Economy, vol. 1: The Process of Capitalist Production*, ed. F. Engels, trans. S. Moore and E. Aveling, New York: International Publishers.

Marx, Karl (1974) *The Ethnological Notebooks*, Assen: Van Gorcum.

Marx, Karl and Engels, Frederick (1848/1952) *Manifesto of the Communist Party*, Moscow: Progress Press.

Marx, Karl and Engels, Frederick (1848/1970) *Manifest Der Kommunistischen Partei* Berlin: Vdietz Verlag.

Massumi, Brian (1992) *A User's Guide to Capitalism and Schizophrenia: Deviations from Deleuze and Guattari*, Cambridge, MA: MIT Press.

Mattelart, Armand (1991/1994) *Mapping World Communication: War, Progress, Culture*, Minneapolis: University of Minnesota Press.

Mattelart, Armand (1996) *The Invention of Communication*, Minneapolis: University of Minnesota Press.

Mattelart, Armand and Mattelart, Michele (1986/1992) *Rethinking Media Theory*, Minneapolis: University of Minnesota Press.

Mazumdar, Charu (1969) 'Peasant Revolutionary Struggle in India', *Liberation* 3(2): 13.

Mercer Kobena (1994) *Welcome to the Jungle: New Positions in Black Cultural Studies*, New York: Routledge.

Messina, A.M. (1989) *Race and Party Competition in Britain*, London: Clarendon Press.

Michaels, Eric (1986) *The Aboriginal Invention of Television in Central Australia*, Canberra.

Michaels, Eric (1987) *For a Cultural Future: Francis Jupurrurla Makes TV at Yuendumu*, Melbourne: Artspace.

Michaels, Eric (1994) *Bad Aboriginal Art: Tradition, Media and Technological Horizons*, Minneapolis: University of Minnesota Press.

Mitchell, Tony (1996) *Popular Music and Local Identity: Rock, Pop and Rap in Europe and Oceania*. London: Leicester University Press.

Mohanty, Manoranjan (1979) 'On Internationalism and Revolution: China and the Indian Revolution', *China Report* March–April.

Morris, Gina (1994) 'So What Is this Asian Kool', *Select* April: 47–52.

Mulvaney, D.J. and Calaby, J.H. (1985) *'So Much that is New': Baldwin Spencer 1860–1929, A Biography*, Melbourne: Melbourne University Press.

Mulvaney, John, Morphy, Howard and Petch, Alison (1997) *My Dear Spencer: The Letters of F.J. Gillen to Baldwin Spencer*, Melbourne: Hyland House.

Namboodiripad, E.M.S. (1994) *The Communist Party in Kerala: Six Decades of Struggle and Advance*, New Delhi: National Book Centre.

Nash, Dennison (1977) 'Tourism as Form of Imperialism', in Smith, Valene (ed.) *Hosts and Guests*, Oxford: Blackwell.

Negri, Antonio (1988) *Revolution Retrieved: Selected Writings on Marx, Keynes, Capitalist Crisis and New Social Subjects 1967–1983*, London: Red Notes.

Negri, Antonio (1997) 'Reappropriations of Public Space', *Common Sense* 21: 31–40.

Nugent, Stephen (1993) *Amazonian Caboclo Society: An Essay on Invisibility and Peasant Economy*. Oxford: Berg.

Oliver, Paul (ed.) (1993) *Black Music in Britain: Essays on the Afro-Asian Contribution to Popular Music*, Milton Keynes: Open University Press.

Omvedt, Gail (1994) *Dalits and the Democratic Revolution: Dr Ambedkar and the Dalit Movement in Colonial India*, New Delhi: Sage.

Parkhill, Peter (1993) 'Of Tradition, Tourism and the World Music Industry', *Meanjin* 52(3): 501–8.

Parry, Benita (1987) 'Problems in Current Theories of Colonial Discourse', *Oxford Literary Review* 9: 27–58.

Perkins, William, Eric (ed.) (1996) *Droppin' Science: Critical Essays on Rap Music and Hip Hop Culture*, Philadelphia, PA: Temple University Press.

Phipps, Peter (1999) 'Tourists, Terrorists, Death and Value', in Kaur, Raminder and Hutnyk, John (eds) *Travel Worlds: Journeys in Contemporary Cultural Politics*, London: Zed Books, pp. 74–93.

Pi-Sunyer, Oriol (1981) 'Tourism and Anthropology', *Annals of Tourism Research* 8: 271–84.

Poster, Mark (1994) 'A Second Media Age?', *Arena Journal* 3: 49–91.

Potter, Howard (1999) 'Confessions in Teleonomy: The Moral Practices of an Anthropology', unpublished dissertation, Goldsmiths College, London.

Prashad, Vijay (1999) 'Red Salute, Comrade Uncle Ho!', Znet commentary distributed on Seminar-12 list, 4 September.

Rai, H. and Prasad, K.M. (1973) 'Naxalism: A Challenge to the Peaceful Transition to Socialism', *Indian Journal of Political Science* 33: 458–78.

Rajagopal, Arvind (1993) 'The Rise of National Programming: The Case of Indian Television', *Media Culture & Society* 15: 91–111.

Ram, Mohan (1971) *Maoism in India*. New Delhi: Vikas Publications.

Ram, Mohan (1972) 'Five Years After Naxalbari', *Economic and Political Weekly* August, Special Issue.

Ree, Jonathon (1998) 'Cosmopolitainism and the Experience of Nationality', in Cheah, Pheng and Robbins, Bruce (eds) *Cosmopolitics: Thinking and Feeling Beyond the Nation*, Minneapolis: University of Minnesota Press, pp. 77–90.

Rosaldo, Renato (1989) *Culture and Truth: The Remaking of Social Analysis*, Boston, MA: Beacon Press.

Rose, Tricia (1994) *Black Noise: Rap Music and Black Culture in Contemporary America*. Hanover: Wesleyan University Press.

Ross, Andrew and Rose, Tricia (eds) (1994) *Microphone Fiends: Youth Music and Youth Culture*, New York: Routledge.

Roy, Arundhati (1997) *The God of Small Things*, London: Flamingo.

Roy, Samaren (1988) *India's First Communist*, Calcutta: Minerva Associates.

Rushdie, Salman (1981) *Midnight's Children*, London: Picador.

Saha, Anamik (1999) 'Asians Can't Rock', unpublished dissertation, Goldsmiths College, London.

Said, Edward (1978) *Orientalism*. Harmonsdworth: Penguin.

Saifullah Khan, V. (1976) 'The Pakistanis', in Watson, J.L. (ed.) *Between Two Cultures*, Oxford: Blackwell.

Satie, Erik (1996) *A Mammal's Notebook*, ed. Ornella Volta, London: Atlas Press.

Savage, Jon (1991), *England's Dreaming: Sex Pistols and Punk Rock*, London: Faber and Faber.

Sayyid, Bobby (1997) *A Fundamental Fear*, London: Zed Books.

Segal, Lynne (1997) 'Generations of Feminism', *Radical Philosophy* 83: 6–16.

Sen Gupta, Bhabani (1972) *Communism in Indian Politics*, New York: Columbia University Press.

Sen, Krishna (1994) *Indonesian Cinema: Framing the New Order*, London: Zed Books.

Seth, Sanjay (1995) 'Interpreting Revolutionary Excess: The Naxalite Movement in India 1967–1971', *Positions* 3(2): 481–507.

Shanin Teodor (ed.) (1983) *Late Marx and the Russian Road*, New York: Monthly Review Press.

Sharma, Sanjay (1994) 'Who's in the House? The Cultural Politics of the New Asian Dance Music', ICCCR South Asia seminar series, University of Manchester, 1 Nov.

Sharma, Sanjay (1996) 'Noisy Asians or Asian Noise?', in Sharma, Sanjay, Hutnyk, John and Sharma, Ashwani (eds) *Dis-Orienting Rhythms: The Politics of the New Asian Dance Music*, London: Zed Books, pp. 32–57.

Sharma, Sanjay and Housee, Shirin (1999) '"Too Black, Too Strong?" Anti-racism and the Making of South Asian Political Identities in Britain', Jordon, T. and Lent, A. (eds) *Storming the Millennium: The Politics of Change*. London: Lawrence and Wishart.

Sharma, Sanjay, Hutnyk, John and Sharma, Ashwani (eds) (1996) *Dis-Orienting Rhythms: The Politics of the New Asian Dance Music*, London: Zed Books.

Sivanandan, A. (1990) *Communities of Resistance*, London: Verso.

Spivak, Gayatri Chakravorty (1987) *In Other Worlds*, New York: Methuen.

Spivak, Gayatri Chakravorty (1988) 'Can the Subaltern Speak?', in Nelson, Cary and Grossberg, Larry (eds) *Marxism and the Interpretation of Culture*, Urbana: University of Illinois Press, pp. 271–313.

Spivak, Gayatri Chakravorty (1990) *The Post-Colonial Critic*, New York: Routledge.

Spivak, Gayatri Chakravorty (1993) *Outside in the Teaching Machine*, London: Routledge.

Spivak, Gayatri Chakravorty (1995) 'Extended Commentary on *Sammie and Rosie Get Laid*' – public discussion at Keele University.

Spivak, Gayatri Chakravorty (1997a) 'On Responsibility', in Mariniello, S. and Bove, P. (eds) *Gendered Agents: Women and Institutional Knowledge*, Durham, NC: Duke University Press.

Spivak, Gayatri Chakravorty (1997b) 'Translator's Forward to Draupadi', in Devi, Mahesweta, *Breast Stories*, Calcutta: Seagull Books, pp. 1–19.

Spivak, Gayatri Chakravorty (1999) *A Critique of Postcolonial Reason: Toward a History of the Vanishing Present*, Cambridge, MA: Harvard University Press.

Street, J (1986) *Rebel Rock: The Politics of Popular Music*, London: Blackwell.

Taylor, Timothy (1997) *Global Pop: World Music, World Markets*, New York: Routledge.

UCENCCL, (1980) *Southall 23 April 1979*. The Report of the Unofficial Committee of Enquiry, London: National Council for Civil Liberties.

Urry, John (1990) *The Tourist Gaze*, London: Sage.

Urry, John (1995) *Consuming Places*, London: Routledge.

Visvanathan, Shiv (1997) *A Carnival of Science: Essays on Science, Technology and Development*, New Delhi: Oxford University Press.

Wagle, H.P. (1993) 'Telecoms' Role in Indian Development', *Transnational Data and Communications Report* March: 29–33.

Wallis, Roger and Malm, Krister (1984/1990) 'Patterns of Change', in Frith, Simon and Goodwin, Andrew (eds) *On Record: Rock, Pop, and the Written Word*, London: Routledge, pp. 160–80.

Werbner, P. and Modood, T. (eds) (1997) *Debating Cultural Hybridity: Multi-Cultural Identities and the Politics of Anti-Racism*, London: Zed Books.

Widgery, David (1986) *Beating Time: Riot 'n Race 'n Rock 'n Roll*, London: Chatto and Windus.

Wiggerhaus, (1984/1994) *The Frankfurt School*, Cambridge: Polity.

Wilson, Kalpana (1998) 'Arundhati Roy and Patriarchy', *Inqilab* 51: 27–31.

Wright, Steve (2000) 'Can Marxists Rap?', *Theory, Culture & Society* 17(1):

Young, Robert J.C. (1995) *Colonial Desire: Hybridity in Theory, Culture and Race*, London: Routledge.

Zuberi, Nabeel (1995) 'Paki Tunes', *Samar* winter: 36–9.

Index

251